BROOKINGS TRADE FORUM

2007

FOREIGN DIRECT INVESTMENT

Susan M. Collins

EDITOR

DATE DUE

BROOKINGS INSTITUTION PRESS
Washington, D.C.

Copyright © 2008
THE BROOKINGS INSTITUTION
1775 Massachusetts Avenue, N.W., Washington, D.C. 20036

ISSN 1520-5479
ISBN-13: 978-0-8157-1298-5

For information on subscriptions, standing orders, and individual copies, contact Brookings Institution Press, P.O. Box 465, Hanover, PA 17331-0465. Or call 866-698-0010. E-mail brookings@tsp.sheridan.com. Visit Brookings online at www.brookings.edu/press/bookstore.htm.

Brookings periodicals are available online through Online Computer Library Center (contact the OCLC subscriptions department at 800-848-5878, ext. 6251) and Project Muse (http://muse.jhu.edu).

BROOKINGS TRADE FORUM

——— 2007 ———

FOREIGN DIRECT INVESTMENT

BROOKINGS TRADE FORUM is a series of annual volumes that provide authoritative and in-depth analysis on current and emerging issues in international economics. The series aims to explore questions on international trade and macroeconomics in an interdisciplinary fashion with both practitioners and academics and seeks to gather in one place papers that provide a thorough look at a particular topic affecting international economic policy. Leading experts in the field will contribute to each volume. This tenth issue contains edited versions of the papers and comments presented at a conference held at the Brookings Institution, May 10–11, 2007. This year's forum examined a variety of dimensions of foreign direct investment. Papers focused on the role of FDI in host country economies, the factors driving FDI, and the concerns about the extent to which potential benefits are shared.

The 2007 Brookings Trade Forum was made possible by a generous grant from the Tokyo Club Foundation for Global Studies and the Nomura Institute of Capital Markets Research.

Shang-Jin Wei, *International Monetary Fund and Brookings Institution*
John Whalley, *University of Western Ontario*
Wing Thye Woo, *Brookings Institution*
Xian Xin, *China Agricultural University*

Conference participants

Garrick Blalock, *Cornell University*
Ralph Bryant, *Brookings Institution*
Linda Cole, *Federal Reserve Board*
Jennifer Derstine, *Department of Commerce*
Rebecca Dillender, *Bureau of Internal Labor Affairs*
William Donnelly, *U.S. International Trade Commission*
Kimberly Elliott, *Peterson Institute for International Economics*
Eylem Ersal, *Georgetown University*
Inbal Hasbani, *Brookings Institution*
Jane Ihrig, *Federal Reserve Board*
Ergys Islamaj, *Georgetown University*
Robert Koopman, *U.S. International Trade Commission*
Ralph Kozlow, *Bureau of Economic Analysis*
Raymond Mataloni, *Bureau of Economic Analysis*
Philip Levy, *American Enterprise Institute*
Cheryl Long, *Colgate University*
Robert Rogowsky, *U.S. International Trade Commission*
Charles Schott, *Department of the Treasury*
Charles Schultze, *Brookings Institution*
Obie Whichard, *Bureau of Economic Analysis*
Falan Yinug, *U.S. International Trade Commission*
William Zeile, *Bureau of Economic Analysis*

SUSAN M. COLLINS

Editor's Summary

Foreign direct investment (FDI) plays a critical and growing role in the global economy. FDI refers to companies based in one country making a substantial physical investment or acquiring a lasting managerial interest in an enterprise based in a foreign country. For a host country, FDI promises a source of new resources and new technologies that could spur economic growth and development. For multinational firms, FDI offers the promise of new markets and less expensive production facilities. But there are clearly risks involved as well as legitimate concerns about the extent to which potential benefits are appropriately shared.

This tenth issue of the *Brookings Trade Forum* examines a variety of dimensions of FDI. On balance, have developing countries benefited from FDI inflows? To what extent has FDI played an important role in China's impressive economic performance? How do tax and productivity differences between source and host countries affect bilateral FDI flows? How have profits been shared between multinational corporations and host country governments in resource-rich economies? Why do U.S. investors appear to earn substantially higher returns on their investment abroad than foreigners earn on their investments in the United States?

The conference was held on May 10 and 11, 2007. This volume provides revised versions of the five papers presented at the conference, as well as the remarks from invited commentators and brief summaries of general discussants for each session.

IN THE FIRST PAPER IN THE VOLUME, Theodore H. Moran addresses three questions: how to evaluate the contribution (positive or negative) of manufacturing FDI to a developing country host economy, how to search for externalities and spillovers (and identify the channels and mechanisms through which spillovers take place), and how to determine whether host governments should devote public sector resources to attracting FDI in manufacturing.

In each area, he argues that the research would benefit from more extensive usage of multiple investigation techniques. Moran notes that industry and sector studies, business cases, management interviews, firm survey data, and cost-benefit analysis of individual projects are relatively rare among recent studies analyzing the impact of FDI. If these approaches are carefully arrayed to avoid selection bias, he believes that they are generalizable and a valuable complement to the more standard regression analyses.

The paper provides a wide-ranging literature review. It concludes that cost-benefit analyses of individual FDI manufacturing projects assessing net contribution at world market prices show that those oriented toward exports make a positive contribution. In contrast, those oriented toward protected national markets tend to subtract from national income.

Business case studies and sectoral analyses corroborate these findings. They also show that multinational corporations (MNCs) use different production processes and business strategies in response to international competition compared with what MNCs use in protected domestic markets. Firm-level studies highlight ways that plants in protected environments differ from those that compete internationally. The production lines are constructed differently and are almost always subscale. The workers do not receive training in those skills that are needed for large-scale automated plants. The operations do not generate the dynamic learning that is essential for infant industries to mature into competitive adulthood.

In export-oriented FDI plants, in contrast, MNC headquarters incorporate economies of scale and orchestrate their developing country affiliates into a coherent supply network within which latest improvements in production technology and quality control procedures can be transmitted on a real-time basis, within days or hours. Industry and case study evidence showing a similar divergence between production for protected domestic markets in developing countries and production for export in competitive international markets—across time periods and across geographical regions—provides some confidence that these results are robust.

Moran argues that failure to adequately account for these differences in production strategy helps to explain why the first generation of econometric studies on the effects of FDI in host economies generated such muddled results. Studies using data from protected economies did not control for the distortions related to import substitution. In these settings, FDI likely resulted in significant negative as well as (perhaps) some positive contributions to the host economy.

Recent, better-designed studies do show robust econometric evidence of externalities and spillovers from FDI, particularly in the vertical direction.

There is also recent evidence of both export and labor market externalities. The best of the new generation of econometric investigations introduce imaginative controls to isolate the impact of FDI and match case study and survey observations about the same phenomenon. However, Moran argues that this work would be even more valuable if it were combined with detailed case studies and well-structured surveys that could help pinpoint the channels through which spillovers take place.

Moran argues that appropriate policy response to these externalities is not to simply subsidize FDI flows up to the value of the social returns. He highlights complex market failures and imperfections in information markets that may warrant subsidies for the provision of vocational skills training and for infrastructure improvements that go beyond FDI attraction. There is also an inherent timing problem: "marketing the country" and securing specific commitments from MNCs require *up-front* outlays that must be expended well before any potential externalities would actually be generated.

Moran draws a number of policy implications of these findings for developing countries. In particular, he argues that weakening the TRIMS Agreement within the World Trade Organization — which bans imposing domestic content or trade-balance mandates on FDI — is counter to developing country interests. He also opposes restoring the host country practice of levying performance requirements on manufacturing multinationals. Similarly, he characterizes as scandalous that eighteen of the nineteen official political risk insurance agencies within the Organization of Economic Cooperation and Development (OECD) provide coverage for multinational manufacturing projects that rely upon trade restraints to survive.

With regard to offering tax breaks and direct subsidies for FDI, Moran emphasizes that developing country authorities certainly understand the misgivings of economists. Their predicament arises from *prisoner dilemma dynamics*: the host that refuses to provide generous locational incentives is undermined by others who will. He concludes that what is needed is an international agreement to cap and rollback locational incentives. To be effective, subnational as well as national authorities would have to be brought under the new disciplines, an undertaking that is likely to be formidable.

Discussants welcomed the paper's broad historical review of the empirical literature on FDI's impact on developing countries as highly informative.

JOHN WHALLEY AND XIAN XIN focus on the role of FDI in China's economic performance. Their study is motivated by the widely shared view that inward FDI flows, together with growth in trade, have been one of the primary mechanisms though which China's economy has become deeply integrated into the wider global economy. In addition to assessing the importance of those FDI flows for China's past and likely future growth, they offer a wide-ranging discussion of some of the issues that have emerged in the recent literature and policy debate on FDI and China.

The first part of the paper provides interesting detail about the magnitude and characteristics of FDI flows to China. FDI inflows to China have increased dramatically over the past quarter century. Not only is China the largest emerging country recipient of such flows, it accounts for nearly half of all the outflows from industrial economies. The paper highlights the relatively high regional concentration as well as the distinction between flows that are *horizontal* (that is, they serve the Chinese market) and flows that are *vertical* (that is, those that are export oriented). It also discusses links between FDI and China's large processing trade.

Chinese outward foreign direct investment has been relatively small until recently. It is heavily concentrated in greenfield and joint venture activities abroad, much of which have been focused in Hong Kong. But since 2005, direct acquisition of foreign firms by Chinese entities involving potentially large transactions have become prominent and with a focus well beyond Hong Kong. Though outward FDI from China is still relatively small, it is growing much more rapidly than is inward FDI, and the size of China's foreign reserves suggests significant room for further increases in outward FDI.

One of the paper's main objectives is to assess the linkages between FDI and growth in China. Building on previous work, the authors undertake a growth-accounting exercise that distinguishes between FDI-related output (from Foreign Invested Enterprises, or FIEs) and indigenous output (from the non-FIE portions of the economy). They argue that although FIEs produce roughly 20 percent of China's output, FIEs have accounted for a disproportionate 40 percent of China's recent growth. Thus they conclude that FDI has played a very substantial role in China's past growth, and they express concerns about the likely deleterious growth consequences of a decline in future FDI inflows.

The paper highlights some of the regional issues that have arisen. China's development has been very geographically concentrated, occurring primarily in a relatively small number of western and coastal provinces. This is widely thought to be a key determinant in China's growing inequality. These same provinces are the largest recipients of inward FDI, raising questions about the link between FDI inflows and relative inequality. Their review of literature concludes that it is difficult to find robust support for a linkage between FDI and relative inequality in China from macrodata. However some evidence of a linkage emerges from more detailed microstudies.

A key issue for the future of China's inward FDI is whether policy change in China might retard further growth in FDI inflows. The authors note that a key factor in attracting foreign investment has been substantial tax preferences. Implementation of a unified and single equal-yield tax rate to all enterprises and the removal of tax preferences toward FIEs might reduce future FDI inflows. The authors conjecture that such tax changes could have a substantial impact but acknowledge the need for more careful analyses. They also hypothesize that a RMB (renminbi) revaluation may reduce China's inward FDI flows. The size of such effects will depend in part on how heavily China's inward FDI has been involved with China's processing trade, since imports used in processing are denominated in foreign currency and the relative effect of production costs will be reduced.

Both of the discussants agreed that FDI has made important contributions to the transformation of China's economy and to its successful performance. However, both raised questions about the data and the methodology used to construct the sectoral growth accounts. They conclude that the paper is likely to have overstated the growth of FIEs relative to non-FIEs.

ASSAF RAZIN AND EFRAM SADKA study the role of taxation and productivity in determining bilateral FDI flows. They first develop a theoretical model that provides a rich and intriguing set of results. This is complemented by an empirical analysis based on data for eighteen OECD countries during the period 1987–2003 that provides some suggestive empirical support for some of the model's key results.

An important contribution of the paper is its carefully specified theoretical framework. It models the decisionmaking of a group of firms that must pay a fixed setup cost to undertake new investments. The approach highlights the distinction between a firm's decision on whether to invest at all (the extensive margin) and its decision of how much to invest, conditional on investing something (the intensive margin). Furthermore, the firms differ in their levels of productivity, introducing a realistic dimension of heterogeneity. In addition, the authors consider greenfield investments (for which firms must compete for a limited supply of entrepreneurs in the host country) and mergers and acquisitions (M&A), which are not subject to a similar constraint.

In this setting, the authors systematically examine the implications of a number of possible shocks, including tax changes and productivity shocks in the host and the source countries. Their results highlight that the effects of particular shocks on the probability that firms will decide to invest in a particular partner country (extensive) may be quite different from those effects on the magnitude of that investment if it occurs (intensive). This distinction has received little attention in prior literature and is likely to lead to important insights, both theoretically and empirically.

I highlight a few of the many theoretical findings in the paper. The model predicts that a tax increase at home will make parent companies more likely to invest abroad but will not affect the amount they invest, should they choose to do so. Firms will be less likely to invest in host countries that are experiencing tax increases, and they will tend to invest smaller amounts. A somewhat more surprising result is that a positive productivity shock in a host country need not make the host a more attractive place to invest, but instead it may reduce the likelihood that firms will decide to invest there. This could occur if the increased host country activity caused a large enough increase in the relevant setup costs associated with new investment.

The empirical application estimates separate equations for depicting the decision on whether to invest and the conditional investment magnitudes. The regression equations control for characteristics in the source and the host countries for each bilateral pair, as well as for "effective" corporate tax rates and labor productivity. The results show that higher host tax rates are associated with lower investment inflows and that higher source country tax rates tend to raise the likelihood of investment outflows. A rise in host country output per worker (interpreted as a positive productivity shock) is associated with a significant rise in investment magnitudes. Contrary to the theoretical finding, a positive productivity shock is also associated with an increased likelihood of investment, but this result is not statistically significant. The authors present simulations, based on the estimation results. It is interesting that these simulations suggest that there are marked differences across countries in the sensitivity of FDI flows to productivity and taxes in other OECD countries.

The discussants found the analysis very thought provoking. Features of the model, such as firm heterogeneity, help to generate useful insights about determinants of FDI. But it would be helpful to provide a clearer real-world interpretation of the setup costs, which play a critical role in the model. Both discussants also suggested a number of extensions, particularly to the empirical portion of the paper that could clarify how to interpret the results.

COUNTRIES THAT ARE RICH in natural resources often negotiate deals with foreign multinational companies to extract the resources. In their paper, Margaret

McMillan and Andrew R. Waxman explore the determinants of the resulting profit-sharing arrangement.

The authors present evidence that suggests that the terms of profit sharing between country governments and U.S. resource-extracting firms vary widely across countries and over time and depend on the quality of governance in host countries. Using firm-level panel data from the U.S. Bureau of Economic Analysis (BEA), their empirical analysis finds that the bargaining power of host governments and extraction companies does impact the relative distribution of rents. Furthermore, they conclude that more democratic governments in countries with higher-quality institutions tend to be able to strike better deals. They note that anecdotal evidence has pointed in this direction for some time. However, there does not appear to be any prior more formal econometric analysis that investigates these relationships.

Between 1982 and 1999, the share of rents going to host country governments in the natural resource extraction industries fell from 52.1 to 28.1 percent. McMillan and Waxman argue that this decline was driven by a reduction in tax collections and that it is consistent with reforms in the mining sector detailed in a recent World Bank report. More intense competition to attract exploration and mining investment appears to have resulted in more generous terms for investors. However, the authors also find that the share of rents paid to developed country governments averaged 40.1 percent—substantially higher than the average of 31.9 percent paid to developing country governments. In their view, this differential is unlikely to be fully explained by differences in country risk.

To quantify the importance of bargaining strength on rent sharing, McMillan and Waxman develop an empirical framework based on Nash bargaining. Their economic measures of bargaining power include sunk costs, technical expertise of the host country, number of competitors, and oil prices.

A central focus of their analysis is to understand how the quality of governance and the development of institutions impact the negotiation process and, in turn, the bargaining outcome. They highlight two competing possible channels. On the one hand, conventional wisdom holds that good governance produces desirable economic outcomes. For instance, other studies have successfully linked good governance with increased FDI inflows. On the other hand, in the case of natural resource extraction, poor governance may lead to higher corporate profitability and a smaller share of rents for the host country. For example, work by Shang-Jin Wei demonstrates how corruption in countries with poor governance can have the same distortionary effect on FDI as taxation, but without the concurrent stream of revenues for the host government.

Their analysis uses data from firm-level surveys on U.S. direct investment abroad, collected each year by BEA of the U.S. Department of Commerce. They use the data collected on majority-owned, nonbank foreign affiliates and non-bank U.S. parents for the benchmark years between 1982 and 1999 and focus on the subset of resource-extracting foreign affiliates. They explore alternative measures of *government take* (the share of profits that goes to the host country government). In addition to controlling for a range of country characteristics, they consider a variety of indicators of governance and institutional quality.

McMillan and Waxman recognize that there are alternative interpretations for their results. Their model suggests that better governance implies that firms will demand a smaller risk premium and that the government will be able to bargain a bigger take. However, better governance may also imply that a government is willing and able to negotiate a better deal for its citizens. They also discuss possible complications associated with the nationalization of extractive industries that would be interesting to explore in future work.

The discussant commended McMillan and Waxman for an interesting paper. However, he highlighted the different ways to interpret their findings, stressing the possibility that poor governance may reflect corruption, which would imply that firms would require a corruption premium to operate, thereby reducing government take. Possible ways to distinguish among alternative interpretations were suggested.

IN "RETURNS ON FDI: DOES THE UNITED STATES REALLY DO BETTER?" Barry Bosworth, Susan M. Collins and Gabriel Chodorow-Reich address two puzzling trends in the recent U.S. external balance. Most of the paper focuses on why large U.S. current account deficits have not caused U.S. net foreign investment income to deteriorate. And if the answer really is that U.S. investors get higher returns abroad than foreign investors do in the United States, then why are the U.S. investors more successful? The authors show that U.S. and foreign investors have earned very similar returns on non-FDI investments and that these returns track U.S. market rates quite closely. In contrast, returns on U.S. direct investment abroad (USDIA) exceed those on foreign direct investment in the United States (FDIUS). This gap is large and persistent, reflecting a low return on FDIUS and, especially in recent years, a high return on USDIA (relative to returns on domestic U.S. investments.

A major conclusion of the paper is that the higher return on USDIA is not an illusion due to bad data. Despite a number of data challenges, the authors conclude that the BEA data are better than the alternatives proposed in recent literature. As disussed further below, a variety of factors are likely to explain part of the returns gap. However, the authors argue that tax-related income shifting has received inadequate attention in this context and present new evidence that is highly suggestive of its importance.

The second puzzle is that net U.S. external debt has grown much more slowly than cumulative current account imbalances would suggest. By the end of 2006, the gap implied nearly $3 trillion in "missing" external liabilities. The authors decompose the data to illustrate that much of this gap can be attributed to the fact that valuation gains on U.S. assets abroad have been substantially greater than the valuation gains on foreign assets in the United States. Valuation gains apply primarily to equity, which account for a larger share of U.S. assets, and there have been, of course, recent gains in foreign relative to U.S. equity markets. It is surprising that U.S. investors also enjoyed valuation gains in their nonequity investments compared with losses for foreign investors, but some of this appears because of inconsistencies in the relevant data.

Because much of the literature on this issue raises concerns about the official measures of relevant variables, the authors spend some time discussing the available data sources and various measurement issues. In particular, they explain why they focus on current cost estimates of international investment positions to measure gross assets and liabilities. This is consistent with standard estimates of returns on domestic capital and avoids the assumption, which they find implausible, that aggregate stock market performances in host countries are a good proxy for the values of foreign affiliates. In contrast. much of the existing literature relies on market value estimates.

The paper examines five possible explanations that have been suggested for the observed gap in returns to FDI. One approach highlights differences between the characteristics of USDIA and FDIUS. While these go in the right direction, the authors caution against overstating the magnitudes of their effects. Higher returns associated with somewhat older U.S. investments abroad is likely to be only a small and diminishing part of the story. More important, USDIA may tend to be riskier than FDIUS, but the claim that this explains most of the gap is unconvincing given the relatively weak correlation between return and sovereign risk.

Considerable recent attention has focused on two potential explanations that assert that a returns differential is implausible and that call the quality of the official data into question. Ricardo Hausmann and Federico Struzenegger argue that official data do not record significant U.S. exports of intangibles, which results in an understatement of the value of U.S. assets abroad and an overstatement of the returns on these assets. In contrast, Daniel Gros is willing to rely on official indicators of net asset position but not those for investment income, in large part because of the treatment of reinvested earnings. While agreeing that there are major difficulties in the measurement of intangibles and that elimination of reinvested earnings does narrow the returns gap somewhat, Bosworth, Collins, and Chodorow-Reich stress a variety of concerns about the assumptions underlying these two proposed alternative methodologies.

A fourth strand of this literature uses alternative measures of returns. In particular, Pierre-Olivier Gourinchas and Hélène Rey construct indicators that include capital gains and losses, unlike the official balance of payments and investment income data. Their estimates of total return are based on performance of country-specific market indexes. However, in these data, the main U.S. return advantage is in *non-FDI* investments. These data highlight issues related to differential performance of equity markets across countries, and not to the puzzle about FDI return differentials. Bosworth, Collins, and Chodorow-Reich question the decision to reject BEA data on capital incomes. Instead, they agree that a focus on total returns is informative in many contexts and advocate that BEA expand its accounts to enable researchers to more fully decompose the returns data.

The final section of the paper presents new empirical analysis of the hypothesis that higher returns on U.S. investment abroad reflect tax-related income shifting by U.S.-owned multinational corporations. This could be done through cross-border transfer pricing among affiliates or through the transfer of intangibles from a parent to an affiliate in a low-tax jurisdiction at a price below that which would reflect appropriate royalties. The authors cite evidence of the latter for MNCs with affiliates operating in Puerto Rico and in Ireland. The authors construct effective tax rates for U.S. majority-owned foreign affiliates operating in fifty-one foreign countries, using firms' income and balance sheet data from BEA. They find that U.S. tax rates were about 12 percentage points above an investment-weighted average of those abroad from 2002 to 2004, which is not much lower than the gap of nearly 15 percentage points from 1999 to 2001. Furthermore, regression analysis finds that cross-country FDI income flows are significantly negatively related to tax differentials. The authors estimate that income shifting may account for an "extra" $28.5 billion earned abroad in 2004, or roughly one-third of the "excess" return earned by U.S. corporations operating abroad.

In his discussion of the paper, Cédric Tille provided additional evidence to support the likely relevance of a relative tax explanation for the return gap. He also highlights that different possible explanations for a yield gap would have quite different implications for the sustainability of the U.S. external balance.

THEODORE H. MORAN

Georgetown University

How to Investigate the Impact of Foreign Direct Investment on Development and Use the Results to Guide Policy

My mentors in graduate school were Raymond Vernon, Charles Kindleberger, and Albert Hirschman. They established their reputations by selecting the most important issues and policy dilemmas on the horizon, getting to know the actors and the settings involved as thoroughly as possible, and deriving insights from intensive investigation of (often) small numbers of cases. They then had to persuade their audience that what they had discovered was not idiosyncratic, atypical, or ephemeral.

Their contributions came at the beginning of the revolution in using regressions on large datasets, which was to become the preeminent investigative technique in economics. Their own work would have had more lasting impact if they had been able to combine—as I urge here—statistical analysis with a dedication to understanding how things worked by looking into the innards of the relationships they were trying to understand.

This paper will argue that the investigation of the impact of foreign direct investment (FDI) in manufacturing on development would be much more valid, more convincing—and less prone to error—if multiple techniques of investigation were used to reinforce (or refute) each other.[1] In addition to statistical

I am grateful to comments from Laura Alfaro, Garrick Blalock, Marc Busch, Beata Smarzynska Javorcik, Wolfgang Keller, Cheryl Long, and Anders Olofsgard. The weaknesses that remain come despite their help.

1. The analysis in this paper is limited to foreign direct investment in manufacturing in developing countries. Foreign direct investment in extractive industries, and in infrastructure, involves distinctive corporate strategies and poses distinctive public policy challenges for host authorities. See Moran (2006, chapter 3). Foreign direct investment in services—potentially of great value for increasing the competitiveness of indigenous firms—is still in the early stages of investigation.

1

regressions, such techniques include industry and sector studies, business cases, management interviews, data collection through firm surveys, and cost-benefit analyses of individual projects that are carefully arrayed to avoid selection bias and ensure generalizability. This argument is, I believe, unexceptional and should not even be controversial. The value of making this assertion arises, alas, because the use of multiple contrasting methodological approaches is quite uncommon—nay, vanishingly rare—among economists in the contemporary period. The weaknesses of this self-imposed narrowness plague current policy debates even among informed practitioners.

This paper examines three topics: how to investigate the impact of manufacturing FDI on a developing country host economy, how to search for externalities and spillovers (and identify the channels and mechanisms through which spillovers take place), and how to evaluate the question of whether host governments should devote public sector resources to attracting FDI in manufacturing. In each area, the paper shows how overlapping kinds of evidence can be useful, and are often indispensable, to carry out accurate investigations, to avoid analytical miscalculations, and to design appropriate policies for developed and developing countries.

How to Evaluate the Impact of Manufacturing FDI on a Developing Country Host Economy

The history of efforts to investigate the outcome from multinational manufacturing investment in developing countries begins with cost-benefit analysis of individual FDI projects, industry studies, multinational business cases, management interviews, and firm surveys. Do these approaches lead to reasonably robust general propositions about the impact of manufacturing FDI on the host economy, or are they no more than impressionistic observations—anecdotal in the pejorative sense—that have a significant probability of being overturned by one or two subsequent observations? Can the results from these kinds of investigations be useful in shaping the design of large-N econometric investigations that use plant-level data as well as in steering clear of mistakes that have spoiled earlier efforts?

Early Assessments Using Cost-Benefit Analysis

The earliest systematic attempts to assess the impact of manufacturing FDI on development were carried out by contemporaries of Vernon, Kindleberger, and Hirschman. The investigators used variations of cost-benefit analysis to measure the effect of the operations of multinational corporations (MNCs) on the host economy. One of the first was conducted by Sanjaya Lall and Paul Streeten under the auspices of the UN Conference on Trade and Development.[2] They analyzed the contribution to the host economy of 147 foreign investor operations in six developing countries. For approximately 62 percent (ninety-two projects), the effect of foreign investment on national income was positive; for the remaining projects (fifty-five, approximately 38 percent), it was nega-tive. The key determinant of whether the social rate of return was positive or negative was the extent of effective protection granted to the investors, across all industries and all countries in the sample. A second study, sponsored by the Organization of Economic Cooperation and Development (OECD) under the direction of Grant Reuber with data from approximately the same time period, uncovered a similar contrast in outcomes drawing on a slightly different set of comparisons.[3] The Reuber group investigated eighty foreign investment proj-ects within thirty host developing countries, comparing the production costs of the subsidiaries with the production costs of the parent companies for forty-five of the projects.[4] Approximately one-quarter of the subsidiaries had production costs that were equal to or lower than those of the parent; the remain-ing three-quarters had higher production costs. The Reuber team separated their sample according to whether the output of the project was destined primarily for the domestic market or for export. For the fourteen export projects identi-fied, more than three-quarters had production costs that were equal to or lower than those of the parent. For the thirty-one remaining projects, twenty-nine had production costs higher than those of the parent. These higher production costs were attributable to three interrelated factors: high levels of protection extended against imports, an uneconomic scale of production, and a high local cost of doing business. They concluded that even under a relatively wide range of shadow exchange rate calculations these projects resulted in a substantial real resource cost to the host countries.

These rudimentary attempts at cost-benefit analysis were given more rigor a decade later by Dennis Encarnation and Louis Wells.[5] They used detailed data from fifty foreign manufacturing projects submitted by prospective for-eign investors to the FDI screening board of a large developing country to calculate the contribution that each would make to national income minus the costs to the national economy, at world market prices, using shadow prices for

2. Lall and Streetan (1977). The data collected from 1970 to 1973 overlap with the data used in the Reuber report (1973).

3. Reuber with others (1973).

4. Reuber with others (1973, p. 179 and appendix C).

5. Encarnation and Wells (1986).

energy, foreign exchange, labor, and domestic capital to account for the opportunity cost of the resources to the host. They found that a majority of the fifty projects (55 to 75 percent, depending upon the shadow price assumptions) would increase national income, while the remainder (25 to 45 percent) would subtract from national income even though the projects were profitable to the foreign multinationals themselves. Their data exhibited a perfect rank-order correlation between the impact of the project on the host and the amount of trade protection afforded to the investor.[6] When trade protection was high, projects subtracted from national income. When trade protection was low, the reverse was true. For eight export-oriented projects, all were beneficial to the host economy.

Subsequent cost-benefit appraisals show similar outcomes. Using data from Kenya during the country's import substitution period, Bernard Wasow found that of thirty-five goods produced by fourteen foreign-owned firms, only three generated benefits to the host economy that exceeded their costs.[7] Under the umbrella of trade protection, more than half of the goods allowed the foreign affiliates to siphon foreign exchange from the host economy, rather than to save or earn hard currency. In the protected host market, there was a multiplication of foreign plants with excess capacity; had they been able to expand production, however, the negative impact on host welfare would have increased as well.

Business Case Studies and Industry Analyses: The Discovery of Distinctive Investor Operations

Business case studies and sectoral analyses not only corroborate these findings, but they provide a clearer understanding of how multinational companies alter their production processes and business strategies in response to international competition on the one hand or domestic protection on the other. The most detailed research comes from the three sectors in which the largest amounts of manufacturing FDI have taken place—the automotive, electronics, and petrochemical industries.

Anne Krueger provided an early model for these industry studies with a microeconomic analysis of India's import substitution policies in the automotive sector.[8] She showed that the Indian approach led foreign investors to build facilities much smaller and less efficient than plants designed to compete in world markets. All thirty-four facilities produced at prices above the compa-

6. Subsidized energy prices also led to project outcomes that reduced national welfare.
7. Wasow (2003).
8. Krueger (1975).

rable foreign price, ranging from 18 percent more than the foreign price to three times the foreign price.[9] The differential was even worse for firms engaged in domestic content generation such as metal fabrication, chemical supply, and other components (prices 123 percent to 309 percent higher) compared with the differential for assemblers (prices 118 percent to 197 percent higher). Her estimates suggested that twenty-seven of the thirty-four operators would not remain in business if levels of effective protection dropped below 50 percent.

Automotive industry studies from other regions, and later periods, reported results similar to those of Krueger.[10] Protected FDI assembly operations in Latin America, Southeast Asia, and eastern Europe had typically less than half the capacity of parent operations in developed countries. The combination of sub-scale size, the requirement to meet domestic content requirements, and trade protection generated prices 150 to 200 percent higher than prices of compara-ble imports—except the studies revealed that domestic output was *not comparable* with imports. To meet domestic content requirements, often with mandatory local partners, international automobile companies standardized the practice of delivering semi knocked down (SKD) or completely knocked down (CKD) kits to be welded and screwed together by hand in miniature assem-bly plants, without benefit of large-scale automotive production and quality-control characteristics found in all cutting-edge factories.[11]

Factories in protected developing country markets turned out earlier-style automobiles—called "repeat models"—with previous-generation performance characteristics. Even well-run plants were not designed to be, or to become, internationally competitive. General Motor's (GM's) otherwise exemplary kit-assembly joint venture in Hungary achieved a maximum output of eight vehicles per hour in contrast to the output of its full-scale operations of ninety vehicles per hour before the prospective loss of trade protection associated with Hun-gary's entry into the EU led GM to buy out its Hungarian partner and shut down the plant entirely in 1999.[12]

Industry executives admitted (or explained) that when host countries required them to operate with indigenous joint venture partners the parent corporation withheld the most advanced technology so as to avoid "leakage" in a horizon-tal direction to potential rivals.[13] In China, product characteristics were ten years

9. Krueger (1975, table V-1, p. 89).

10. Bale and Walters (1986); Samuels (1990); UNCTC (1991).

11. For an engineering comparison of CKD and SKD auto plants with standard full-scale assem-bly operations, see Ngo and Conklin (1996, appendix 3: Note on the Automobile Assembly Process of Mekong Corporation and the Vietnam Motor Vehicle Industry).

12. Klein (1995); Kalotay (2002, pp. 1042–049).

13. Beamish (1988). Multinational investors show a marked difference in behavior between freely choosing a local partner to help penetrate a host country market and being required to form

behind the industry frontier, in Latin America, sometimes even farther back.[14] The investors' reluctance to deploy the latest technology to China was not merely precautionary. Audi's Chinese partner in the First Automobile Works "expropriated" the production technology after the European multinational's license expired in 1997. When host countries required them to meet explicit domestic content requirements, parent corporations subtracted from their kits the most simple fixtures and components, designating these for local procurement in the host economy.

In the electronics industry, William Cline's dissection of Brazil's policy in the informatics sector mirrors what Krueger found in the Indian automobile sector.[15] Brazil's strategy of restricting computer imports and limiting foreign ownership to 30 percent allowed international companies to sell less-capable models for two to three times world prices. Cline estimated the cost to consumers to have been about $500 million per year in the mid-1980s, not including the competitive disadvantage suffered by user-companies like Embraer (aerospace) and Petrobras (petroleum exploration and development) whose international rivals could enjoy cutting-edge products with no price penalty.

To meet import substitution goals, international computer companies, sometimes using the same knocked down kit assembly pattern as the automotive sector, shipped previous-generation components and technologies to generate a second round of oligopoly rents from production in protected markets. Operating in Mexico with a mandatory local partner and 25 to 35 percent domestic content requirement, Hewlett-Packard (HP) charged prices 160 percent higher for locally assembled computers that were at least one technology cycle (that is, two to four years) behind those in the United States.[16] The HP factory was approximately one-tenth minimum efficient scale for computer assembly, which precluded the introduction of automated, computerized production lines or large-batch quality-control procedures that were being perfected in Southeast Asian export plants. The kit for the previous-generation computer brought all sophisticated inputs in from elsewhere; the domestic content requirements were filled with purchases of simple coils, wires, and packaging.

Thus, besides documenting the inefficiency of using FDI for import substitution, studies using firm-level data showed that the plants were *not miniature replicas* of what could be found along the industry frontier. The production

---

a joint venture as a condition of entry. They frequently partner with a local firm to set up domestic operations but then take full control if they decide to incorporate the host site into the parent's internal sourcing network.

14. Wang (2004).
15. Cline (1987).
16. Austin (1990).

lines were physically constructed differently. The workers did not receive training in the same skills as those needed for large-scale automated plants. The
operations in the host country did not generate the dynamic learning that was
essential for infant industries to mature into competitive adulthood. In the
petrochemical industry, for example, a sector known for high fixed costs and
low variable costs, the competitiveness of foreign-owned facilities in the developing world was acutely dependent upon capturing all economies of scale. In
a study of fifteen foreign direct investment projects in petrochemicals, Peter
Gray and Ingo Walter found that, from an engineering point of view, all six
boutique plants built to serve protected local markets were not only high cost
but were ill designed to be used as building blocks in an infant industry strategy.[17] Two of the six were considered outright failures by the parent investors.
The remaining four survived only with ongoing protection in the host market.

These industry studies show that the MNC reaction to trade protection in
developing countries was *noticeably different from what was coming to be called
tariff jumping FDI* among the developed countries. Confronted by U.S. tariff
and nontariff barriers, Japanese auto companies began building plants in the
United States that reproduced the most advanced high-quality-control production techniques available in the Japanese home market. In protected developing
country markets, in contrast, manufacturing MNCs were not able to reproduce
plants with the size and sophistication similar to home country facilities.

Parent-Affiliate Relationships: Fragmentation versus Integration

At the same time, industry studies revealed that the relationship between
multinational parent and subsidiary was becoming increasingly fragmented
within the import substitution framework. But they also showed that the parent-
subsidiary relationship was growing ever more closely integrated when the
former relied on the latter to secure the firm's position in international markets. Rather than merely searching for low-wage assembly sites, MNC
headquarters began to orchestrate their developing country affiliates into a
coherent supply network within which latest improvements in production technology and quality-control procedures could be transmitted on a real-time
basis, within days or hours.[18]

Volkswagen designed the facilities producing the inputs for its basic vehicle platform (engines, axles, chassis, and gear boxes) in Brazil, Mexico,
Argentina, and eastern Europe so that they could incorporate engineering

17. Gray and Walter (1984).
18. For a more extensive review of evidence of this intimate parent-affiliate relationship, see
Moran (2001).

upgrades online within sixteen hours of each other. General Motors placed cylinder head equipment that could accept continuous changes without rebuilding the production line in its high-performance engine export plant at Szentgotthard in Hungary. Ford designated its new export assembly facility in Hermosillo as the site to teach managers worldwide quality-control techniques that rival those of the Japanese. The output of this Mexican plant achieved higher scores for reliability (according to independent tracking agencies) than those of Ford plants in the United States.[19]

International electronics firms synchronized production changes in their Asian supply chains with the pace of the new product introduction in the home market.[20] Telecommunications and semiconductor multinationals assigned high-precision manufacturing and quality-control procedures to their plants in Malaysia as soon as they appeared. "As far as assembly and testing are concerned," observed a Texas Instruments executive, "we have more expertise here than we have in the U.S."[21] Using plant-level data from the disk drive industry, David McKendrick, Richard Donner, and Stephan Haggard traced the organization of "new product transfer teams" within Seagate and Read-Rite for each new generation of magnetic platters and associated high-performance motors.[22] Product developers at headquarters meet with fifteen process engineers and managers brought in from wholly owned affiliates in Singapore, Malaysia, or Thailand some fifty days before launch, who are followed two weeks later by twenty-four production supervisors, to be trained on the pilot line. When the assemblers return to Southeast Asia, they are accompanied by eleven managers and engineers from headquarters to perform tests on the new production line. After the official launch, ten more U.S. supervisors oversee local operations to trouble-shoot problems until high-volume, high-reliability output is achieved with minimal downtime or rejection rates.

It became a trick question in business school literature to ask whether would-be consultants in the classroom would advise a particular host to provide a tax break to an investor who would promise to introduce the very latest techniques into the local export plant—the correct answer was "no, of course not" because it would be clearly in the self-interest of the parent to incorporate such latest techniques on its own since the parent's competitive position in global markets depended upon highest performance from the affiliate.

19. Womack, Jones, and Roos (1991, chapter 10).
20. Borrus, Ernst, and Haggard (2000).
21. Lim and Fong (1991, p. 115).
22. McKendrick, Donner, and Haggard (2000).

Avoiding Selection Bias:
From Anecdotal Observations to Robust Generalizations

To what extent might these observations about the differential impact of manufacturing FDI on the host economy—drawn from the international automotive, electronics, and petrochemical industries—be generalizable to manufacturing FDI more broadly?

Business cases, and even industry studies, are routinely referred to as anecdotal, suggesting that generalizations based on them may be discredited with no more than a handful of additional observations and that there is a high probability that such additional observations will differ.[23] The fact that the automotive, electronics, and petrochemical sectors show a similar divergence between production for protected domestic markets in developing countries and production for export in competitive international markets across time periods and across geographical regions provides some confidence, however, about further observations within these industries. But might there be some kind of selection bias that renders the results from these industries different from manufacturing FDI more generally? Or does evidence from FDI in manufacturing in other sectors point in the same direction? Already, the cost-benefit analyses that recorded negative host country economic effects from FDI in protected domestic markets and positive host country economic effects from export-oriented FDI have included data from such sectors as industrial equipment, agribusiness, textiles, canned goods and juices, pharmaceuticals, chemicals, and petrochemicals, as well as automotive equipment and electrical equipment. And, dating from the period of the earliest cost-benefit investigations, solid theoretical research emerged backing the expectation that domestic content requirements and other forms of trade protection are likely to lead to a proliferation of subscale and inefficient plants.[24]

With regard to the quality of the relationship between parent and developing country affiliate, two separate studies by Edwin Mansfield and Anthony Romeo and Jeong-Yeon Lee and Mansfield surveyed a total of sixty-five firms from a wide range of sectors and showed systematic differences as a function of whole or shared ownership.[25] Parent firms deployed new technology and production processes more rapidly within wholly owned MNC supply channels than they did among joint ventures or licensees. The data showed a mean lag of three to four years before technology was transferred to joint ventures or licensees in developing countries. In Vijaya Ramachandran's sample of

23. King, Keohane, and Verba, (1994).
24. Eastman and Stykolt (1970).
25. Mansfield and Romeo (1980); Lee and Mansfield (1996).

industries in fourteen sectors, the potency of the interaction between head-quarters and affiliate was significantly stronger within wholly owned networks than it was for joint venture or licensees across all sectors.[26] Contemporary data from China exhibited the same contrast in plant operations, notwith-standing the Chinese success in attracting extraordinary large numbers of foreign investors. Drawing on a sample of 442 multinational investors, Guo-qiang Long showed that wholly owned or majority parent-owned foreign affiliates were much more likely to be using the most advanced technology available to the parent than are ventures with 50-50 ownership or majority domestic ownership.[27] Thirty-two percent of the wholly owned foreign affili-ates and 40 percent of the majority foreign-owned affiliates used technology as advanced as in the parent firm, whereas only 23 percent of the 50-50 shared ownership firms and 6 percent of the majority Chinese-owned firms did.

Business strategy literature provides ample testimony from senior MNC man-agers that control over ownership is used to limit opportunistic behavior, prevent appropriation of proprietary assets, and minimize transaction costs in dealing with host country partners.[28] Supporting such testimony, Magnus Blomstrom, Ari Kokko, and Mario Zejan found a negative correlation between host coun-try policies that stipulate that foreign firms provide access to the parent's patents, perform research and development onsite, or transfer skills to local personnel and ensure that technology inflows from headquarters to affiliate.[29] Japanese MNCs displayed a negative coefficient for intrafirm technology trans-fer, according to Shujiro Urata and Hiroki Kawai, when host authorities imposed technology sharing requirements as a condition for international investors to set up a local affiliate.[30] Using Bureau of Economic Analysis benchmark sur-vey data of U.S. multinationals from 1982, 1989, and 1994, and from the nonbenchmark year 1997, Mihir Desai, Fritz Foley, and James Hines noted that whole or majority ownership occurs most frequently when parent firms coor-dinated production among different offshore sites, transfered technology and other intangible property among affiliates, and managed tax planning on an international basis.[31] Their data suggested that lifting local ownership restric-tions provides a clear payoff to host governments in terms of expanded trade

26. The results came from industries as diverse as metal products, chemicals, rubber, food, tex-tiles, and medical products, as well as transport equipment and electronics. Potency was operationalized by Ramachandran (1993) as the number of parent company employees sent to a given host country to bring a given technology on line and the number of host country employees sent to the parent country for training.

27. Long (2005).
28. Gomes-Casseres (1989); Beamish and Delios (1997).
29. Blomstrom, Kokko, and Zejan (1992).
30. Urata and Kawai (2000).
31. Desai, Foley, and Hines (2002).

within multinational sourcing networks: each 4 percent increase in sole ownership of affiliates was associated with 3 percent higher intrafirm trade volumes. Thus evidence showing a contrast in firm behavior, and in impact on the host economy, as a function of inward orientation toward a protected market (often with performance requirements like domestic content and joint venture mandates) and outward orientation toward international markets (typically free of performance requirements) emerges across industries, regions, and time periods. This evidence from affiliate operations is backed by consistent management testimony about the motivation for the contrasting investor behavior and is supported by theoretical models to explain the favorable and the unfavorable consequences for the host economy.

An Exception in Korea or Taiwan?

Recent reevaluation of Korean performance in high-performance electronics demonstrates that Korea's experiences with FDI is not so much a bona fide exception as an exception that proves the rule.[32] In industries where technology was stable and could be replicated through licenses and for-hire foreign engineers, such as shipbuilding and steel, Korea followed a model of excluding FDI, requiring domestic production of inputs, and creating "national champion" companies through government funding. In industries in which the international technological frontier was continuously pushed outward, especially computers, semiconductors, telecommunications, and high-performance consumer electronics, Korea followed a script much closer to that of Hong Kong or Singapore than conventional wisdom has suggested. Foreign multinationals built the industrial base for electronics in Korea in the decade from the mid-1960s to the mid-1970s, during which foreign-owned production accounted for one-third of the domestic market and more than half of all exports. Korean companies grew up as suppliers to the foreign investors and gradually entered export markets via original equipment manufacturer (OEM) relationships with the foreign assemblers (that is, foreign-owned affiliates). The Korean suppliers credited technology acquisition to contract manufacturing, which occurred three times more often than it did through licenses or joint venture partnerships.[33]

In the 1980s, nationalistic policies pushed most foreign electronics assemblers out of Korea, but the OEM channel nonetheless remained the crucible that shaped the performance of Korean-owned firms. At the turn of the decade, 50 to 60 percent of all color TVs and VCRs were still exported from Korea by means of OEM contracts with assemblers who provided the specifications for

32. Hobday (1995, 2000).
33. Rhee, Ross-Larson, and Pursell (1984).

contract manufacturing.[34] All three of the companies that became Korean national champions—Samsung, Lucky Goldstar, and Hyundai—grew up as contract manufacturers for multinationals and after three decades still relied on OEM contracts for 60 percent of their electronics exports. They expanded their own design expertise because of learning-by-doing work for foreign purchasers, not because of mandatory joint venture partnerships. They depended upon duty-free imports of inputs for their own assembly, not domestic content requirements.

The Taiwan experience shows a similar pattern. Indigenous electronics firms began by selling components for calculators, clocks, and VCRs to the local affiliates of IBM, Hitachi, and Philips; the more successful graduated to contract manufacturing of printed circuit boards, monitors, and power supplies. All the major Taiwanese computer makers, including ACER, Tatung, and MiTAC, entered export markets as OEM suppliers to foreign multinationals, learning advanced design and own-brand marketing as they went. Not one of the three became successful because of forced joint-ownership with a multinational. All eschewed government obligations on domestic content. Thus, as discussed in the final section of this paper, the argument that developing countries need more "policy space" to impose performance requirements on FDI such as domestic content or joint venture, among others—"like Korea and Taiwan did"—is simply not well informed by the facts.[35]

A First Look at Backward Linkages

Sectoral studies and business cases also showed a stark contrast in the spread of backward linkages from multinational affiliates to indigenous suppliers in the host economy. With FDI oriented toward protected local markets, the smaller-sized and less advanced production techniques of the multinational affiliates not only penalized the efficiency of their own plants but also hindered local companies from becoming competitive suppliers. In the automotive sector, the multinational kit assemblers fulfilled their domestic content obligations with parts for which economies of scale were least evident. The opportunities for local firms were concentrated in stamped or molded plastics, windows, simple electrical fixtures. Domestic companies were virtually precluded from becoming cost-effective producers of transmissions, axles, and even exhaust systems. In the electronics sector, local suppliers had to fabricate computer cas-

34. These assemblers included Sony, Panasonic, Mitsubishi, Zenith, Toshiba, Philips, RCA, and Hitachi.

35. For the argument that more "policy space" is needed for developing countries to regulate FDI, using Korea as an alleged model, see Birdsall, Rodrik, and Subramanian (2005).

ing from fiberglass or aluminum because their operations were not large enough to support the use of newer composite materials that were becoming the norm in international markets. Transistor wiring was hand-soldered, with predictable negative consequences for reliability.

For export-oriented FDI, however, MNCs began to farm out procurement contracts in a vertical direction to low-cost local suppliers. In the automotive industry, certification as an original equipment manufacturer or replacement equipment manufacturer (REM) emerged as the principal channel for the creation of a host country auto parts industry. In the electronics industry, contract manufacturing of printed circuit boards and other subassemblies became a major source of domestic industrial growth first in Southeast Asia, including Korea and Taiwan, and later in Latin America after the trade-and-investment liberalization of the 1990s.

This contrast between FDI operations oriented toward protected local markets or exports plays an important role in the search for externalities.

How to Investigate for Externalities from Manufacturing FDI in the Developing Country Host Economy

The first generation of econometric analysis, examining data from the 1980s and 1990s, failed to demonstrate the existence of externalities. Industry or sector studies, business school cases, management interviews, and firm surveys analyzed evidence from the same period and from more recent periods and showed multiple kinds and types of externalities. But what is the reality? Why has the search for externalities produced such disparate outcomes? How can investigative methods be improved to provide more thorough and rigorous identification of externalities and better understanding of when and how beneficial spillovers might occur?

Positive externalities, which are spillovers from the presence of foreign investors that benefit the host economy without having to be paid for, come in various forms. Executives, managers, engineers, and workers may leave foreign-owned plants after having acquired skills and expertise. Nonrelated firms may observe MNC strategies, duplicate their purchases of equipment, replicate their production or management practices, or copy their quality-control practices. Foreign investors may provide advice, designs, direct production assistance, or marketing contacts to suppliers, which the latter then deploy more broadly than simply providing cheaper or more reliable inputs to the foreigners.

It is possible to imagine in the abstract a world in which executives, managers, engineers, and workers never leave the foreign plants where they have obtained on-the-job training; in which indigenous firms do not imitate production processes or marketing techniques introduced by foreigners; in which foreign affiliates do not provide advice and assistance to help suppliers reduce costs, improve quality, or penetrate new markets; or in which those suppliers fail to improve their operations in ways that cannot be fully captured by the foreign purchasers. However, this is not a world that emerges from the testimony of participants, whether they are in international corporations or indigenous companies. The evidence from the actors themselves makes a clear distinction between the spread of externalities in the vertical as opposed to the horizontal direction.

Horizontal Externalities:
Evidence from Industry and Business Case Studies

In the horizontal direction, international companies report diligent efforts to avoid leakage of technology and know-how to potential rivals.[36] The preoccupation with maintaining whole or majority ownership, as outlined in the section above, is largely driven by a desire to prevent host country entrepreneurs from becoming competitors. The decision to internalize corporate operations across borders, as opposed to licensing technology or exporting goods and services, is motivated by a strategy to prevent erosion of market position. The evidence suggests, however, that these self-protective efforts on the part of multinationals are not perfectly successful—especially in cases when the technology and management skills needed to launch a successful business are relatively simple, stable, and can be learned on the job. Multinational corporations have a long history as incubators of senior managers in the industrial sectors or in Latin America and Southeast Asia.[37] Local banks and financial sector institutions in both regions are filled with alumni of Citibank and Banque Nationale de Paris (BNP).[38] Within six years of the beginning of FDI-led export growth in Mauritius, 50 percent of all export processing zone (EPZ) firms were indigenously owned. They were founded, managed, and staffed, in many cases, by employees who had received on-the-job training in foreign enterprises and then had left to set up their own companies.[39]

36. Vernon, Wells, and Rangan (1995).
37. Katz (1987).
38. McKendrick (1994).
39. Rhee, Katterbach, and White (1990, p. 39). The figure of 50 percent represents the share of all EPZ equity capital. The authors report that indigenous firms were founded by former employees of the foreign multinationals, but they do not provide exact data.

Contemporary survey data provide details about the spread of production techniques and management practices in the horizontal direction. One-quarter of the managers of Czech firms and 15 percent of the managers of Latvian firms reported that they learned about new technologies by observing foreign firms as the latter entered their industry sector.[40] Twelve percent of the Czech managers and 9 percent of the Latvian managers indicated that they discovered new marketing procedures and outlets from watching the performance of foreigners. Nonetheless, in general, the transfer of production and management skills in a horizontal direction appears to take place despite the best efforts of foreign investors to prevent it. Along this axis, the popular phrase "technology transfer" can legitimately be considered an oxymoron, as far as the wishes and efforts of the multinational corporations are concerned. In a vertical direction, however, the story is far different. The surprise in the data comes from where it is least expected, in export-oriented MNC manufacturing plants.

Vertical Externalities: Industry and Business Case Study Evidence

The developing country governments that imposed performance requirements such as domestic content and joint venture mandates on foreign manufacturing investors justified their actions with the fear that otherwise the foreigners would engage in little more than "screwdriver" operations that had few backward linkages into the host economy. Confirming their worst apprehensions, early export-oriented MNC plants—often set up in EPZs or free trade zones, with wholly owned subsidiaries free to procure inputs from wherever they wished—were largely self-contained operations that assembled imported components with minimal local purchases. Beginning in the first half of the 1980s, however, plant-level studies began to show growing amounts of purchases from local suppliers. These local suppliers included foreign-owned component producers from the home country, induced by the original MNCs to follow them to the host country. But they also consisted of a growing number of indigenous firms. As discussed below, the spread of backward linkages to locally owned firms varied as a function of the sophistication of the local corporate community, the business-friendly character of the local investment environment, the access of indigenous firms to duty-free imports, and the length of stay of the foreign investors in the host economy.

Using data on firms based in Singapore, Linda Lim and Pang Eng Fong traced the path of backward linkages from individual foreign electronics exporters into the host economy and documented the forms of assistance explicitly pro-

40. Figures are from the sample conducted in 2003 by Beata Smarzynska Javorcik and Mariana Spatareanu (2005).

vided to locally owned firms.[41] Company A, the subsidiary of a U.S. semiconductor manufacturer, bought goods and services from 200 local companies in Singapore. Six of the top ten local suppliers, by value of sales to the MNC, were component affiliates of U.S., Japanese, or European investors from the home market; the other four were indigenous Singapore firms. To ensure quality and reliability of components, the U.S. semiconductor investor provided detailed specifications and engineering help to the latter. For Company B, which was the subsidiary of a European consumer electronics manufacturer, four of the eight largest suppliers were foreign-owned, and four were indigenous. For the latter, the European purchaser provided assistance in quality-control procedures and helped automate their production lines. In both cases, the local firms became sellers to unaffiliated buyers. For Company B, the foreign affiliate introduced the Singapore producers to regional sister plants, following which the Singapore companies began to sell in international markets more generally.

In Malaysia, Rajah Rasiah's study of international telecommunications and semiconductor investors, which included two months of factory-floor residency, followed the foreigners as they assigned technicians to suppliers' plants to help set up and oversee large-volume production and testing procedures.[42] In some instances, the multinational firms sent engineers to participate in joint design with supplier personnel of subassemblies and components. Over time, the contract manufacturing phenomenon became *more intimate than mere shopping around for cheap inputs*. Of particular note is Rasiah's account of the development of a vertical supplier group in a separate industrial sector, machine tools.[43] The founders of seven of the nine leading Malaysian machine tool firms started as workers in the semiconductor and telecommunications MNCs then struck out on their own. Ten percent of the workforce in these seven companies was also drawn from the MNCs. Initially, the foreigners supplied molds and dies to their former employees for products that required simple machining and stamping. As in the case of components for telecommunications and semiconductor assembly, over time, engineers from both sides worked together to design specialized machine tool equipment for the mounting of semiconductor wafers. Duplicating what Lim and Fong discovered in Singapore, the foreigner investors opened a channel for the machine tool suppliers to export to affiliated buyers abroad. All seven machine tool firms began to sell to unrelated parties, moving from the status of "captive producer" for the multinational corporation to that of independent player in the marketplace.

41. Lim and Fong (1982).
42. Rasiah (1995).
43. Rasiah (1994).

In the automotive sector, the indigenous auto part industry in Mexico ramped up production quite rapidly after the automotive multinationals shifted from import substitution to using Mexican sites as export platforms. Wilson Peres Nuñez estimated that more than 115 local component firms surpassed the $1 million mark in sales within five years after the foreigners began to build world-scale plants.[44] Indigenous Mexican firms constituted more than half of the thirty largest auto part exporters (excluding engines). U.S., Japanese, and European investors provided production audits and zero-defect procedures to help improve quality control among the suppliers. Once those suppliers qualified as OEMs or REMs, they were certified for sales throughout the industry. Archanun Kohpaiboon reported that, to reduce unit costs and lower defect rates in Thailand, foreign auto companies assigned technicians who "ate and slept with local workers" in the factories of their local suppliers.[45] By 2003, according to the Thai Automotive Industry Association, the fourteen largest U.S., Japanese, and European automotive multinationals had certified 709 host country firms for OEM status (287 foreign owned, 68 joint ventures, and 354 Thai owned), followed by 1,100 second- and third-tier suppliers.[46]

Contemporary business surveys provide details about deliberate coaching for suppliers across many industry sectors as part of the effort of foreign investors to acquire inputs in the host economy. The survey data of Javorcik and Spatareanu showed that 90 percent of 119 majority-owned multinational investors in the Czech Republic acquired inputs from at least one Czech supplier.[47] The median affiliate acquired inputs from ten local firms; an affiliate in the top quartile acquired inputs from at least thirty Czech firms. One-tenth of those surveyed acquired all of their intermediate inputs from local suppliers. This evidence provides a reminder, however, that great care must be taken to identify with rigor what constitutes genuine externalities.

In the view of Javorcik and Spatareanu, the vertical relationships between foreign affiliates and indigenous suppliers took three distinctive forms. First, the multinationals may simply identify the cheapest and most reliable host country suppliers and purchase growing amounts of inputs from them—that is, the foreigners are cherry picking from among Czech firms that are already fully equipped to produce goods and services needed by the foreigners. Second, the multinationals may provide explicit assistance to potential suppliers to help improve their performance so that it meets acceptable standards of cost and reliability. Third, the multinationals may announce certain criteria that poten-

44. Nuñez (1990, chapter 6).
45. Kohpaiboon (2005).
46. Kohpaiboon (2005).
47. Javorcik and Spatareanu (2005).

tial suppliers must meet that act as a stimulus for local firms to upgrade their activities on their own. A common example of this latter phenomenon was the decision of Czech firms to obtain ISO 9000 (quality-control) certification, once foreigners stipulated this as a precondition for qualifying to bid on procurement contracts.

Statistical analysis alone would show a positive correlation between the presence of foreign investors and higher-than-average productivity among local suppliers for all three types of relationships. But the first scenario—the cherry picking scenario in which firms supplying multinationals have higher productivity than others—would not merit the externality label, whereas the second, in which the foreigner provides explicit assistance to the supplier, would qualify if the benefits are not all exclusively captured by the purchaser. One-fifth of the 119 multinationals reported that they did provide some kind of clearly defined assistance. Most frequently this assistance took the form of financing and advance payment; next was the training of employees, followed by quality-control help. Other forms of assistance included lending and leasing of equipment, production technology and organization of production lines, aid with financial planning and management strategy, and initiation to exporting. More tricky to label is the third relationship (which Javorcik and Spatareanu called a "positive productivity shock") in which the foreign presence provides the incentive for the local firms to acquire ISO 9000 certification. Forty percent of the Czech firms that underwent the arduous ISO qualification process reported that their motivation was to gain access to the advance payments, production help, and external marketing assistance that came with being a supplier to multinational corporations. Javorcik and Spatareanu left unresolved the question of whether local firms motivated by multinationals to upgrade their capabilities might be considered a genuine externality.

The buildup of indigenous supplier networks depends upon important preconditions. The extent of backward linkages, spillovers, and possible externalities differs according to the duration of the foreign investor residence in the host country, the sophistication of the local business community, and the business climate within which indigenous firms operate. The early data from Singapore and Malaysia show much lower levels of local procurement than do data from later years. René Belderbos, Giovanni Capannelli, and Kyoji Fukao found that the proportion of local content (from both foreign-owned and indigenous suppliers) was directly related to the length of the Japanese multinationals' operating experience in any given Asian host economy.[48] In their estimation, one additional year of local operating experience increases the local content

48. Belderbos, Capannelli, and Fukao (2000).

ratio by 0.6 percentage point. Ari Kokko showed that spillovers between foreign affiliates and local firms in Mexico differed depending upon the productivity difference between the two: when the local firms had much lower productivity, there were few signs of spillovers. Ari Kokko, Ruben Tansini, and Mario Zejan found the same difference among Uruguayan manufacturing investors. Nonetheless, even in relatively poorer developing countries, there is evidence that some managers and workers do move from foreign affiliates to set up parallel operations in low-skill operations like garment and toy manufacturing, as demonstrated by the Mauritius case cited above. Mauritius was not alone: within two decades of export-led growth, the proportion of EPZ firms in the Dominican Republic that were locally owned had grown to 20 percent. Local procurement, however, appears to depend directly upon the business conditions surrounding the domestic business community. International firms in Mauritius engage in more subcontracting with indigenous firms, for example, than what takes place in other African countries, such as in Madagascar, Senegal, or Tanzania. In addition, Mauritian firms also engage in more subcontracting with each other than is common in these other countries as well. Manju Kedia Shah suggests that both outcomes quite likely may be explained by the fact that business-operating conditions for all firms in Mauritius benefit from a higher rating than what is in other countries, including favorable tax rates and tax administration, superior access to finance, lower economic and regulatory policy uncertainty, better customs and trade regulations, and more reliable electricity and telecommunications.[49]

Weaknesses in Early Statistical Studies

Why did the first generation of econometric studies fail to show that FDI generated externalities for the host economy? The reason lies in the discovery that FDI in manufacturing and assembly comes in two distinct forms, both of which have far different impacts on the host economy:

—First are the plants that are fully controlled by the parent and oriented toward export markets.

—Second are those plants that are oriented toward protected domestic markets and required to meet domestic content requirements and operate with majority ownership on the part of host nationals.

This discovery helps explain why the first generation of econometric studies showed such jumbled results.

---

49. Shah (2006, p. 2, figure 1); Shah and others (2005, p. 29, table 3-2).

In the oft-cited study of manufacturing FDI in Venezuela, Brian Aitken and Ann Harrison asked whether foreign equity participation raised the productivity of the recipient plants and found a robust positive correlation only for small enterprises.[50] Searching for productivity spillovers from foreign investors to domestically owned plants in the same industry (that is, in the horizontal direction only), they found a negative correlation. They concluded that the impact of manufacturing FDI in Venezuela was neither clearly positive nor clearly negative and surmised that the net effect was quite small. This study is frequently cited to cast doubt on the benefits from foreign direct investment and to refute the contention that the presence of foreign firms generates externalities for a host economy. But the data on industrial plants come from a period (1976 through 1989) when Venezuela followed a dedicated import substitution strategy and the Venezuelan Superintendencia de Inversiones Extranjeras imposed a heavy layer of controls of foreign firms.[51] Business International reported that the country's policy toward foreign ownership during this era involved "strict joint venture requirements/only foreign minority position tolerated and this on a limited basis"; host country policy toward domestic content included "general requirements for specified percentage of local content/strictly enforced requirements for fully utilizing local components and materials."[52] Foreign firms faced restrictions on repatriation of profits and were obliged to exchange bolivares at the official rate rather than at the free market rate. In addition, they were forbidden from exercising confidentiality and exclusive-use-of-trade-secrets in their mandatory joint ventures. Only with discretionary authorization from the Superintendencia could foreigners undertake majority-owned FDI, but how frequently majority-owned operations might be reflected in the industrial plant database is impossible to ascertain. In short, the trade-and-investment regime in Venezuela during the period of this study replicated rather faithfully those anticompetitive conditions under which several studies found foreign direct investment subtracting from host country welfare, when all inputs and outputs were valued at world market prices.[53] Indeed, the most interesting discovery is that Aitken and Harrison uncovered any favorable impact whatsoever.

On the basis of these cost-benefit studies of FDI projects in such a highly distorted setting, one would be justified in supposing that Venezuela was quite probably experiencing a large dose of negative as well as (perhaps) some pos-

50. Aitken and Harrison, (1999).
51. Balasubramanyam, Salisu, and Sapsford (1996, appendix); Wheeler and Mody (1992, tables A-1 and A-2.)
52. Wheeler and Mody (1992, p. 76).
53. Lall and Streetan (1977); Reuber and others (1973); Encarnation and Wells (1986); Wasow (2003).

itive contributions to the host economy. But this is impossible to know because of the way the investigation is designed. What would be needed would be to separate out export-oriented FDI (if any) from import-substitution FDI, to separate out foreign investors free to source from wherever they wish (if any) from foreign investors operating with domestic content requirements, and to separate out foreign investors obliged to operate as minority shareholders from foreign investors with whole or majority ownership.

Data from FDI in Morocco might appear to offer a clearer picture of the relationship between foreign investment and development. Between 1983 and 1985, Moroccan regulations governing FDI allowed foreign manufacturing firms for the first time to take an ownership position of more than 49 percent and eased trade restrictions. Mona Haddad and Ann Harrison proposed that data from 1985 through 1989 would show the impact of FDI under conditions of trade and investment liberalization.[54] They found that there was no significant relationship between higher productivity growth in domestic firms and greater foreign presence in the sector, suggesting that foreign investment did not bring positive spillovers to the host economy. Firms with whole or majority foreign ownership demonstrated higher levels of total factor productivity than did their domestic counterparts, but the rate of growth of productivity was higher for the latter.[55] Controlling for firm size, they found that foreign investors did not exhibit higher levels of labor productivity. They concluded that the evidence did not show foreign investors making a large and dynamic contribution to the development of the Moroccan economy, which was similar to the results in the Venezuelan case. When they varied measures of relative trade protection, technology spillovers from foreign investors to domestic firms remained insignificant and generally negative.[56] Morocco's trade reform during this period, however, was limited to phasing out quantitative restrictions while leaving in place a complicated tariff system with nominal rates ranging from 17 to 44 percent by sector and effective rates rising for each stage of processing. Other researchers continued to place Morocco in the import-substitution category during this period.[57] Indeed, Haddad and Harrison attributed the higher rate of total

54. Haddad and Harrison (1993).

55. The data from Morocco showed a positive and statistically significant relationship between the extent of foreign ownership of a firm's assets and firm-level productivity: each increase by one standard deviation in the extent of foreign ownership of a given firm brought that firm 4 percent closer to best practices in the industry. This test of the Moroccan data comes from a later analysis by Harrison (1996). In the original article on Morocco, Haddad and Harrison had suggested that firms with majority foreign ownership behaved generally in the same way as did firms with minority foreign ownership.

56. Once again, Haddad and Harrison tested only for horizontal spillovers not vertical spillovers.

57. Balasubramanyam, Salisu, and Sapsford (1996).

factor productivity growth for indigenous firms to their superior ability to cope with the continuing distortions in the protected local market.

As for foreign direct investment, the data do not show how much new FDI might have flowed into Morocco in the four-year period 1985 to 1989 as a response to the new-found freedom to gain majority ownership, but the aggregate changes in the share of foreign ownership by sector were small: five percentage points in leather; four percentage points in scientific instruments; three in machinery, textiles, and apparel. Only in a nonmanufacturing category (mining of phosphates) was there a more substantial FDI inflow, with the foreign share rising by seven percentage points. Most of the FDI stock in manufacturing was left over from the previous period during which strict FDI regulations oriented production toward the protected domestic market. Genuine liberalization of the Moroccan economy did not occur until the mid-1990s, following which FDI exports of electronics and other manufactured goods rose from U.S.\$4 million to some \$633 million, with overall EPZ exports approaching \$3 billion by 2006.[58] It would be enlightening to undertake a reevaluation of the impact of FDI on Morocco in the contemporary period, following procedures as outlined next, which avoid mixing the distinctively different forms of inward- and outward-oriented FDI.

Improving Current Econometric Methodology: Horizontal Externalities

How can contemporary econometric investigations be strengthened to provide a more accurate assessment of whether manufacturing FDI generates externalities in the host economy? How can such research be designed to identify those channels through which externalities are created when they occur? Looking first at the impact of FDI in the horizontal direction on the performance of indigenous firms, the standard econometric methodology has been to examine the relationship between the presence of foreign firms and the total factor productivity of indigenous firms in the same sector.[59] Perhaps the foreign firms demonstrate superior technologies or management techniques that the local firms can then imitate; or they generate competitive pressures that push local firms to upgrade their practices; or they train managers, workers, and engineers who move from foreign-owned to locally owned plants. But a positive correlation alone cannot be taken as proof that FDI is responsible for raising the performance of local firms—it could be that the foreign firms are simply settling in sectors where standards of productivity are already high. So, the next step might be to trace how the total factor productivity of local firms

58. Economist Intelligence Unit (2007).
59. Hanson (2005).

changes when levels of FDI in the sector increase. Once again, however, a positive correlation between the two might arise because there is some external reason that causes more foreign investment to enter into the sector and total factor productivity of local firms to rise, such as changes in host country tax legislation or contract enforcement. These business-friendly reforms might simultaneously act as an inducement to foreign investment while also allowing domestic firms to operate more efficiently. To infer that the arrival of foreign investors causes domestic firm productivity to rise would be mistaken. Furthermore, as Beata Smarzynska Javorcik and Mariana Spatareanu pointed out, the arrival of foreign firms is likely to produce two contradictory impacts simultaneously in the horizontal direction—the rise in the performance of indigenous firms through the demonstration of technology and management techniques by foreign-owned firms and through the spread of foreign-trained workers, managers, and engineers, and, at the same time, damage to the performance of indigenous firms through the shrinking of their market share and the draining off of their workers, managers, and engineers.[60]

Econometric studies that merely try to establish a horizontal correlation between changes in total factor productivity of indigenous firms and rising numbers of foreign investors in the same industry, Javorcik and Spatareanu argued, are not going to be able to disentangle these two contrary impacts. To measure spillovers and externalities in the horizontal direction, researchers using econometric techniques will have to figure out how to control for the level of competition as well as for the movement of personnel, technology, and management practices between foreign investors and indigenous firms. This constitutes a major challenge for future research on horizontal externalities. Research on developing countries can benefit from such efforts to separate true spillovers from competitive effects using developed country FDI data.[61]

Improving Current Econometric Methodology: Vertical Externalities

Shifting from the horizontal to the vertical, the use of econometric techniques to investigate when foreign investors create externalities in their relations with local suppliers is fraught with similar difficulties. As discussed above, a positive correlation between a foreign investor presence and higher total factor productivity in upstream or downstream local firms might occur because the foreigners were attracted to regions or sectors in which indigenous investors

---

60. Javorcik and Spatareanu (2005).
61. Haskel, Pereira, and Slaughter (2002); Keller and Yeaple (2007). Wolfgang Keller and Stephen Yeaple use data on the mark-up rate among firms, for example, to control for change-in-degree-of-competition effects.

would be able to operate more efficiently. Or the positive correlation might be due to other factors that attract foreign firms and also increase the efficiency with which domestic companies can operate, so that inferring a causal connection would be unjustified.

The challenges of introducing controls that enable the researcher to separate out the foreign investor impact on indigenous firms are not insurmountable, however, as the work of Garrick Blalock and Paul Gertler reveals.[62] They used data on manufacturing establishments in Indonesia collected by region since 1988, of which about 70 percent have export-oriented operations. First, to deal with the possibility that multinationals might make their investments in locations that are near to the most efficient suppliers but might not make those suppliers any more efficient after entering, Blalock and Gertler included establishment fixed effects in the production function. This controls for unobserved firm-specific productivity factors such as managerial capabilities and local characteristics. As a result, only changes related to suppliers' average productivity enter the estimation. Multinationals may very well locate their plants where suppliers are most efficient, but the technique employed by Blalock and Gertler investigates whether the performance of suppliers gets even better after the foreign firms enter. Second, to deal with the possibility that multinationals might make their investments in locations that are near suppliers whose productivity is growing or expected to grow, they included industry-year fixed effects in the production function. This controls for changes over time in factors common to all firms in the same industry such as regulation and terms of trade. It also allows them to look at the overall growth of productivity in a particular sector over a given year and then to compare the growth in productivity in that particular sector in a region that had a large inflow of FDI with that in another region in which the inflow of FDI was noticeably less. Third, to deal with the possibility that multinationals might make their investments in regions where area conditions themselves are allowing suppliers' productivity to grow, they included region-year fixed effects in the production function (they call these "island-year" fixed effects, as in the island of Java versus the island of Sumatra). This controls for changes in location-specific factors that are common to all firms in the same region and that might affect firm productivity, such as local regulation, infrastructure, and labor markets. They thereby isolated the overall productivity of the particular region (for example, Java), which enabled them to compare suppliers to a sector in that region in which FDI is growing with suppliers to a sector in which FDI is stagnant during a particular time period.

---

62. Blalock and Gertler (forthcoming). Similar research sophistication and similar results are found in Javorcik (2004).

Marching through these three steps, Blalock and Gertler found that the productivity of Indonesian supplier firms increased when the share of output purchased by foreign investors rose. What these three steps of investigation cannot rule out, however, is that foreign investors expected that the productivity of some specific suppliers in a particular sector in a particular region would grow over time—that is, the foreign firms chose to locate their operations in a particular place because they anticipated that suppliers there would undergo some idiosyncratic positive transformation that was not part of industrywide or regionwide changes promoting greater productivity growth. To address this potential concern, they employed a simultaneity correction for the estimation of production functions that used capital investment or energy consumption as a proxy for idiosyncratic shocks.[63] They found that the effect of downstream FDI was statistically identical to that measured without the simultaneity correction. These steps give increasingly solid confidence that the higher productivity of local suppliers that they observed originates from the presence of FDI and not from some other unobserved factor. Their calculation of the chain of welfare effects was that rising numbers of foreign investors led to improvement in the performance of local suppliers, resulting in lower prices, increased output, higher profitability, and increased entry at the supplier level. The lower prices in the supplier market, in turn, resulted in lower prices, increased output, higher profitability, and increased competition throughout the Indonesian host economy, benefiting other final goods producers as well as consumers.

But regression analysts must always wonder whether correlation (even overlapping layers of correlation) demonstrates causation. Do foreign investors actually bring about higher levels of indigenous productivity, and if so, how and why? Here, Blalock and Gertler took the logical additional investigative step, which is unusual for econometricians, and interviewed the foreign investors and Indonesian suppliers about their relationships with each other.[64] Both sides affirmed that concrete transfer of technology and management did take place in the vertical direction and identified the mechanisms through which this transfer occurred. An American MNC described a step-by-step program to find and qualify indigenous suppliers. Affiliate engineers would first visit the target factories to survey their operations and suggest modification. Next, the MNC would send sample output from a selected domestic factory for appraisal at home in the United States. If the product passed inspection, the American investor would send managers from the would-be local supplier to overseas training classes to learn the parent's systems for inventory control, quality con-

63. Olley and Pakes (1996).
64. Blalock and Gertler (2005).

trol, and cost accounting. This would be followed by small-scale orders from the MNC, building to regular purchases in large quantities as the supplier established a record of delivering on time and within specification. The managers of an affiliate from a Japanese MNC reported a similar certification process, adding that their usual procedure was to introduce qualified suppliers to sister affiliates of their industrial group within Indonesia and abroad.[65] Since other members of the Japanese MNC corporate network did the same, the Japanese managers in Indonesia became acquainted with Malaysian and Thai suppliers from whom they procured inputs for Indonesian operations. This strategy reduced search costs for the network and enabled suppliers to achieve economies of scale. Many candidates, the Japanese managers noted, did not survive the certification ordeal. From the perspective of Indonesian suppliers, Indonesian firms identified visits from engineers, efficiency specialists, and product design experts as channels for assistance. Not all MNCs provided usable advice, however, and one Indonesian firm broke off a relationship with an American buyer who demanded cost reductions but offered no technical support for achieving them.

These interviews provide a real-life picture of the diffusion of technology and management techniques between foreigners and local firms that is reflected in the econometric analysis and support the supposition that there is a link between the presence of foreign investors and the improvement in supplier productivity. But the number of observations was very small, and the collection methods do not pretend to offer a representative sample of foreign and local firms. A well-structured randomized survey would yield better, more valuable results, accompanied by details about the characteristics of the respondents that would allow other tests to determine when diffusion was more or less likely and larger or smaller. The combination of econometric analysis and sophisticated survey techniques offers great promise for future research, an observation given added resonance from looking at export externalities.

Improving Current Econometric Methodology: Export Externalities

The study by Brian Aitken, Gordon Hanson, and Ann Harrison provides a particularly valuable example in which multiple investigative techniques lead to greater value added. Using panel data on 2,104 Mexican manufacturing plants from the period 1986 to 1990, which followed the country's liberalization of trade and investment in 1985, they investigated whether there were spillovers from multinational corporations to domestic firms that led the latter to export.[66] Their task was particularly challenging since the more intuitive

65. Lim and Fong (1982); Rasiah (1994, 1995).
66. Aitken, Hanson, and Harrison (1997).

hypothesis is that firms are especially likely to export from wherever the overall concentration of export activity is larger—because the accumulation of exporters may allow construction of specialized transportation infrastructure, perhaps, or because access to information about the tastes of foreign purchasers may be more widespread, or because there may be some other local comparative advantage that benefits all exporters. For each location, therefore, they independently measured the overall concentration of economic activity, the concentration of export activity in general, and the concentration of MNC export activity. By controlling for the overall concentration of activity in a region, they eliminated the impact of unobserved fixed factors that might affect the export behavior of all firms. By treating local export activity and local MNC activity as endogenous variables, moreover, they controlled for the existence of region-industry-specific shocks that might make all of the firms in a particular region and industry more likely to export. In the end, after taking into account other factors that affect the decision to export (as might be the case for Mexican states with port facilities, or Mexican states located near the U.S. border, or Mexican states located near the capital city), they found that the probability of doing "more-than-expected" exporting is positively correlated with the local concentration of MNC activity but uncorrelated with the local concentration of overall export activity.

Despite this careful, powerful demonstration that the presence of MNCs leads to exports on the part of local firms, the demonstration-processes, learning-procedures, or other mechanisms—the concrete spillovers they feature in the title of their article—by which the foreign investors engender higher levels of exports remain totally opaque.

—Is the stimulus to local exporters direct or indirect? Do the MNCs themselves provide coaching in external marketing, an introduction to specific foreign buyers, or information about overseas demand? Or, alternatively, does MNC behavior simply demonstrate (without coaching) the processes through which penetration of foreign markets can be achieved, processes that can be copied and imitated by local companies?

—Is the transfer of export-related skills and knowledge horizontal or vertical? What is the relative likelihood of Mexican seafood-packing exporters growing up alongside U.S. and Japanese seafood-packing exporters (horizontal spillovers) in comparison with Mexican auto parts companies transforming themselves from suppliers to U.S. and Japanese auto plants in Mexico into OEM exporters to the international automotive industry (vertical spillovers)?

—Do the FDI-stimulated local exporters experience larger returns to scale, acquire new learning-by-doing skills, or gain reputational effects as they enter international markets, or not?[67]

Industry studies, business cases, management interviews, and firm surveys could provide answers at the same time as they boost confidence about the inference of causation. For researchers to move in this direction, the leading economics journals would have to begin to accept—indeed reward—research that combines multiple kinds of investigation.

Improving Current Econometric Methodology:
Labor Market Externalities

The investigation of possible labor market externalities similarly demonstrates that the introduction of ever greater statistical controls (that is, ever more narrow constrictions) on large plant-level datasets is valuable and often indispensable but with diminishing returns in comparison with what the simultaneous use of other investigative techniques might impart. How do wages paid by foreign investors to workers compare with wages paid by local firms? What accounts for the differences? Are there spillovers from labor payment practices of MNCs to labor payment practices of indigenous firms? Survey data collected by the International Labor Organization regularly show that wages paid by foreign firms are higher than those provided by domestic companies. Responses to World Bank questionnaires suggest that international companies offer permanent contracts (at higher rates than those received by temporary hires) to a larger share of their workers than do local firms. But, as in the case of productivity comparisons, the higher compensation paid by foreigners might arise solely because multinationals are located in higher-wage sectors, because they are attracted to higher-wage regions of the host country, or because the foreign-owned plants are larger or newer than the average plant.

To investigate the determinants of payments to labor, Robert Lipsey and Fredrik Sjöholm availed themselves of the same detailed information from the Indonesia Central Statistical Office as did Blalock and Gertler.[68] Drawing on

67. In addition to Lim and Fong (1982), Rasiah (1994, 1995) and Hobday (1995, 2000), Blalock and Gertler (2004) found strong evidence that firms experience an increase in productivity of 2 to 5 percent following the initiation of exporting. The timing of the increase points to learning from exporting rather than self-selection of higher performing firms into export markets. In interviews, the foreign investors indicated that they help their suppliers export precisely because exporting keeps the suppliers current with best practice and also because exporting expands and smoothes suppliers' demand so they can justify investment in the latest capital equipment. For the contrary view, see Clerides, Lach, and Tybout (1998); Bernard and Jensen (1999); Delgado, Fariñas, and Ruano (2002).

68. Lipsey and Sjöholm (2004a, 2004b).

18,652 plant observations from 1996, they found that foreigners paid 33 percent more for blue-collar workers and 70 percent more for white-collar workers than domestic companies did. The information for each of the plant observations included industry details, type of ownership, value added, energy consumption, and geographical location, as well as separate labor characteristics for white-collar and blue-collar employees, by number of employees of each, gender, distribution by level of education, and wages.

First, introducing controls for region and industry sectors, the premium paid by foreign-owned firms remained at 25 percent for blue-collar workers and 50 percent for white-collar workers. Next, adding controls for plant size, energy inputs per worker, other inputs per worker, and the proportion of workers that was female, the wage premium of the foreign firm remained at 12 percent for blue-collar and 22 percent for white-collar workers. Their analysis thus suggested that approximately one-third of the premium paid by foreigners was explained by region and sector and one-third by plant size and use of other inputs. But their data indicated that multinational investors were paying wages to their blue-collar and white-collar workforce above and beyond what might be due to superior productivity arising from greater scale of production and more inputs per worker, and the origin of this final one-third of the wage premium was unaccounted for.

Turning to labor market spillovers, their analysis of the data showed that the higher wages paid by foreign firms did lead to payment of higher wages in domestically owned plants. Holding labor force quality constant, they found a positive spillover within broad industry groups at the national level and a smaller, but still positive and significant, spillover within narrower industry groups and at the province level. These results introduce a puzzle quite at variance with popular discourse: rather than engaging in "exploitation" of workers, why do foreign investors pay more than they "have to" in developing country markets, and what are the dynamics that make this wage premium turn up among local firms as well? Labor market literature introduces a complicating reverse-causality hypothesis that higher MNC wages might derive from team-spirit, pride, or enhanced dedication, in which higher pay generates higher productivity instead of the opposite. Could this be the explanation?

Further investigation of this puzzle would be especially helpful, given the common allegation that multinational firms use their power to drive down worker wages and generate a race to the bottom among all firms in the host economy. A well-structured survey of the determinants of human resource practices within foreign affiliates and their host country counterparts could be a particularly valuable complement to the econometric analysis. The initiative to use survey data as a complement to econometric investigation would probably have to originate among senior scholars since such an approach would be too risky for pretenure academics to do.

How to Assess the Need for Public Sector Support—including Subsidies and Incentives—to Attract FDI

A key question faced by every developing country is whether host authorities should expend public funds to attract manufacturing FDI, by offering special support, providing subsidies, bestowing incentives. Economists are rightly skeptical about the desirability of showering multinational corporations with tax breaks and other subsidies. But standard economist reasoning follows an unimaginative script—not inaccurate, but unimaginative—that short-circuits any analysis of where the real problems lie and what practical policy responses might be available. The decision tree is simple: does FDI generate externalities? If not, do not subsidize FDI. If so, subsidize FDI up to the social value of the externalities. As shown next, what is needed is more thorough investigation of what are the obstacles—including market failures—that impede flows of FDI that are potentially laden with externalities and the most appropriate methods to overcome those obstacles.

Once again, it is useful to begin—Albert Hirschman–like—by looking closely at a complicated real-life case study to investigate what generalizable insights of use might emerge to analysts and policymakers alike. The most thoroughly researched case study of the challenges of attracting manufacturing FDI—and of the role of public expenditures as part of the host country investment promotion strategy—is the effort of Costa Rica to persuade Intel to build a semiconductor plant in Belen County, Heredia.[69] This case from 1996 is held up as a model by the Foreign Investment Advisory Service (FIAS) of the World Bank and is used as a training tool by other multilateral agencies.[70] Close examination of this experience offers insights both more subtle and more useful for general-purpose design of investment promotion policies, however, than conventional treatment indicates.

Before approaching potential semiconductor investors, Costa Rica had undertaken micro- and macroeconomic reforms in the 1980s that offered investors low inflation, a realistic exchange rate, sensible fiscal policy, and a reasonable business environment. Unusual in Central America, the country had a long his-

69. Spar (1998).
70. Multilateral Investment Guarantee Agency (2006).

tory of political stability, with well-respected legal and regulatory institutions. Drawing on these favorable traits, Costa Rica had managed to attract FDI in the garment and footwear sectors. As domestic wage rates rose, Costa Rican authorities feared competition from cheaper production sites and turned their attention to trying to diversify the FDI base with more sophisticated manufacturing operations. With backing from the U.S. Agency for International Development, the government reorganized its investment promotion agency CINDE (la Coalición Costarricense de Iniciativas de Desarrollo) in 1992 and staffed it with well-trained and well-compensated professionals who were able to decipher the concerns of the semiconductor, biotech, and other advanced sectors as well as prepare customized investment feasibility studies. CINDE identified Intel, which was looking for a site to build a new semiconductor plant, as the country's preeminent target. But when CINDE approached Intel with carefully crafted proposals, the agency discovered that Costa Rica was not even on Intel's long list of possible sites, let alone the short list (which included Indonesia, Thailand, Brazil, Chile, and Mexico). It took two years of what Debra Spar characterized as "assiduous" campaigning to obtain the first invitation to visit Intel headquarters.[71] CINDE persisted and with a high-intensity effort—the republic's president was asked to order ministries to make special expenditures from their budgets to support Intel's proposed operations—secured the largest foreign investment ($300 million) in the history of Central America. The final item that Costa Rica agreed to, to get Intel's signature on the investment contract, was the provision of twelve years of tax holidays for the multinational's operations.

The conventional lesson that this case is used to illustrate is that markets do not supply relevant and timely information on their own, that multinational searches are costly and incomplete, and that would-be hosts have to take active steps (the term of art is proactive steps) to "market the country." FIAS uses this case study to urge host countries to keep the websites of investment promotion agencies up to date, with current economic and legislative materials and real-time contacts to key ministries, agencies, and presidential assistants. While this is sensible advice, the Intel case study provides more profound insight into the challenges facing would-be host governments. What kind of information is most crucial to help a multinational investor decide to commit massive resources to a plant in a new locale that will play a central role in the company's global strategy (in the case of Intel, 22 to 25 percent of its output)? And when can high-level host leaders, including perhaps the president, weigh in and deploy

71. Spar (1998).

their clout in allocating domestic resources most effectively? Is providing tax breaks and subsidies to the new investor the answer?

The Intel case shows that improving the functioning of information markets on even the most rudimentary level—to position the country on Intel's horizon— is not easy and requires prior expenditure of public funds for a well-staffed investment promotion agency. But a closer look at the details reveals, as common sense would suggest, that the doubts and hesitations that a multinational investor faces when considering a new investment derive from more than a paucity of general information, such as economic statistics, relative wage information, or legislative texts. The doubts and hesitations derive from paucity of information of a particular kind: a multinational investor like Intel (especially the first investor in a given sector) cannot know for sure whether this might be a profitable investment site—indeed, cannot even reduce most of the uncertainty involved in site selection—without "test driving" it. The challenge for the would-be host is to overcome the anxieties of a risk-averse investor who, having to make an irreversible commitment to a plant upon which headquarters will depend for the success of its international competitive position, will not know until the company tries out the proposed facility whether the MNC will—in George Akerloff's famous phrase—be "stuck with a lemon"?[72]

When uncertainty about quality hinders market functioning, as Akerloff points out, outcomes can be improved when the seller takes measures to reassure the buyer about the reliability of his purchase. This is most straightforward when there is asymmetric information (the used car dealer knows which used cars are okay and which are not), and the reassurance can take the form of some guarantee (such as a warranty or a promise to fix or replace). For a host country like Costa Rica trying to attract an investor like Intel, however, the obstacle to market functioning is not information asymmetry, strictly speaking, since the host government itself does not know for sure that the local economy will be a suitable site for semiconductor assembly. The best the host can do is to try to reassure the party considering a new plant in a novel sector by taking steps to reduce the most significant sources of risk and uncertainty. Intel executives told CINDE that their principal concerns were obstacles that might reduce the corporation's lead time over rivals.[73] The first obstacle was the possibility of power shortages or electrical failures. The second obstacle was potential bottlenecks in service at the national airport. The third obstacle was possible shortages of workers trained appropriately for the new semiconductor plant.

---

72. Akerloff (1970). For investments as irreversible commitments, see Dixit and Pindyck (1994).

73. Spar (1998).

Here is where CINDE deployed presidential power to direct the state utility to dedicate a new substation in the electrical grid to supply the Intel plant, to instruct the Ministry of Transportation to speed construction of a new air cargo terminal for Intel's use, and to create a special cooperative program between Intel's manpower experts, the national vocational training institutes, and the Ministry of Education. The provision of tax breaks was more pro forma. Once Costa Rica addressed the multinational's principal concerns, Intel negotiators notified CINDE that their country had gained a place on the company's short list. All other finalists, the Intel negotiators then pointed out, had agreed to a tax holiday for the first eight years of operation and a 50 percent exemption for the next four. Costa Rica assented to the same conditions without fanfare.

The structure of Costa Rica's negotiations with Intel is not unusual.[74] Multinational investors frequently demand public expenditures to reduce the most questionable aspects of project feasibility—measures to ensure the reliability of infrastructure and the availability of skilled manpower are often high on the list. Rather than advising against public sector intervention in the abstract, FIAS and other multilateral agencies typically urge that the host try to provide support in a form that benefits investors in the economy more generally, not just the MNC in question. In the Intel case, CINDE argued that air cargo and electrical capacity were fungible, that the new facilities would not subtract from what was available to other firms, and that the services were being offered to Intel at commercial rates (a subject of some domestic debate). With regard to manpower training, the Ministry of Education managed to ensure that the new cooperative training program would turn out workers with skills that could be used throughout the information technology and electronics sector. As for the tax breaks, other business cases reveal that the standard MNC negotiating technique is to line up several approximately equivalent production sites for headquarters's scrutiny and then require the host authorities at the sites to bid against each other, with packages of locational subsidies acting—in the words of one veteran negotiator—as a tie breaker.[75]

74. Hausmann and Rodrik (2003). In an earlier work, I posed the hypothesis that the market failure in attracting FDI in a novel sector sprang from appropriability problems: the first mover takes all the risks but (if successful) does not enjoy a period of market exclusivity long enough to compensate for this exposure. This is the market failure that is proposed by Ricardo Hausmann and Dani Rodrik (2006). The Costa Rica case does not support this interpretation, however, because of the following: senior Intel executive testimony pointed to the parent's uncertainty about efficient, reliable production as the binding constraint, not fear of follow-the-leader behavior by others; other semiconductor investors did not rush into Costa Rica after the Intel plant proved successful. As noted infra, the Intel decision to invest did have a demonstration effect on other multinational investors but not on investors whose entry would reduce the profitability of Intel. For my earlier hypothesis, see Moran (1998).

75. Uyterhoeven (1992, 1993).

How is the expenditure of public funds to attract multinational investors related to confirmation that externalities will justify such expenditure? Here again the Intel case study throws a snag into standard economic reasoning, which is obvious as soon as it is pointed out. Once Intel built its plant, backward linkages and externalities began to appear. Two years after Intel's arrival, a survey of eighty indigenous Intel suppliers in 2000 (thirty-seven suppliers of services, forty-three of goods) indicated that 35 percent of the former and 17 percent of the latter received training from Intel.[76] The largest local suppliers concentrated on metalwork, plastic injecting molding, packaging, and engineering services. More important for upgrading the FDI base, Intel's choice of Costa Rica had a large demonstration effect on other multinationals. Within three years of the Intel investment, the country tripled its stock of FDI to $1.3 billion with an annual export level of more than $3 billion. Of sixty-one multinationals with operations in Costa Rica, 72 percent said that the Intel investment played an important "signaling role" in their own decision to invest (thirty-six in electronics, thirteen in medical devices, three in business services, and nine in other sectors).[77] The electronics sector became the largest export cluster in the country, with 55 companies (forty-two foreign, thirteen indigenous) employing some 12,000 workers with exports of $1.65 billion.[78] Management interviews indicated that success with clean rooms in the electronics industry attracted the interest of medical companies: for example, Baxter Healthcare preceded Intel; Abbot Laboratories (now Hospira) and Boston Scientific came afterward. The quality of the workforce played the same role with business services: Proctor & Gamble made Costa Rica the center for "shared services back office," followed by Western Union's technical support center and Sykes' call center for hire. Overall, by 2006, Costa Rican FDI exports of manufactured products and business services exceeded $5 billion.

More than access to capital, FDI provided access to the international industry frontier in increasingly sophisticated activities. Costa Rica became a model of "dynamic comparative advantage," in which a host economy whose leading industries initially were composed of coffee and bananas moved (because of FDI) to low-skilled, labor-intensive exports like garments and footwear then upgraded foreign investor operations to a broad spectrum of medium- to higher-skilled endeavors. The catch was that during the period when the decision was made to refurbish CINDE and launch the drive to attract Intel the prospect of spillovers and demonstration effects was largely wishful thinking, according

76. Larrain, López-Calva, and Rodríguez-Clare (2001).
77. Larrain, López-Calva, and Rodríguez-Clare (2001).
78. Multilateral Investment Guarantee Agency (2006).

to CINDE officials.[79] Only the likelihood of above-average wage rates for Intel employees appeared to be a sure thing (2,900 workers with a premium of approximately 50 percent more than other manufacturing jobs), and estimates of other positive benefits were purely hypothetical.

The idea that host authorities are going to know with much certainty when externalities will be delivered from FDI operations, or be able to calibrate how much to subsidize their provision, is farfetched. Perhaps the most reasonable fashion to deal with the quandary of not knowing what the payoff from incentives will be is to direct investment promotion efforts toward FDI sectors that common sense suggests might be relatively externality-laden—sectors that are higher skill intensive, are higher value added, promise more local research and development, or have demonstrated records of extensive local procurement in other developing countries, for example. Moreover, as suggested above, the host will be well advised to provide incentives in forms that are most likely to benefit investors more broadly than the specific MNC in question, such as upgrading worker skills and improving infrastructure reliability across-the-board.

Implications for Developed and Developing Country Policies

The implications of the preceding analysis are rather simple and straight-forward. The puzzle is why they are missing from the learned body of economic literature on foreign direct investment and development.[80] The inability to find one single "universal" relationship between manufacturing FDI and host country development represents not an investigative failure but an important discovery, crucial for both analytical and policy conclusions.

Manufacturing FDI is most likely to make a positive contribution to national income under reasonably competitive conditions. The willingness of a multinational firm to place an affiliate along the frontier of best practices in the industry, and keep it there with continuous improvements and updates, depends upon the ability of the parent to control that affiliate with minimal risk of technology leakage or external interference in operations. Manufacturing FDI in a distorted economic environment—in particular in a host economy using trade protection to substitute local production for imports and imposing domestic content, joint venture, or other technology-shifting requirements on multina-

79. Alonso (2001).

80. Or, worse, they are turned on their head into a complaint: "Policy making has come to ignore the ambiguous and inconclusive academic literature"; see Lipsey (2006).

tional investors—is likely to result in inefficient plants that subtract from national income. The Developing countries should note, therefore, that their interests are not served by weakening the Agreement on Trade-Related Investment Measures (TRIMS Agreement) within the World Trade Organization, which had banned the imposition of domestic content or trade-balance mandates on FDI, or by restoring the host country practice of levying performance requirements on manufacturing multinationals. For this reason, the allegedly prodevelopment agenda advanced at the Hong Kong Trade Ministerial in 2005, which afforded developing countries greater leeway to place domestic content requirements upon foreign investors and to maintain them until 2020, represents a dramatic step backward.[81] Developing countries would advance their own development agenda more effectively, in fact, if they tightened the TRIMS Agreement—to bring joint venture requirements under multilateral discipline— rather than loosening it.

Contrary to the prescription of Nancy Birdsall, Dani Rodrik, and Arvind Subramanian, regulation of manufacturing FDI—leaving aside the complicated issue of intellectual property rights—is not a sphere where developing countries need more policy space.[82] In the roster of areas in which host country policies toward multinational corporations (not just manufacturing multinationals) might be given more or less freedom to maneuver, imposition of performance requirements is a prime candidate for less, rather than more, policy space.[83] The analysis in the first section of this paper is particularly important for least developed countries. Contradicting the justification given for the attack on the TRIMS Agreement in Hong Kong, the counterproductive impact of performance requirements holds for poorer developing countries as well as for more advanced developing countries. There is no evidence that least developed economies gain from placing greater restraints on manufacturing investors or from undergoing longer, slower periods of transition for liberalization of trade and investment. To be sure, to help poorer countries take full advantage of trade-and-investment liberalization, the developed world may want to redou-

---

81. WTO (2005).

82. Birdsall, Rodrik, and Subramanian (2005).

83. The TRIMS Agreement is one of three areas in which developing countries would actually benefit from *less* policy space: to impose performance requirements on foreign investors; to participate in bribery, corrupt payments, and nontransparency; and, as indicated infra, to award tax breaks and locational incentives to attract foreign investors. In three other areas, they would benefit from *greater* policy space: to avoid multilateral trade sanctions to enforce labor standards; to establish health, safety, and environmental regulations without paying compensation to foreign investors; and to engage in international arbitration procedures that emphasize conciliation with investors during cross-border financial crises (rather than mere commercial contract enforcement). See Moran (forthcoming).

ble both the provision of aid for trade and the provision of aid for investment (including aid for investment promotion and aid for regulatory and institutional reforms). But the observation that the liberalization of trade and investment does not produce maximum benefits in a vacuum does not imply that least developed countries are served by placing greater restrictions on multinational investors than are middle-income developing countries.

Despite rich country rhetoric about wanting to assist the development of poor countries through encouragement of FDI, it is a scandal to find that eighteen of the nineteen official political risk insurance agencies within the OECD—including those in the United Kingdom, Canada, France, Germany, Japan, and the United States—provide coverage for multinational manufacturing projects that rely upon trade restraints to survive.[84] Worst of these is the U.S. Overseas Private Investment Corporation, which insures foreign investors against the threat that the host authorities may remove anticompetitive barriers that they have used to confer high profits upon the policy holder and pays the claim when the host reneges on its promise of on-going protection by liberalizing the economy.[85] Nor have the developed countries exercised their responsibility to require that the Multilateral Investment Guarantee Agency of the World Bank group—or the multilateral financial agencies like the Inter-American Development Bank, the Asian Development Bank, and the European Bank for Reconstruction and Development—screen out welfare-reducing import substitution projects from their FDI guarantee portfolios. As long as manufacturing FDI projects show a positive commercial rate of return they are eligible for official guarantees even if the broader economic impact on the host economy is negative.

Designing policies to best capture externalities is likely to remain vexing. From an analytic point of view, identifying and measuring externalities—in both horizontal and vertical directions—will always be difficult, although earlier sections of this paper show that great strides are already being taken, and new multidisciplinary breakthroughs are within grasp. From a host policy point of view, the unfortunate truth is that attracting foreign direct investment in the hope of securing externalities costs money. The evidence introduced above suggests that would-be hosts are unlikely to have the luxury of basing policy on the pristine principle: improve the overall business climate and MNCs will show up. Just to improve the functioning of information markets alone, the annual budget for CINDE is $11 million; for the Dominican Republic's investment promotion agency (IPA), $9 million; for the IPA in Mauritius, $3 million. The

84. Center for Global Development (2007).
85. O'Sullivan (2005). See Memorandum of Determinations by OPIC, "Expropriation Claim of Joseph Companies Incorporated of Minneapolis: Jamaica—Contract of Insurance No. E197," 1999 (www.investmentclaims.com/decisions/JosephCompanies-OPIC-Jamaica-Aug1999.pdf).

bigger ticket expenditures associated with meeting infrastructure and human resource needs of international firms require much more. The combination of marketing the country and securing specific commitments from MNCs to fill ready-made industrial parks and export zones with new plants, moreover, requires up-front outlays that must be expended well before the generation of externalities is anything more than a gleam in the eye of host authorities.

Complicating the task for would-be hosts is the fact that the allocation of public dollars to promote investment, in a world of scarce resources, requires targeting—more effort is needed to attract FDI in software development, less in garments; more is needed to attract FDI in frozen shrimp, less in bananas; more to attract FDI in call centers, less in tourism, or vice versa—and subjects the allocators to the political and economic challenges of picking winners and losers among sectors and even firms. Contemporary advice to host authorities exhibits a distinctly schizophrenic quality, switching back and forth abruptly from the interventionist urgings of Joseph Stiglitz, Ricardo Hausmann, and Dani Rodrik to the industrial policy skepticisms of Marcus Noland and Howard Pack.[86] As suggested above, host country authorities may have no more than common sense to guide them in trying to keep the allocation of public expenditures as free from political contamination as possible and aimed at sectors where spillovers appear most likely to emerge, without discrimination between foreign-owned and indigenous-owned recipients.[87]

With regard to tax breaks and direct subsidies, the predicament for developing countries springs from prisoner dilemma dynamics, not from the failure of host authorities to comprehend the misgivings of economists. The host that refuses to provide generous locational incentives is undermined by others who will. Complicating any solution is the unpleasant detection of growing competition between developed country and developing country plant sites. Conventional wisdom held that multinational corporations do not compare rich country and poor country locales in deciding where to set up operations. But contemporary research is showing otherwise: Mexico, Thailand, and Slovakia compete with Ireland, Canada, and North Carolina.[88] John Mutti has uncovered a particularly high elasticity for alternative sites for internationally traded goods—tax breaks that reduce the cost of capital by 1 percent raise MNC production in the manufacturing sector of the host by approximately 3 percent.

---

86. Noland and Pack (2003). Compare World Bank (2006); UNCTAD (2005).

87. The effort to attract FDI in new sectors must also be ready for surprises. As Hausmann and Rodrik (2006) pointed out, both salmon farming and fresh grape exports were unexpected successes that market forces in Chile alone might have overlooked.

88. Mutti (2003); Altshuler, Grubert, and Newlong (1998).

"Just Say No" is not a realistic approach for controlling giveaways to multinational corporations. What is needed (as previously indicated in the roster of areas where developing country policy space needs to be narrowed) is an international agreement to cap and roll back locational incentives. To be effective, alas, subnational as well as national authorities—from Alabama to Minas Gerais—will have to be brought under the new disciplines, an undertaking that will be formidable indeed.

Comments and Discussion

Laura Alfaro: Ted Moran has written an engaging paper that asks three important questions: How to investigate the impact of manufacturing foreign direct investment (FDI) on a developing country host economy? How to search for externalities and spillovers (and identify the channels and mechanisms through which spillovers take place)? How to evaluate the question of whether host governments should devote public sector resources to attracting FDI in manufacturing? Many readers will find Moran's overview of the evolution of the literature on the effects of manufacturing FDI to be a further, valuable contribution of this paper.

Moran believes that it is important that researchers who attempt to answer the questions he poses use, in addition to statistical regressions, multiple forms of evidence and other techniques including industry or sectoral studies, business cases, interviews, firm surveys, and cost-benefit analyses of individual projects. I could not agree more. I will use my comments to expand further on the need of an integrated approach, as Moran calls for, to study the effects of FDI on host countries: the need for macrolevel work to uncover the role of local conditions and absorptive capacities and the role of theory in not only guiding empirical work but also illuminating policy implications, for example, such as those that relate to what is and is not an externality. I also offer some observations on data issues and requirements that call for even more integrated work and some thoughts on why so little work seems to use different methodologies.

Why have researchers paid so much attention to the role of FDI in the development of host countries? There is widespread belief in both policy and academic circles that FDI can have valuable positive effects beyond the capital financing it might bring and the jobs it might create. Because FDI embodies technology and know-how as well as foreign capital, host economies can potentially benefit through knowledge spillovers (such as accelerated diffusion of new technologies, introduction of new products and processes, employee training, and access to international production networks) as well as through backward and forward linkages between foreign and domestic firms. Such arguments have led governments in developed and developing countries alike to devise and offer incentives that encourage FDI. Yet, empirical evidence at the microlevel remains ambiguous generally, although consistently more pessimistic for developing countries. Holger Görg and David Greenaway reviewed the microevidence on externalities from foreign-owned to domestically owned firms, paying particular attention to panel studies, and concluded that the effects were mostly negative.[1]

Why did FDI fail to generate positive externalities in panel studies? According to Moran, the first generation of cost-benefit analyses, industry studies, and multinational business cases provided an important explanation: the extent of a competitive environment (on the basis of import substitution–type policies). Indeed, the work by Vudayagi Balasubramanayam, Muhammed Salisu, and David Sapsford found FDI flows to be associated with faster growth in countries that pursued outward-oriented trade policies.[2] Many of the panel studies were conducted in countries (for example, in Colombia, India, Morocco, and Venezuela) that were pursuing inward-oriented policies. An important paper in this literature is the work by Brian Aitken and Ann Harrison, who found that the overall effect of foreign investment in Venezuela was small.[3] The fact that Venezuela, during the period of study from 1976 to 1989, was characterized by inward-oriented policies leads Moran to conclude that "manufacturing FDI is most likely to make a positive contribution to national income under reasonably competitive conditions."

But are reasonable competitive conditions enough of an answer? For this, the macroliterature on the effects of FDI and growth offers important insights. At the macrolevel, we find evidence not of an exogenous positive effect of FDI on economic growth but of positive effects conditional on local conditions and policies, notably, the policy environment, human capital, local financial markets, sector characteristics, and market structure.[4] I would argue that it is important to consider the findings of the macrolevel studies when answering the important questions raised by Moran. First, firm-level panel studies tend to cover specific and quite different types of countries (transition, developing, emerging, and industrialized), and in addition, different periods under study

1. Görg and Greenaway (2004).
2. Balasubramanayam, Salisu, and Sapsford (1996).
3. Aitken and Harrison (1999).
4. For the policy environment, see Balasubramanayam, Salisu, and Sapsford (1996); human capital, Borensztein, De Gregorio, and Lee (1998); local financial markets, Alfaro and others (2004); sector characteristics, Alfaro and Charlton (2007); market structure, Alfaro and others (2006).

make it difficult to understand the role of country-specific conditions. Because they generally span multiple countries and longer periods of time, macrolevel studies tend to afford an understanding of the role of local conditions in enabling positive benefits of FDI to materialize. Furthermore, as Robert Lipsey noted, one of the main reasons to examine productivity spillovers from foreign-owned to domestically owned firms is to understand the contribution of FDI to host country economic growth.[5] If higher productivity is achieved by foreign firms at the expense of lower productivity in domestic firms, there might not be any spillovers. But there might still be growth effects attributable to the operation of the foreign firms that can be analyzed in terms of the impact of FDI on a country's output or growth. Issues related to, for example, data, methodology, and determining causality notwithstanding, these studies have by virtue of their scope and duration produced evidence that suggests a relationship between local conditions and whether the benefits of FDI materialize.

But is even this enough? Can positive effects of FDI be educed by the right local conditions or, more generally, by the right economic environment? Through what mechanisms does FDI contribute to a country's development efforts? Many empirical studies have looked for the presence of externalities without trying to understand the mechanisms through which they might occur. Their focus has been on revealing indirect evidence of externalities by looking for associations between the increased presence of multinational corporations (MNCs) in a country or sector and productivity improvements in local firms or upstream sectors, for example. We need to investigate mechanisms to establish the robustness of these findings and devise appropriate policy interventions to maximize FDI externalities.

Papers by Beata Javorcik and Garrick Blalock and Paul Gertler explored the transfer of positive externalities from FDI to local firms in upstream industries (suppliers) and made an important contribution to the literature in this respect.[6] Moran shares these authors' belief that foreign firms have an incentive to minimize technology leaks to competitors while transferring knowledge that will improve the productivity of their local suppliers, in which case spillovers generated by FDI are more likely to be vertical rather than horizontal.

An obvious follow-up question is whether all vertical (supply) relations imply positive FDI spillovers? Here again, important information can be derived from an integrated approach that considers conducting surveys of multinationals. The cherry-picking behavior of many foreign firms with respect to local firms that can already supply goods is not associated with potential positive exter-

5. Lipsey (2002).
6. Javorcik (2004); Blalock and Gertler (2007).

nalities.[7] Foreign firms seem also to help some suppliers improve their performance, which again implies an externality only if these benefits are not fully internalized by the firm. Surveys administered to suppliers and MNCs in Costa Rica revealed few cases in which a positive technology transfer from an MNC to suppliers had clearly occurred.[8] The interviews also revealed that MNCs often lack technical knowledge about the production processes of the inputs they use. When they do have such knowledge, it tends to be about production processes for sophisticated inputs that, because they are unlikely to be supplied by local firms, are usually sourced from highly specialized international suppliers. Instead of examples of knowledge spillovers through technology transfers, the interviews revealed many instances in which local firms had decided to upgrade the quality of their production processes in order to become suppliers to MNCs.

A related question is whether MNCs' interactions with domestic suppliers always have the potential to develop into positive linkages. To answer that question, an integrated approach that links theory and evidence is needed. Theoretical work by Andrés Rodríquez-Clare suggested that under certain conditions (such as benefits of specialization, increasing returns, and transportation costs) increased demand for specialized inputs would lead to the local production of new types of these inputs, thereby generating positive externalities for other domestic firms that use those inputs.[9] According to this view of linkages, MNCs could even generate a negative backward linkage effect. If, for example, MNCs were to behave as enclaves, importing all their inputs and restricting their local activities to hiring labor, demand for inputs might decrease as the MNCs increase in importance relative to domestic firms, leading to a reduction in input variety and specialization.

As discussed in Laura Alfaro and Andrés Rodríguez-Clare, it is important to consider the different key assumptions of the model and how the violation of these assumptions might affect the potential for multinationals to create linkages.[10] One important assumption is nontradability of the intermediate goods used by domestic firms. Were goods perfectly tradable (that is, were there no transportation costs), it would not make sense to talk about a firm introducing a good to a developing country: given demand, all existing goods would be automatically available everywhere. First, only demand for nontradable inputs generates meaningful linkages. Ideally, researchers would take into account only purchases of nontradable inputs, but data constraints make this impossible in most cases. Second, only demand for intermediate goods that exhibit

7. Javorcik and Spatareanu (2005).
8. See Alfaro and Rodríguez-Clare (2004).
9. Rodríquez-Clare (1996).
10. Alfaro and Rodríguez-Clare (2004).

increasing returns (as opposed to constant returns to scale, for example) entails linkages. One could thus imagine a situation in which domestic firms use mostly inputs with increasing returns and multinationals use mostly inputs with constant returns, in which case the conclusion of a positive linkage effect by multinationals would be incorrect. Here again, researchers might face important data constraints. Third, demand for inputs with a low elasticity of substitution generates linkages with a stronger effect on productivity than does demand for inputs that have good substitutes. A final concern is that skilled workers seem to be hired in greater numbers by multinationals than by domestic firms. Positive linkage effects by multinationals might be less likely in the face of greater competition between MNCs and domestic firms for scarce skilled labor.

Is this mechanism valid? The traditional interpretation of the finding frequently reported in the empirical literature, that is, that the share of inputs bought domestically by MNCs is lower than the share for local firms, has been that MNCs generate fewer linkages than do domestic firms.[11] Theory, however, suggests that the share of inputs bought domestically is not a valid indicator of the linkages that MNCs can generate. The appropriate measure of linkages is the ratio of the value of inputs bought domestically to the total number of workers hired by the firm—which can also be defined as the share of inputs sourced domestically times intensity (inputs per worker). Most likely, MNCs have a lower share (as they are more likely to import inputs), but foreign firms are also likely to have higher intensity coefficients (as they are more likely to use more advanced, roundabout technologies).

Do foreign and domestic firms exhibit differences in the linkage coefficient? Using plant-level data for Brazil (1997–2000), Venezuela (1995–2000), Mexico (1993–2000), and Chile (1987–99), Alfaro and Rodríguez-Clare found, consistent with earlier evidence, that the share of inputs sourced domestically was lower for foreign firms in all countries but also that the intensity coefficient for foreign firms was higher in all countries.[12] Overall, the linkage coefficient in Brazil, Chile, and Venezuela was higher for foreign firms. In Mexico, we could not reject the hypothesis that foreign and domestic firms have similar linkage potential. Another important result was that entering foreign firms tended to have a lower linkage coefficient but that the linkage tended to increase over time, highlighting the importance of the duration of study (as well as the timing, such that studies closer to the liberalization periods are more likely to produce negative results).

11. Barry and Bradley (1997); Görg and Ruane (2001).
12. Alfaro and Rodríguez-Clare (2004).

In contrast to what has sometimes been implied in the empirical literature on FDI externalities, a positive backward linkage effect does not necessarily imply a positive externality from MNCs to suppliers.[13] In fact, such a positive linkage effect should lead to a positive externality from MNCs to other firms *in the same industry* (that is, a positive horizontal externality). That the empirical literature finds precisely the opposite, a negative or zero horizontal externality and a positive vertical externality is puzzling.

Why is it that we do not observe a positive externality from MNCs to other firms in the same industry? Quality of data, measurement errors in productivity, and endogeneity issues in the presence of multinationals are all possible answers. But another possible answer to this puzzle is that there might be some negative horizontal externality that offsets the positive effect MNCs might otherwise have on other firms in the same industry, consequent to increases in the variety (or even quality) of domestic inputs, which have been precipitated by, for example, the competition effect occasioned by the entry of MNCs (as argued by Aitken and Harrison) or MNCs' pirating of the best workers from domestic firms.[14]

An important challenge for the literature, according to Moran, is to control for competition effects. Data availability imposes a significant restriction on efforts to address this issue through econometric work, particularly in developing countries. This leads to the issue of the availability of data for tackling important questions behind FDI. Firm-level data are available in few countries and in very few of the developing countries in which this question might have the greatest policy relevance. Such data that are available are rarely available for very long periods (or similar periods across countries), and some of the datasets do not have all the information one would want. Because inputs and outputs are typically poorly measured and physical outputs not really observed, researchers tend to use nominal variables deflated by a broad price index, which might introduce some biases into the productivity measures.[15] Again, the solution to these issues is to employ an integrated approach: different methodologies, different techniques, and talking to firms.

So why then is an integrated approach so seldom used? This seems to be driven in part by journal biases, but there are also important issues in some of the nonstatistical work: potential sample biases, generalizability of results, and so forth. Surveys are expensive and difficult to administer. Because few developing countries have good census data, it is difficult to judge whether surveys are representative samples. Interviewed business managers might convey a

13. Alfaro and Rodriguez-Clare (2004).
14. Aitken and Harrison (1999).
15. For a discussion of poor measurement of inputs aond outputs, see Tybout (2001)

(positively) biased perception of the role of the multinational corporation (by overestimating positive effects to the host country, particularly if they think doing so might bring subsidies), and they are not always willing to disclose data and information about their firms. Business cases are difficult and time consuming to write: researchers need to develop important skills seldom taught in graduate schools, and they need to learn or intuit how to strike the right balance between documenting the general picture and recording essential details. In my view, the new round of empirical analysis has dealt with some of these issues, and we now see consistent evidence with previous work. So I think we might now see a widespread adoption of an integrated approach.

What are the policy implications of the integrated approach? FDI can play an important role in economic growth, most likely through suppliers, but local conditions matter and can limit the extent to which FDI benefits materialize. It is not clear that incentives to MNCs are warranted. More sensible policies might involve eliminating barriers that prevent local firms from establishing adequate linkages; improving local firms' access to inputs, technology, and financing; and streamlining the procedures associated with selling inputs. But we might also seek to improve domestic conditions, which should have the dual effect of attracting foreign investment (according to Alfaro, Kalemli-Ozcan, and Volosovych) and enabling host economies to maximize the benefits of such foreign investment.[16]

Beata Smarzynska Javorcik: There are several aspects of Ted Moran's approach to research that I really admire, and this paper is no exception. First of all, I admire his courage to ask broad and important questions that are very difficult to tackle. He manages to resist the temptation to look at narrow and insignificant issues just because they can be answered rigorously. Second, I really like the fact that he acknowledges that the perfect may be the enemy of the good and that even anecdotal case studies and imperfect econometric studies can tell us something interesting and useful about the world. Finally, I really appreciate the reality check, as each of his papers asks: Do the conclusions of econometric studies make sense? Are they consistent with what people on the ground tell us?

In this brief discussion, I would like to touch upon three issues. I will start by giving my interpretation of the message conveyed in Moran's paper. Then, I will talk about services, a topic that is missing in his paper but ought to be receiving some attention. Finally, I will close with some comments on policy implications.

---

16. Alfaro, Kalemli-Ozcan, and Volosovych (forthcoming).

Reinterpretation of Moran's Findings

The starting point of his paper is a puzzle presented by the empirical literature on spillovers from foreign direct investment. The puzzle is that studies that are very similar in terms of the data and the methodology often have found seemingly contradictory results. Rather than summarizing the large body of research on this subject, I will illustrate this point by focusing on three papers that, in my view, are representative of the patterns found in the literature. All three studies were careful about their methodology, presented a number of robustness checks, and have been frequently cited in the literature.

The first study, published by Brian Aitken and Ann Harrison, caused a stir in the literature by suggesting that FDI inflows may not only fail to produce positive productivity externalities but may also result in negative spillover effects.[1] Using a panel of more than 4,000 Venezuelan plants from 1976 to 1989, the authors identified two effects of FDI on domestic enterprises. First, they found that increases in foreign equity participation were correlated with increases in total factor productivity in recipient plants with fewer than fifty employees but not in other plants. Second, they showed that increases in FDI presence negatively affected the total factor productivity of domestic plants in the same industry. Their interpretation of the latter finding was that the expansion of foreign affiliates reduced the market share of local producers, which in turn forced them to spread their fixed costs over a smaller volume of production and resulted in a lower observed total factor productivity.

In contrast, Jonathan Haskel, Sonia Pereira, and Matthew Slaughter produced evidence consistent with positive intra-industry FDI spillovers in the United Kingdom.[2] Using a plant-level panel covering the manufacturing sector from 1973 through 1992, they found that a 10 percentage points increase in foreign presence in a U.K. industry raised the total factor productivity of that industry's domestic plants by about 0.5 percent. They also showed that these effects tended to be more important for plants at the lower end of the performance distribution.

More recently, Beata Javorcik found evidence suggesting that spillovers are more likely to benefit the supplying industries rather than the industries in which multinationals operate.[3] She argued that while multinationals have an incentive to prevent knowledge from leaking to their local competitors they may have an incentive to provide assistance to their local suppliers in upstream sec-

1. Aitken and Harrison (1999).
2. Haskel, Pereira, and Slaughter (2002).
3. Javorcik (2004).

tors. Using firm-level panel data from Lithuania covering the period from 1996 to 2000, she found that the total factor productivity of Lithuanian firms was positively correlated with the extent of potential contacts with multinational customers in downstream sectors but not with the presence of multinationals in the same industry. An increase of 1 standard deviation in foreign presence in the sourcing sectors was associated with a 15 percent rise in productivity of Lithuanian firms in the supplying industry. The study determined that the productivity effect originated from investments with joint foreign and domestic ownership but not from fully owned foreign affiliates, a finding that was consistent with the evidence showing that a larger amount of local sourcing had been done by jointly owned projects.

How should we interpret these seemingly conflicting results? One could dismiss the whole literature on the grounds that the total factor productivity is a poor measure of performance. One could attribute the inconsistency in the findings to the poor quality of the data. If the data from developing countries tend to be of lower quality than are data from industrialized economies, then maybe the results based on the former should not be trusted. One could also question the identification strategies and point out potential endogeneity problems. However, doing so would not bring us any closer to understanding the effects of FDI on host economies.

Rather than dismissing the spillover literature, Moran's answer is to search for clues by looking at host country conditions. He points out that Aitken and Harrison's finding that only some plants benefited directly from an increase in foreign ownership share indicates that FDI in Venezuela presented limited potential for productivity spillovers. He argues that this situation was due to heavy restrictions imposed by the government on foreign investors, which included strict joint venture and local content requirements. Moreover, foreign investors were forbidden from exercising confidentiality and exclusive use of trade secrets in their mandatory joint ventures, which no doubt dampened their incentives for technology transfer. Further, during the time period considered in the study, Venezuela was pursuing an import substitution strategy, thus indigenous producers were not exposed to significant competition from abroad. This can explain why FDI inflows could have had a large negative effect on market shares of indigenous producers.

Following this line of thinking, it is worth noting that in contrast to Venezuela, foreign affiliates operating in the United Kingdom tended to exhibit higher value added per worker relative to British firms in the same industry. They were also responsible for a large share of the research and development effort undertaken.[4]

4. Griffith, Redding, and Simpson (2004).

These observations indicate that foreign affiliates in the United Kingdom were a potential source of knowledge spillovers. Moreover, the sophistication of the British firms and the openness of the country to international trade also suggest that the negative "market stealing" effect described by Aitken and Harrison was unlikely to be large in the United Kingdom. The fact that lesser performers seemed to benefit more from spillovers is also not surprising given the sophistication of the British manufacturing sector and thus the limited room for learning.

The same type of interpretation can be applied to Lithuania, the country considered by Javorcik. There, one would expect both the "market stealing" effect as well as opportunities for learning from multinationals. Only five years before the beginning of the period under study, Lithuania started its transition from central planning to a free market economy and opened its doors to FDI. On the one hand, this meant that indigenous manufacturers were going to be strongly affected by competition from FDI inflows, which did not bode well for intra-industry spillovers. On the other hand, this situation also meant that indigenous producers having had limited exposure to foreign clients in the past could now develop new supply relationships with foreign investors in Lithuania that had the potential to lead to significant knowledge transfers.

Thus one can rephrase Moran's conclusion as suggesting that researchers should not be asking *whether* spillovers from FDI exist but rather *under what condition* do they occur. Policymakers should not assume that positive externalities from FDI are automatic. More research is certainly needed to understand how to facilitate FDI spillovers.

FDI Inflows into Services

Moran's paper is almost entirely devoted to the effects of FDI inflows into manufacturing industries, yet FDI inflows into the service sector have gained in importance during the past decade and may constitute another channel through which the presence of multinationals benefits the host economy. One distinctive feature of services is that they serve as an essential input into an exceptionally wide range of activities, including manufacturing. Given the limited scope for cross-border trade in services inputs, one would expect the performance of downstream sectors to be tied more directly to the quality and availability of services supplied by providers operating domestically than is the case for physical intermediate inputs. And indeed recent empirical work by Jens Arnold, Javorcik and Aaditya Mattoo confirmed the existence of such a link.[5]

5. See Arnold, Javorcik, and Mattoo (2007).

This view is also reflected in the results of a recent firm survey: A majority of the 350 Czech enterprises interviewed in 2004 on behalf of the World Bank believed that liberalization of the service industry, including opening the sector to foreign entry, contributed to improvements in the quality, range, and availability of services inputs in their country. The share of positive perceptions ranged from 55 percent of the respondents when asked about the quality of accounting and auditing services to 82 percent queried about telecommunications. With regard to the variety of products offered, the positive views of liberalization varied between 56 percent of respondents evaluating accounting and auditing services to 87 percent of respondents asked about telecommunications. The corresponding figures for the effect on services availability ranged from 47 percent in accounting and auditing to 80 percent in telecommunications.[6]

FDI inflows into services may facilitate FDI spillovers. A theoretical model and a calibration exercise undertaken by Laura Alfaro and others suggested that without access to financing local entrepreneurs were unable to become suppliers to multinationals and benefit from productivity spillovers associated with such relationships.[7] In a cross-country growth regression, the same authors found that FDI inflows contributed to a faster economic growth only in the presence of well-developed financial markets.[8] In another cross-country study, Harrison, Inessa Love, and Margaret McMillan showed that FDI inflows are associated with a reduction in financing constraints of indigenous firms.[9] Improvements in services infrastructure in sectors other than banking, resulting from opening the sector to FDI, may have similar effects. It is certainly a question worth exploring in the future.

Policy Implications

Moving on to policy implications, I agree with Moran that spillovers can serve as a justification for FDI incentives. However, the use of incentives may make sense only if some basic conditions are fulfilled. A country struggling to run a reliable electricity network is unlikely to attract multinationals through fiscal incentives. Moreover, it is crucial to recognize that the cost of incentives may not be worth the benefits, as is clearly shown in Haskel, Pereira, and Slaughter's study mentioned earlier.[10]

6. See Arnold, Javorcik, and Mattoo (2007).
7. Alfaro and others (2006).
8. Alfaro and others (2004).
9. Harrison, Love, and McMillan (2004).
10. Haskel, Pereira, and Slaughter (2002).

Information asymmetry is another frequently used justification for FDI incentives. It is costly to obtain information about business conditions in developing countries, especially since indigenous and foreign firms operating there have no incentive to share this information. Therefore, it may make sense to subsidize the first flagship FDI project. Having a prominent multinational in the country is often the best way of advertising the country as a good place to do business. But it makes less sense to subsidize subsequent investors. Another way of dealing with information asymmetry is to provide information through investment promotion agencies (IPAs). In the past two decades, the world has witnessed an explosion in the number of IPAs. For instance, the 2005 census of investment promotion agencies revealed that 85 percent of the responding IPAs in developing countries were established in 1980 or later.[11] The good news is that investment promotion appears to be effective. According to a recent study by Torfinn Harding and Javorcik, sectors explicitly targeted by IPAs in developing countries see their FDI inflow double in the posttargeting period relative to the pretargeting period and to nontargeted sectors.[12] A similar conclusion was reached by Andrew Charlton and Nicholas Davis in the context of OECD countries.[13] There is also evidence of FDI diversion due to investment incentives offered by other countries in the same geographic region, which suggests that regional cooperation in this area may be beneficial.[14]

Unfortunately, the advice international economists can give policymakers is still quite limited. We have a limited idea on how to facilitate spillovers from FDI and on how the costs of FDI promotion policies and incentives compare with the benefits they bring. One thing is certain though, unless we follow Moran's advice and use multiple approaches to examine these questions, we are not going to get any closer to answering these questions in a convincing manner.

Discussion: Susan Collins opened the general discussion by remarking that she found the piece interesting and enjoyed reading it. She went on to note that attention should be focused on FDI in services and commented that one of the points made in the paper was that foreign firms use different styles when investing in other countries. To strengthen this idea, she alluded to a Trade Forum discussion held two years ago in the Trade Forum conference on offshoring during which a number of case studies talked about call centers and the different operating practices used by offshore sites as well as ones that were outsourced elsewhere

11. See Harding and Javorcik (2007).
12. Harding and Javorcik (2007).
13. Charlton and Davis (2006).
14. See Harding and Javorcik (2007).

within the United States (in house). In particular, she pointed out that call centers in developing countries were the most mechanized and routinized. Collins also brought up the issue of selectivity, which was also one of the key points made in Assaf Razzin's paper discussed earlier. Last, firm selectivity is based on a variety of characteristics, not just taxes or productivity, but other country characteristics as well. Many of these issues have to do with determinants of the desired ownership structure of a source country's firm, in that, it influences what they do, how they set up business, and the extent to which one might expect productivity spillovers, both horizontally and vertically.

Deborah Swenson commented that it is difficult to find evidence of horizontal spillovers because firms do not want to disclose what they are doing. Another reason, highlighted in the chapter, for not finding any spillovers was the export dimension of local firms in the Brian Aitken and Ann Harrison case study of manufacturing FDI in Venezuela. Swenson pointed to earlier work of hers on China that looked at the expansion of domestic exports by local private firms as opposed to state-owned enterprises (SOEs), joint ventures, or multinationals. From the China data, using geographical variation across cities and industries, she found that expansion of multinational activities preceded the growth in domestic exports in subsequent years, suggesting there are informational spillovers.

Swenson highlighted intriguing work by Dani Rodrick with Ricardo Hausmann on self-discovery, which observed that countries with comparative advantages in broad industries have very distinct export profiles. Therefore, multinationals may be providing one of these conduits for self-discovery that would not otherwise be there, which may have implications for how countries become more integrated. Another study by James Rausch and Vitor Trindade argues that information is one of the main things that segments countries, to the extent it becomes more widely available. This may present additional globalization effects by bringing together wage effects. As a final point, Swenson spoke about the difficulties in data collection when there are too few case studies. She went on to say that the environment is important, but incorporating these issues into econometrics is very difficult.

Kimberly Elliot raised the issue of controlling skills. She commented that a lot of theory suggests foreign investors need a higher-skilled workforce, which in turn may have some bearing on local wage effect. She pointed to an earlier paper done by Ann Harrison on Indonesia and the apparel industry. In the paper, wages effects were influenced by activists' pressure on firms. Elliot also commented that local conditions are important elements to consider in how FDI effects are positive or negative. If restrictions on investment are only in countries where conditions are right, you are going to be piling distortions on top of distortions with countries with bad conditions then trying to incentivize investments. Because of this, a cautious approach on incentives must be taken.

Margaret McMillan applauded the paper, particularly the literature review because it reiterates why we should care about FDI and issues related to it. To her surprise, the BEA data showed that U.S. multinationals account for 80 to 90 percent of all private R&D in the United States. She continued by remarking it would be interesting to investigate previous studies to give us an upper bound on the potential impact on FDI and a lower bound on the domestic economy.

Beata Javorcik agreed with McMillan's comment and suggested looking at 2003 data, which showed that multinationals accounted for about half of global R&D spending. This could be used as a motivation for why multinationals would have the potential to become a source of knowledge transfer to developing countries. Javorcik went on to say that if one looks at R&D budgets of large multinationals, such as Ford Motor Company or Pfizer, their budgets are larger than the annual budget of what Russia or European countries spend on all their R&D activities during the same year.

On a similar note, Garrick Blalock agreed with the point made by Laura Alfaro, that technology transfer to a supplier is not an externality. He then posed the question: The problem is then how do you tease out the market structure effects that fan out from that? Blalock commented that he does not think it feasible to do this to a level of econometric rigor required by journals. In his opinion, not all evidence should have to pass this sort of rigor.

In the context of China, Cheryl Long reflected on a paper she cowrote. To her surprise, after analyzing data using an array of techniques, splitting the samples, determining whether the firm is in the export processor zone or not, and whether it is forward or backward or horizontal, the research was unable to find spillover effects in FDI. Long commented that if you look at the experience of China's growth, you cannot deny that FDI did not play a role. She commented on the fact that China is exporting capital to the rest of the world and asked how can one argue that it is necessary to have FDI coming in? Last, Long agreed with earlier comments made on the difficulties in measuring specific variables, which often do not meet the rigors or standards of journals.

Theodore Moran concluded by offering a few responses to comments made by the participants. He agreed that when looking at investment promotion agencies, for example, there is certainly a difference in quality and ways to measure it.

References

Aitken, Brian J., and Ann E. Harrison. 1999. "Do Domestic Firms Benefit from Direct Foreign Investment? Evidence from Venezuela." *American Economic Review* 89, no. 3 (June): 605–18.

Aitken, Brian J., Gordon H. Hanson, and Ann E. Harrison.1997. "Spillovers, Foreign Investment, and Export Behavior." *Journal of International Economics* 43, no. 1–2 (August): 103–32.

Akerloff, George A. 1970. "The Market for 'Lemons': Quality Uncertainty and the Market Mechanism." *Quarterly Journal of Economics* 84, no. 3 (August): 488–500.

Alfaro, Laura, and Andrew Charlton. 2007. "Growth and the Quality of Foreign Direct Investment: Is All FDI Equal?" Working Paper 07-072. Harvard Business School.

Alfaro, Laura, and Andrés Rodríguez-Clare. 2004. "Multinationals and Linkages: An Empirical Investigation." *Economia* 4, no. 2: 113–70.

Alfaro, Laura, Sebnem Kalemli-Ozcan, and Vadym Volosovych. Forthcoming. "Why Doesn't Capital Flow from Rich to Poor Countries? An Empirical Investigation." *Review of Economics and Statistics*.

Alfaro, Laura, Areendam Chanda, Sebnem Kalemli-Ozcan, and Selin Sayek. 2004. "FDI and Economic Growth: The Role of Local Financial Markets." *Journal of International Economics* 64, no. 1 (October): 89–112.

———. 2006. "How Does Foreign Direct Investment Promote Economic Growth? Exploring the Effects of Financial Markets on Linkages." NBER Working Paper 12522. Cambridge, Mass.: National Bureau of Economic Research (September).

Alonso, Eduardo. 2001. "Trade and Investment Promotion: The Case of CINDE in Costa Rica." Paper presented at the Inter-American Development Bank. Washington, September 18.

Altshuler, Rossane, Harry J. Grubert, and Scott Newlong. 1998. "Has U.S. Investment Abroad Become More Sensitive to Tax Rates?" Working Paper 6383. Cambridge, Mass.: National Bureau of Economic Research.

Arnold, Jens M., Beata S. Javorcik, and Aaditya Mattoo. 2007. "Does Services Liberalization Benefit Manufacturing Firms? Evidence from the Czech Republic." Policy Research Working Paper 4109. Washington: World Bank.

Austin, James E. 1990. "Mexico and the Microcomputers." Abridged. Case 390-093. Harvard Business School.

Balasubramanayam, Vudayagi N., Muhammed Salisu, and David Sapsford. 1996. "Foreign Direct Investment and Growth in EP and IS Countries." *Economic Journal* 106, no. 434 (January): 92–105.

Bale, Harvey E., Jr., and David Walters. 1986. "Investment Policy Aspects of U.S. and Global Trade Interests." *Looking Ahead*. NPA Pamphlet 9 (Washington: National Planning Association).

Barry, Frank, and John Bradley. 1997. "FDI and Trade: The Irish Host-Country Experience." *Economic Journal* 107, no. 445: 1798–811.

Beamish, Paul W. 1988. *Multinational Joint Ventures in Developing Countries*. London: Routledge.

Beamish, Paul W., and Andres Delios. 1997. "Incidence and Propensity of Alliance Formation by U.S., Japanese, and European MNEs." In *Cooperative Strategies: Asian-Pacific Perspectives*, edited by Paul W. Beamish and J. Peter Killing, pp. 91–113. San Francisco: New Lexington Press.

Belderbos, René, Giovanni Capannelli, and Kyoji Fukao. 2000. "The Local Content of Japanese Electronics Manufacturing Operations in Asia." In *The Role of Foreign Direct Investment in East Asian Economic Development*, edited by Takatoshi Ito and Anne O. Krueger, pp. 9–47. University of Chicago Press for the National Bureau of Economic Research.

Bernard, Andrew B., and J. Bradford Jensen. 1999. "Exceptional Exporter Performance: Cause, Effect, or Both?" *Journal of International Economics* 47, no. 1: 1–25.

Birdsall, Nancy, Dani Rodrik, and Arvind Subramanian. 2005. "How to Help Poor Countries." *Foreign Affairs* 84, no. 4 (July–August): 136–52.

Blalock, Garrick, and Paul J.Gertler. 2004. "Learning from Exporting Revisited in a Less Developed Setting." *Journal of Development Economics* 75, no. 2: 397–416.

———. 2005. "Foreign Direct Investment and Externalities: The Case for Public Intervention." In *Does Foreign Direct Investment Promote Development?* edited by Theodore H. Moran, Edward M. Graham, and Magnus Blomstrom, pp. 73–106. Washington: Center for Global Development and Institute for International Economics.

———. 2007. "Welfare Gains from Foreign Direct Investment through Technology Transfer to Local Suppliers." *Journal of International Economics* 71, no. 1: 206–20.

Blomstrom, Magnus, Ari Kokko, and Mario Zejan. 1992. "Host Country Competition and Technology Transfer by Multinationals." Working Paper 4131. Cambridge, Mass.: National Bureau of Economic Research.

Borensztein, Eduardo, José De Gregorio, and Jong-Wha Lee. 1998. "How Does Foreign Direct Investment Affect Economic Growth?" *Journal of International Economics* 45, no. 1: 115–35.

Borrus, Michael, Dieter Ernst, and Stephan Haggard, eds. 2000. *Rivalry or Riches? International Production Networks in Asia*. New York: Routledge.

Center for Global Development. 2007. "Commitment to Development Index 2006." Washington.

Charlton, Andrew, and Nicholas Davis. 2006. "Does Investment Promotion Work?" Mimeo. London School of Economics.

Clerides, Sofronis K., Saul Lach, and James R. Tybout. 1998. "Is Learning by Exporting Important? Micro-Dynamic Evidence from Colombia, Mexico, and Morocco." *Quarterly Journal of Economics* 113, no. 3: 903–47.

Cline, William R. 1987. *Informatics and Development: Trade, and Industrial Policy in Argentina, Brazil, and Mexico*. Washington: Economics International.

Delgado, Miguel A., Jose C. Fariñas, Sonia Ruano. 2002. "Firm Productivity and Export Markets: A Non-Parametric Approach." *Journal of International Economics* 57, no. 2: 397–422.

Desai, Mihir A., C. Fritz Foley, and James R. Hines, Jr. 2002. "International Joint Ventures and the Boundaries of the Firm." Working Paper 9115. Cambridge, Mass.: National Bureau of Economic Research (August).

Dixit, Avinash K., and Robert S. Pindyck. 1994. *Investment under Uncertainty*. Princeton University Press.

Eastman, Harry, and Stefan Stykolt. 1970. "A Model for the Study of Protected Oligopolies." *Economic Journal* 70, no. 278: 336–47.

Economist Intelligence Unit. 2007. *EIU Country Profile 2007: Morocco*. London.

Encarnation, Dennis J., and Louis T. Wells, Jr. 1986. "Evaluating Foreign Investment." In *Investing In Development: New Roles for Private Capital?* edited by Theodore H. Moran, pp. 61–86. Washington: Overseas Development Council.

Gomes-Casseres, Benjamin. 1989. "Ownership Structures of Foreign Subsidiaries: Theory and Evidence." *Journal of Economic Behavior and Organization* 11, no. 1 (January): 1–25.

Görg, Holger, and David Greenaway. 2004. "Much Ado about Nothing? Do Domestic Firms Really Benefit from Foreign Direct Investment?" *World Bank Research Observer* 19, no. 2: 171–98.

Görg, Holger, and Frances Ruane. 2001. "Multinational Companies and Linkages: Panel-Data Evidence for the Irish Electronics Sector." *International Journal of the Economics and Business* 8, no. 1: 1–18.

Gray, H. Peter, and Ingo Walter. 1984. "Investment-Related Trade Distortions in Petrochemicals." *Journal of World Trade Law* 17, no.4 (July–August): 283–307.

Griffith, Rachel, Stephen J. Redding, and Helen Simpson. 2004. "Foreign Ownership and Productivity: New Evidence from the Service Sector and the R&D Lab." *Oxford Review of Economic Policy* 20, no. 3: 440–56.

Haddad, Mona, and Ann E. Harrison. 1993. "Are There Positive Spillovers from Direct Foreign Investment? Evidence from Panel Data for Morocco." *Journal of Development Economics* 42, no. 1 (October): 51–74.

Hanson, Gordon. 2005. "Comment." In *Does Foreign Direct Investment Promote Development?* edited by Theodore H. Moran, Edward M. Graham, and Magnus Blomstrom, pp. 175–178. Washington: Center for Global Development and Institute for International Economics.

Harding, Torfinn, and Beata S. Javorcik. 2007. "Developing Economies and International Investors: Do Investment Promotion Agencies Bring Them Together?" Mimeo. Washington: World Bank.

Harrison, Ann E. 1996. "Determinants and Effects of Direct Foreign Investment in Cote d'Ivoire, Morocco, and Venezuela." In *Industrial Evolution in Developing Countries: Micro Patterns of Turnover, Productivity, and Market Structure*, edited by Marc J. Roberts and James R. Tybout, pp. 163–187. Oxford University Press for the World Bank.

Harrison, Ann E., Inessa Love, and Margaret S. McMillan. 2004. "Global Capital Flows and Financing Constraints." *Journal of Development Economics* 75, no. 1: 269–301.

Haskel, Jonathan E., Sonia C. Pereira, and Mathew J. Slaughter. 2002. "Does Inward FDI Boost the Productivity of Domestic Firms?" Working Paper 8724. Cambridge, Mass.: National Bureau of Economic Research.

Hausmann, Ricardo, and Dani Rodrik. 2003. "Discovering El Salvador's Production Potential." Working Paper. September.

———. 2006. "Doomed to Choose: Industrial Policy as Predicament." Paper prepared for the first Blue Sky seminar, Center for International Development, Harvard, September 9.

Hobday, Michael. 1995. *Innovation in East Asia: The Challenge to Japan*. London: Aldershot.

———. 2000. "East versus Southeast Asian Innovation Systems: Comparing OME- and TNC-Led Growth in Electronics." In *Technology, Learning, and Innovation*, edited by Linsu Kim and Richard R. Nelson, pp. 129–69. Cambridge University Press.

Javorcik, Beata Smarzynska. 2004. "Does Foreign Direct Investment Increase the Productivity of Domestic Firms? In Search of Spillovers through Backward Linkages." *American Economic Review* 94, no. 3: 605–27.

Javorcik, Beata Smarzynska, and Mariana Spatareanu. 2005. "Disentangling FDI Spillover Effects: What Do Firm Perceptions Tell Us?" In *Does Foreign Direct Investment Promote Development?* edited by Theodore H. Moran, Edward M. Graham, and Magnus Blomstrom, pp. 45–72. Washington: Center for Global Development and Institute for International Economics.

Kalotay, Kálmán. 2002. "Central and Eastern Europe: Export Platform for Investors?" *Journal of World Investment* 3, no. 6 (December): 1037–059.

Katz, Jorge M., ed. 1987. *Technology Generation in Latin American Manufacturing Industries*. New York: St. Martin's Press.

Keller, Wolfgang, and Stephen R. Yeaple. 2007. "Multinational Enterprises, International Trade, and Productivity Growth: Firm-Level Evidence from the United States." Working Paper. (April).

King, Gary, Robert O. Keohane, and Sidney Verba. 1994. *Designing Social Inquiry: Scientific Inference in Qualitative Research*. Princeton University Press.

Klein, Karen. 1995. "General Motors in Hungary: The Corporate Strategy behind Szentgotthard." Washington: Georgetown University, Pew Economic Freedom Fellows Program.

Kohpaiboon, Archanun. 2005. "Industrialization in Thailand: MNEs and Global Integration." Ph.D. dissertation, Australian National University.

Kokko, Ari, Ruben Tansini, and Mario Zejan. 1996. "Local Technological Capability and Productivity Spillovers from FDI in the Uruguayan Manufacturing Sector." *Journal of Development Studies* 32, no. 4 (April): 602–11.

Krueger, Anne O. 1975. *The Benefits and Costs of Import Substitution in India: A Microeconomic Study*. University of Minnesota Press.

Lall, Sanjaya, and Paul Streetan. 1977. *Foreign Investment, Transnationals, and Developing Countries*. Boulder, Colo.: Westview Press.

Larraín, Felipe B., Luis F. López-Calva, and Andrés Rodríguez-Clare. 2001. "Intel: A Case Study of Foreign Direct Investment in Central America." In *Economic Development in Central America*, vol. 1, *Growth and Internationalization*, edited by Felipe B. Larraín, chapter 6, pp. 197–250. Harvard University Press.

Lee, Jeong-Yeon, and Edwin Mansfield. 1996. "Intellectual Property Protection and U.S. Foreign Direct Investment." *Review of Economics and Statistics* 78, no. 2: 181–86.

Lim, Linda Y. C., and Pang Eng Fong. 1982. "Vertical Linkages and Multinational Enterprises in Developing Countries." *World Development* 10, no. 7: 585–95.

———. 1991. *Foreign Direct Investment and Industrialization in Malaysia, Singapore, Taiwan and Thailand.* Paris: Organization for Economic Cooperation and Development.

Lipsey, Robert E. 2002. "Home and Host Country Effects of FDI." NBER Working Paper 9293. Cambridge, Mass.: National Bureau of Economic Research.

———. 2006. "Measuring the Impacts of FDI in Central and Eastern Europe." Working Paper 12808. Cambridge, Mass.: National Bureau of Economic Research.

Lipsey, Robert E., and Fredrik Sjöholm. 2004a. "FDI and Wage Spillovers in Indonesian Manufacturing." *Review of World Economics* 140, no. 2: 321–32.

———. 2004b. "Foreign Direct Investment, Education, and Wages in Indonesian Manufacturing." *Journal of Development Economics* 73, no. 1: 415–22.

Long, Guoqiang. 2005. "China's Policies on FDI: Review and Evaluation." In *Does Foreign Direct Investment Promote Development?* edited by Theodore H. Moran, Edward M. Graham, and Magnus Blomstrom, pp. 315–36. Washington: Center for Global Development and Institute for International Economics.

Mansfield, Edwin, and Anthony Romeo. 1980. "Technology Transfer to Overseas Subsidiaries by U.S.-based Firms." *Quarterly Journal of Economics* 95, no 4: 737–50.

McKendrick, David. 1994. "Building the Capabilities to Imitate Product and Managerial Know-how in Indonesian Banking." *Industrial and Corporate Change* 3, no. 2: 513–35.

McKendrick, David, Richard F. Donner, and Stephan Haggard. 2000. *From Silicon Valley to Singapore: Location and Competitive Advantage in the Hard Disk Drive Industry.* Stanford University Press.

Moran, Theodore H. 1998. *Foreign Direct Investment and Development: The New Policy Agenda for Developing Countries and Economies in Transition.* Washington: Institute for International Economics.

———. 2001. *Parental Supervision: The New Paradigm for Foreign Direct Investment and Development.* Washington: Institute for International Economics.

———. 2006. *Harnessing Foreign Direct Investment for Development: Policies for Developed and Developing Countries.* Washington: Center for Global Development.

———. Forthcoming. *Toward A Development-Friendly International Regulatory Framework for Foreign Direct Investment.*

Multilateral Investment Guarantee Agency. 2006. *The Impact of Intel in Costa Rica: Nine Years After the Decision to Invest.* Washington: World Bank Group.

Mutti, John H. 2003. *Foreign Direct Investment and Tax Competition.* Washington: Institute for International Economics.

Ngo, Huan, and David W. Conklin. 1996. "Mekong Corporation and the Vietnam Motor Vehicle Industry." Case 96-H002. University of Western Ontario, Richard Ivey School of Business.

Noland, Marcus, and Howard Pack. 2003. *Industrial Policy in an Era of Globalization: Lessons from Asia.* Washington: Institute for International Economics.

Nuñez, Wilson Peres. 1990. *Foreign Direct Investment and Industrial Development in Mexico.* Paris: Organization for Economic Cooperation and Development, Development Centre.

Olley, G. Steven, and Ariel Pakes. 1996. "The Dynamics of Productivity in the Telecommunications Equipment Industry." *Econometrica* 64, no.6: 1263–297.

O'Sullivan, Robert C. 2005. "Learning from OPIC's Experience with Claims and Arbitration." In *International Political Risk Management: Looking to the Future,* vol. 3, edited by Theodore H. Moran and Gerald T. West, pp. 30–74. Washington: World Bank.

Ramachandran, Vijaya. 1993. "Technology Transfer, Firm Ownership, and Investment in Human Capital." *Review of Economics and Statistics* 75, no.4: 664–70.

Rasiah, Rajah. 1994. "Flexible Production Systems and Local Machine-Tool Subcontracting: Electronics Components Transnationals in Malaysia." *Cambridge Journal of Economics* 18, no. 3 (June): 279–98.

———. 1995. *Foreign Capital and Industrialization in Malaysia.* New York: St. Martin's Press.

Reuber, Grant L., and others. 1973. *Private Foreign Investment in Development.* Oxford, U.K: Clarendon Press.

Rhee, Yung Whee, Katharina Katterbach, and Janette White. 1990. *Free Trade Zones in Export Strategies.* Industry Series 36. Washington: World Bank, Industry and Energy Department, Industry Development Division (December).

Rhee, Yung Whee, Bruce Ross-Larson, and Garry Pursell. 1984. *Korea's Competitive Edge: Managing Entry into World Markets.* Johns Hopkins University Press.

Rodríguez-Clare, Andrés. 1996. "Multinationals, Linkages and Economic Development." *American Economic Review* 86, no. 4: 852–73.

Samuels, Barbara C., II. 1990. *Managing Risk in Developing Countries: National Demands and Multinational Response.* Princeton University Press.

Shah, Manju Kedia. 2006. "Subcontracting in Sub-Sahara Africa." Working Paper. Washington: World Bank (February).

Shah, Manju Kedia, and others. 2005. *Madagascar Investment Climate Assessment: Technical Report.* Washington: World Bank, Africa Private Sector Group (June).

Spar, Debora L. 1998. "Attracting High Technology Investment: Intel's Costa Rican Plant." Occasional Paper 11. Washington: World Bank Group, Foreign Investment Advisory Service.

Tybout, James R. 2001. "Plant- and Firm-Level Evidence on 'New' Trade Theories." NBER Working Paper 8418. Cambridge, Mass.: National Bureau of Economic Research.

[UNCTAD] United Nations Conference on Trade and Development. 2005. *Investment Policy Review: Kenya*. New York: United Nations.

[UNCTC] United Nations Center on Transnational Corporations. 1991. *The Impact of Trade-Related Investment Measures on Trade and Development*. New York: United Nations.

Urata, Shujiro, and Hiroki Kawai. 2000. "Intrafirm Technology Transfer by Japanese Manufacturing Firms in Asia." In *The Role of Foreign Direct Investment in East Asian Economic Development*, edited by Takatoshi Ito and Anne O. Krueger, pp. 49–77. University of Chicago Press for the National Bureau of Economic Research.

Uyterhoeven, Hugo E. R. 1992–93. *Adam Opel AG, A and B*. Case 9-392-100, Case 9-392-101. Harvard Business School.

———. 1993. *Adam Opel AG, Supplement*. Case 9-392-127. Harvard Business School.

Vernon, Raymond, Louis T. Wells, and Subramanian Rangan. 1995. *The Manager in the International Economy*. 7th ed. New York: Prentice Hall.

Wang, Xiaolu. 2004. "People's Republic of China." In *Managing FDI in a Globalizing Economy: Asian Experiences*, edited by Douglas H. Brooks and Hal Hill, pp. 79–118. New York: Palgrave Macmillan for the Asian Development Bank.

Wasow, Bernard. 2003. "The Benefits of Foreign Direct Investment in the Presence of Price Distortions: The Case of Kenya." Working Paper (May).

Wheeler, David, and Ashoka Mody. 1992. "International Investment Locations Decisions: The Case of U.S. Firms." *Journal of International Economics* 33, nos. 1–2: 57–76.

Womack, James P., Daniel T. Jones, and Daniel Roos. 1991. *The Machine That Changed the World*. New York: Harper Perennial.

World Bank. 2006. *Fostering Higher Growth and Employment in the Kingdom of Morocco*. Washington.

[WTO] World Trade Organization. 2005. "Agreement on Trade-Related Investment Measures." In *Ministerial Declaration*, Annex F: Special and Differential Treatment (84). Hong Kong, December 18.

JOHN WHALLEY
University of Western Ontario

XIAN XIN
China Agricultural University

China and Foreign Direct Investment

That China's economy is now deeply integrated into the wider global economy and that inward foreign direct investment (FDI) flows and trade growth have been mechanisms for this integration over the last fifteen years is hardly news. But the dimensions and speed of change continue at a torrid pace. Here we discuss the size and geographical concentration of the FDI and raise several key issues linking FDI and wider economic performance. One is whether FDI-led growth can continue as the prime developmental path for China, or do constraints on global aggregate flows, rising wage rates, or limits on the ability of markets abroad to absorb Chinese exports, at some point, serve to restrict growth. If so, when will any one of these factors slow growth and what could become an alternative growth path? Another issue is whether regionally concentrated, location-specific FDI has been a prime contributor to the growing inequality in China that threatens to politically constrain growth. Yet another is whether proposed or likely policy change, such as removing the substantial tax preferences toward FDI under a proposed unified tax, or a significant renmimbi revaluation, or both together, could also serve to limit FDI inflows.

In what follows, we first document the dimensions of inflows of FDI into China in recent years, emphasizing its links to China's large processing trade. FDI inflows to China now account for nearly half of all Organization for Economic Cooperation and Development (OECD) outflows, are split between horizontal (serving the Chinese market) and vertical (export oriented), and are highly regionally concentrated. We then go on to discuss the contribution of FDI inflows to China's growth drawing on an earlier growth accounting paper, which argues that a plateauing of FDI inflows to China could reduce growth

The authors would like to thank Nicholas R. Lardy, Susan Collins, and other participants for their helpful comments and suggestions. We are also grateful to Edgar Cudmore and Li Wang for help with data and comments on an earlier draft.

61

rates by 3 to 4 percentage points.[1] We then use this as a bridge to discuss potential constraints on China's future growth linked to FDI and trade. We note that for more than twenty years Western economists have been predicting the demise of Chinese high growth, which has not happened. Sections follow on regional concentration of FDI and inequality in China and the potential impact of tax preference removal and renminbi revaluation on FDI inflows.

Inward and Outward FDI in China

FDI inflows have grown rapidly in recent years, and China now accounts for nearly 50 percent of OECD outflows, while Chinese outward foreign direct investment has been relatively small.

Inward FDI

Foreign direct investment was prohibited in China until restrictions were lifted as part of China's open door policy of 1979, when a new foreign investment law was adopted. In its early stages, FDI was restricted to China's "Four Special Economic Zones" and limited to equity joint ventures. Most of the FDI went into hotel construction and energy. In 1984 a new foreign investment law accelerated FDI growth, and a number of preferential policies were also used by both central and local governments to attract investment.

A sharp increase in FDI only occurred after 1992 when China reaffirmed the policies of openness and market-oriented reforms introduced earlier. Significant tax preferences toward FDI introduced in 1991 and 1994 were also instrumental in the post-1992 surge. The resulting growth in China's inward FDI has been spectacular. In 1985 annual FDI inflows were less than U.S.$2 billion, while in 2006 they were around U.S.$70 billion, thirty-five times those of twenty years earlier.[2] Between 1985 and 1991, the annual growth rate of FDI inflows into China was 14 percent, with annual amounts during this period being less than U.S.$4.5 billion. The sharpest increase in FDI inflows occurred in the early 1990s—U.S.$11 billion in 1992 and U.S.$28 billion in 1993, with growth rates of over 150 percent in both years.[3]

By 1997 China had FDI inflows of U.S.$49 billion, and they increased again after China joined the WTO in 2001. During years 2001, 2002, and 2003, world FDI inflows declined sharply by 41 percent, 26 percent, and 10 percent, respec-

1. Whalley and Xin (2006).
2. MOFCOM (2007).
3. NBSC (2006 and various years).

tively, but China saw FDI inflows grow at much lower rates—15 percent, 13 percent, and 1.4 percent.[4] But in 2004 and 2005, China again saw inward FDI grow at 13 percent and 19.4 percent, respectively.[5] A small decrease of 4 percent in 2006 was the result of inward FDI in financial services falling by 47 percent. China is now the world's largest developing country FDI recipient and was the world's second largest FDI recipient overall after the United States in 2004, third in 2005, and fourth in 2006. By contrast, FDI inflows into India were only U.S.$5.5 billion in 2004 and U.S.$6.6 billion in 2005.[6]

A feature of China's inward FDI is the large and increasing share involved with manufacturing. Before China's accession to the WTO, less than 60 percent of inward FDI went to the manufacturing sector. After accession in 2001, the manufacturing share of inward FDI reached more than 70 percent in 2005, while the share of FDI going to the real estate sector decreased. Because labor productivity in China's Foreign Invested Enterprises (FIEs) is sharply higher than elsewhere in the economy, maybe by a factor of four compared to the rest of the industrial sector, one can argue that the primary attraction of FDI is access to a high-quality, low-wage labor pool, which can be used effectively with foreign technology in processing trade of various forms. In 2005 FIEs accounted for only 3 percent (25 million out of a 778.8 million labor force) of China's workforce (including agriculture), but over 20 percent of GDP and over 58 percent of exports.[7]

The size distribution of the FIEs funded by FDI is a further feature. Between 2001 and 2005, 553,000 FIEs using FDI had been established, with around 47 percent (260,000 enterprises) of them still in operation in 2005. Among these 260,000 functioning FIEs, 186,000 are industrial enterprises, although the large majority are small. Only 56,000 FIEs with annual sales income of more than 5 million yuan (U.S.$0.61 million equivalent) are tracked by statistical agencies in China for data purposes.[8]

A key link between FDI and overall world economic performance is that a large portion of China's trade is conducted via FIEs. The Ministry of Commerce of the People's Republic of China (MOFCOM) estimates that 46 percent of the output of FIEs in the manufacturing sector is for export, while only 17

---

4. United Nations (2006).

5. China's official inward FDI data did not include FDI inflows to financial services (including banking, securities, and insurance) before 2005 since FDI inflows to these service sectors are relatively small. FDI Inflows to financial services soared to U.S.$12.1 billion in 2005 and declined to U.S.$ 6.45 billion in 2006 (MOFCOM, 2007).

6. United Nations (2006).

7. NBSC (2006).

8. NBSC (2006).

percent is produced by non-FIEs for export.[9] The export growth rate of FIEs in most years since the early 1990s has been more than 30 percent, with some years showing more than 40 percent—a much higher growth rate than that for non-FIEs. Whalley and Xin (2006) note the sharp change in share of China's exports from FIEs, rising from less than 2 percent in 1990 to nearly 60 percent in 2005. Without growth in FIE exports, China's export growth rate would have been only about 10 percent in most years after 1990, with negative growth in some years.

Along with rapid export growth, FIEs have also accounted for progressively more of China's imports. FIEs are heavily involved in component import, assembly, and re-export as part of the processing trade. In 2005 the ratio of imports by China's FIEs to total imports was about 60 percent, although compared to exports, the ratio of imports by FIEs to China's total imports is more volatile. This ratio was 55 percent in 1998, declined to 37 percent by 2001, and rebounded by almost 20 percentage points in 2002.[10]

Lemoine (2000) reports that most of the vertical and export-oriented FDI inflows to China originate from elsewhere in Asia (primarily from Hong Kong, Korea, and Taiwan).[11] But while Hong Kong, Macao, and Taiwan accounted for 66 percent of FDI inflows between 1979 and 1992, and later this share declined, it still was around 40 percent in 2004. Many of these businesses are owner managed from initial investments, with the core business growth occurring inside rather than outside China. Fung (2004) also reports that, in contrast to the 1990s, the majority of foreign investment inflows to China now take the form of wholly foreign-owned entities rather than joint ventures. He reports that in 2002, 64 percent of FDI was of this form. Also, FDI in China from North America and Europe is claimed to be more heavily horizontal and aimed more at the Chinese domestic market than at exports. Fung (2004) reports an estimate that U.S.-origin FIEs sold more than 80 percent of their products locally in 2002, while Japanese-origin FIEs sold only 47.2 percent of their production locally.

A large amount of China's FDI-related trade is conducted through intermediaries and distribution arrangements centered around Hong Kong, Korea, and Taiwan. Fung (2004) notes that 28.3 percent of China's exports in 2002 were re-exported via Hong Kong and 21.9 percent of Chinese imports were imported via Hong Kong. Trade through agents is a reflection of trade in textiles and

9. MOFCOM (2004).

10. Authors' calculations based on NBSC (2006 and various issues).

11. Eichengreen and Tong (2005) demonstrate that China's emergence as a destination for foreign direct investment also affects the ability of other countries to attract FDI. Their results suggest that China's rapid growth and attractions as a destination for FDI also encourage FDI flows to other Asian countries, as if producers in these economies belong to a common supply chain.

apparel and the impact of the quota restraints imposed by the bilateral Multi-Fiber Arrangement (MFA) on China in the U.S. and EU markets. As Whalley (2006) notes, the termination of the MFA in January 2005 has seen large increases in China's exports of clothing to the United States and European Union, accompanied by sharp falls in exports to Hong Kong as these quotas are removed. But at the same time, this Hong Kong trade also involves many more products than apparel, notably electronics.

A considerable amount of China's trade is also related to processing and assembly, with sourcing via overseas retailers in OECD and other markets. Labor adds chiefly to the value of process exports, whose content itself has less value than non-process exports. Processed exports are typically products for final rather than intermediate sale, such as consumer electronics and clothing. Fung (2004) reports official estimates that 55.2 percent of China's exports in 2003 were processed exports, while 39.5 percent of the country's imports were inputs for processing. Feenstra and Hanson (2005) report similarly that 55.6 percent of China's exports between 1997 and 2002 were processed. The most recent official data indicate that in 2005, 78 percent of China's FIE exports were processed exports and 60 percent of FIE imports were inputs to processing. FIE-processed exports and imports accounted for 83 percent and 84 percent of China's total processed exports and imports, respectively, in 2005 indicating the importance of FDI to processing trade.[12]

There has been substantial growth in China's technology trade within this component. As Fung (2004) notes, 2003 data from China's national statistics report 25.2 percent of China's exports and 28.9 percent of imports as high technology products. Two-way trade in high technology products would thus seem to be substantial. MOFCOM (2006) estimates that 88 percent of China's exports of high technology products are conducted by FIEs and that 43 percent of China's FIE exports were high technology products in 2005 (of which 94 percent were processed exports).

While Tomiura (2005) finds that relatively few Japanese firms outsource directly to China, Xing (2006c) found that Japanese-affiliated manufacturers in China operating as subsidiaries sold about one-third of their products back to Japan. In industrial machinery, more than half of the products were exported to the Japanese market either as final goods or intermediate inputs. In the textile and transportation equipment sectors, ratios of re-export increased between 1997 and 2002. In 1997 only 31 percent of textile products were produced for the Japanese market, while the share rose to 47 percent in 2002. In transportation equipment, Japanese-affiliated manufacturers also exported 47 percent of

12. MOFCOM (2006)

Table 1. Shares of FDI in China by Province and City, 2000, 2003, and 2005
Percent[a]

Province and city	2000	2003	2005
Eastern China	**86.50**	**85.73**	**88.78**
Guangdong	27.97	14.78	20.50
Jiangsu	15.93	19.95	15.75
Shandong	7.37	11.36	14.73
Shanghai	7.84	10.33	11.12
Zhejiang	4.00	9.41	8.64
Beijing	4.17	4.14	5.85
Tianjin	2.89	2.90	4.03
Liaoning	5.07	5.33	3.82
Fujian	8.51	4.91	3.42
Hebei	1.68	1.82	0.85
Hainan	1.07	0.80	0.07
Central China	**7.65**	**11.02**	**8.00**
Hunan	1.68	1.92	1.90
Jiangxi	0.56	3.04	1.71
Hubei	2.34	2.96	1.25
Anhui	0.79	0.69	0.89
Henan	1.40	1.02	0.86
Heilongjiang	0.26	0.61	0.67
Jilin	0.36	0.36	0.55
Shanxi	0.26	0.40	0.16
Western China	**4.59**	**3.25**	**3.22**
Sichuan	1.08	0.78	1.01
Guangxi	1.30	0.79	0.62
Inner Mongolia	0.26	0.17	0.44
Chongqing	0.61	0.49	0.37
Shaanxi	0.72	0.63	0.32
Yunnan	0.32	0.16	0.29
Ningxia	0.04	0.03	0.07
Guizhou	0.06	0.09	0.06
Gansu	0.15	0.04	0.03
Xinjiang	0.05	0.03	0.01
Qinghai	0.00	0.05	0.01
Tibet	0.00	0.00	0.00

Source: NBSC (2006 and various issues) and MOFCOM (2006).
a. Boldface indicates total FDI for that province.

their products to Japan in 2002, a percentage much higher than the 27 percent re-export ratio in 1997. Re-exports increased by 23 percent in 2000, and continued to grow in 2001 and 2002 with 36 percent and 16 percent growth, respectively. This suggests growing Japanese-affiliate production in China for the Japanese market via FDI.

Finally, the geographical concentration within China of both China's trade and FDI inflows is pronounced. The majority of FDI inflows still go to the eastern and southeastern coastal areas, although the picture is changing. As table 1 indicates, in 2000 nearly 44 percent of FDI was located in two provinces—Guangdong and Jiangsu; by 2003 the share in Guangdong had fallen sharply, but five provinces still accounted for 56 percent of FDI in 2003 and 59 percent in 2005.[13] Fung (2004) also notes that Guangdong accounted for 31.7 percent of China's imports in 2003, and 34.9 percent of China's exports in the same year. These two figures are relatively stable and are 30 percent and 32 percent in 2005 for imports and exports, respectively. Among both these exports and imports, more than 60 percent are conducted via FIEs in 2005.[14]

All these studies and data thus suggest that China has indeed become a significant production base for both final products consumed abroad (and largely in OECD markets) and intermediate inputs purchased by foreign firms using FDI. Both Roach and Rauch characterize China as now a vital part of a global supply network in certain key industries, engaged in both importing and exporting various components and parts. Foreign direct investment is at the heart of this role.[15] This suggests increasing vertical integration between the OECD and Chinese industrial activity, and the creation of linkage between firms through FDI. A significant portion of this is affiliate activity, and a further portion involves owner-operated firms from Taiwan and Hong Kong.

Outward FDI

In contrast to inward FDI, Chinese outward foreign direct investment has been relatively small until recently (U.S.$5.5 billion in 2004, $12.3 billion in 2005, and $16.1 billion in 2006),[16] and also heavily concentrated on both greenfield and joint venture activity abroad, much of it focused on Hong Kong. But, in the last year or two, direct acquisition of foreign firms by Chinese entities involving potentially large transactions has become prominent, in some instances in the U.S.$15–20 billion range and with a focus well beyond Hong Kong. Examples include the Lenovo buyout of IBM's personal computer business, CNOOC's bid for Unocal, a prospective bid by MinMetals for Noranda, the Haier Group bid for Maytag, and others.[17] In part, the motivation is for the Chinese acquirer to combine the potential foreign distribution system with growing lower-wage Chinese manufacturing output, which slowly displaces higher-wage supplies abroad.

13. NBSC (2006).
14. NBSC (2006).
15. Roach (2003, pp. 2–3); Rauch (2001).
16. NBSC (2006).
17. Antkiewicz and Whalley (2006).

Chinese outward FDI has previously been concentrated outside the OECD (table 2), and data on the size of this investment have been hard to interpret because of the large amount flowing through intermediary tax havens such as the Cayman Islands. By the end of 2003, 84.3 percent of China's accumulated outward FDI was in Asia, 8.2 percent in Latin America (and mainly in the Cayman Islands), around 2 percent each in Europe, Africa, and North America, and 0.8 percent in Oceania. The top five destinations for China's cumulative outward FDI by 2003 were Hong Kong, Cayman Islands, Macao, the United States, and the Virgin Islands. China's outward FDI share in different regions has changed rapidly in recent years. The largest changes have occurred in Latin America, where the share rose to 52.7 percent from 32.1 percent between 2003 and 2005, of which 42.1 percent went to the Cayman Islands. The share in Europe and in North America increased slightly but went down in Africa and in Oceania.

China's outward FDI has been heavily concentrated in five sectors: leasing and business services (28.9 percent of China's accumulated outward FDI by 2005); distribution, wholesale, and retail (20.0 percent); mining (15.1 percent); transport, storage, and post (12.4 percent); and manufacturing (10.1 percent).[18] In 2006 Chinese outward investment was only U.S.$16.1 billion, only one-fifth of FDI flowing into China, even though the growth rate of outward FDI shares outpaced that of inward FDI for several prior years (in 2006, 32 percent and –4 percent, respectively; in 2005, 123 percent and 20 percent , respectively).[19]

A recent joint study undertaken by the Chinese Academy of International Trade and Economic Cooperation (CAITEC) and the Welsh Development Agency (WDA) used a questionnaire to investigate key factors involved in Chinese outward FDI. These included expanding markets, implementing long-term development strategies for firms, increasing access to technology, accessing advanced management methods, avoiding trade barriers, taking advantage of foreign preferential investment policies, achieving cost reductions, acquiring material inputs (resources), and transferring excess production capacity abroad. The use of overseas investment as a way around official Chinese restrictions on access to foreign exchange and foreign capital markets was also cited as a factor.[20]

Other studies have pointed to non-economic reasons for Chinese enterprises' investing abroad, such as the possibility of gaining residency rights and other benefits in the host country for managerial staff (including health services, social

18. NBSC (2006).

19. Department of International Cooperation (DIC), Ministry of Commerce of the People's Republic of China, 2007. See www.fdi.gov.cn/pub/FDI/wztj/jwtztj/t20070213_74079.htm.

20. CAITEC (2005).

Table 2. China's Outward FDI

Region and country	Accumulated outward FDI, end of 2003		Outward FDI, 2004		Outward FDI, 2005		Accumulated outward FDI, end of 2005	
	Amount (U.S.$ millions)	Share (percent)	Amount (U.S.$ millions)	Share (percent)	Amount (U.S.$ millions)	Share (percent)	Amount (U.S.$ millions)	Share (percent)
Total	39,446.5	100.0	5,498.0	100.0	12,261.2	100.0	57,205.6	100.0
Asia	33,254.1	84.3	3,000.3	54.6	4,374.6	35.7	40,629.0	71.0
Hong Kong	30459.0	77.2	2628.4	47.8	3419.7	27.9	36507.1	63.8
Indonesia	67.1	0.2	62.0	1.1	11.8	0.1	140.9	0.2
Japan	118.2	0.3	15.3	0.3	17.2	0.1	150.7	0.3
Macao	563.8	1.4	26.6	0.5	8.3	0.1	598.7	1.0
Singapore	257.2	0.7	48.0	0.9	20.3	0.2	325.5	0.6
Republic of Korea	253.2	0.6	40.2	0.7	588.8	4.8	882.2	1.5
Thailand	191.0	0.5	23.4	0.4	4.8	0.0	219.2	0.4
Vietnam	191.6	0.5	16.9	0.3	20.8	0.2	229.2	0.4
Africa	886.2	2.2	317.4	5.8	391.7	3.2	1,595.3	2.8
Algeria	75.1	0.2	11.2	0.2	84.9	0.7	171.2	0.3
Sudan	113.7	0.3	146.7	2.7	91.1	0.7	351.5	0.6
Guinea	13.4	0.0	14.4	0.3	16.3	0.1	44.2	0.1
Madagascar	36.2	0.1	13.6	0.2	0.1	0.0	49.9	0.1
Nigeria	-4.7	0.0	45.5	0.8	53.3	0.4	94.1	0.2
South Africa	47.0	0.1	17.8	0.3	47.5	0.4	112.3	0.2
Europe	922.3	2.3	170.9	3.1	505.0	4.1	1,598.2	2.8
United Kingdom	53.8	0.1	29.4	0.5	24.8	0.2	108.0	0.2
Germany	112.1	0.3	27.5	0.5	128.7	1.0	268.4	0.5
France	17.4	0.0	10.3	0.2	6.1	0.0	33.8	0.1
Russia	184.9	0.5	77.3	1.4	203.3	1.7	465.6	0.8
Latin America	3,240.7	8.2	1,762.7	32.1	6,466.2	52.7	11,469.6	20.0
Bahamas	-51.8	-0.1	43.6	0.8	23.0	0.2	14.7	0.0
Cayman Islands	2486.7	6.3	1286.1	23.4	5162.8	42.1	8935.6	15.6
Mexico	111.2	0.3	27.1	0.5	3.6	0.0	141.9	0.2
Virgin Islands (U.K.)	372.0	0.9	385.5	7.0	1226.1	10.0	1983.6	3.5
North America	815.9	2.1	126.5	2.3	320.8	2.6	1,263.2	2.2
Canada	65.7	0.2	5.1	0.1	32.4	0.3	103.3	0.2
United States	470.9	1.2	119.9	2.2	231.8	1.9	822.7	1.4
Oceania	327.3	0.8	120.2	2.2	202.8	1.7	650.3	1.1
Australia	269.4	0.7	125.0	2.3	193.1	1.6	587.5	1.0
New Zealand	36.6	0.1	-4.9	-0.1	3.5	0.0	35.2	0.1

Source: NBSC (2006, table 18-20, and various issues).

security, access to education). But the decision by a Chinese company to buy a foreign company is also often linked to an intent to move the manufacturing component to China to benefit from lower labor costs while keeping existing distribution networks of the acquired business in the host country—similar to the considerations of foreign firms that outsource activities in China.

Recent widely publicized Chinese bids for large firms in OECD countries are also portrayed in Chinese media as involving a prestige factor, such as coverage of Lenovo's takeover of IBM, an example of a Chinese company going abroad to buy a recognizable foreign brand, or of Haier's factory in South Carolina, an example of a Chinese corporation seeking to build its brand's identity by establishing manufacturing plants in the target country.

However, recent Chinese outward FDI also reflects official Chinese government policy to encourage domestic enterprises to invest abroad. Government regulatory approval processes for overseas investment projects have been significantly simplified in recent years helping to increase this outward flow. Chinese companies are also supported by low-interest loans if their overseas activity involves, among other things, resource exploration and acquisition of advanced foreign technology. This use of low-interest loans made available to Chinese state-owned enterprises (SOEs) reflects China's large and growing foreign reserves. These reserves today stand at close to U.S.$1 trillion, reflecting both large Chinese trade surpluses in recent years and inward foreign investment. With worries over the country's money supply, and the prospect of possible further falls in the U.S. dollar, as well as the impact on the large holdings of U.S. treasuries in the reserve portfolio, deploying Chinese reserves in this way is seen in China as reasonable policy.

Chinese government policy is now chiefly to allow large SOEs to use outward-oriented investment in order to secure access to resources and raw materials (especially iron ore, coal, oil, and natural gas), to acquire new technology for transfer back to China, to expand Chinese export markets, and to strengthen international relationships with and gain more influence in other countries. In 2003 SOEs accounted for only 43 percent of total Chinese investments abroad with limited liability; shareholding and private companies taken together account for another 43 percent. With the recent large-scale acquisition activity abroad, these proportions seem poised to change.

The OECD has shown some political resistance to these transactions, raising questions related to subsidization, lack of transparency, and national security. National security issues regarding foreign acquisitions are not new, and in the United States go back to the Exxon-Florio provisions of the American Defense Production Act of 1998, following concerns in the late 1980s over Japanese buyouts. Issues of subsidization of foreign acquisitions through low-interest loans from central banks and the transparency of organizational form of acquiring entities (state-owned enterprises), however, are new.

For now, outward FDI from China is still relatively small but growing much more rapidly than inward FDI, and the size of China's foreign reserves suggests this could change significantly in future years. The linkage to distribution and marketing networks seems even more critical with this outward investment than with inward FDI.

Inward FDI and Growth Performance in China

We discussed how much of China's strong growth performance can be attributed to inward FDI in a recent joint paper.[21] Here we used an extension of the growth accounting approach long associated with Solow (1957) and Dennison (1967), extending the original Solow framework by using a two-stage production growth accounting approach.

Solow's original purpose was to investigate the contribution of technical progress relative to factor accumulation in U.S. long-term growth, which he put at 87.5 percent. Dennison (1967) later used Solow's framework to explore the factors, explaining why growth rates differed across OECD countries, and Jorgenson and Griliches (1967) investigated the role of embodied technical progress on growth, concluding it was substantial. Young (1995) later used this growth accounting approach to analyze growth experiences more broadly in Asia, finding that the higher growth in the newly industrializing countries of East Asia was not due to rapid technological progress and other factors affecting the Solow residual, but rather to capital accumulation. The Solow framework has recently been extended to open economies by Kohli (2003a and 2003b) to capture terms of trade effects in growth performance of open economies.

Following the trade literature, at the first stage we use a GDP function in which the outputs of the FIE and non-FIE portions of the Chinese economy aggregate to yield GDP,

$$O(t) = g[FIE(t), NFIE(t)], \qquad (1)$$

where $O(t)$ refers to aggregate output and $FIE(t)$ and $NFIE(t)$ are outputs of the FIE and non-FIE portions of the economy.

In the second stage we use separate production functions for each sector, that is,

21. Whalley and Xin (2006).

$$FIE(t) = A^F(t)f[FDI(t), L^F(t)] \tag{2}$$

$$NFIE(t) = A^N(t)h[K(t), L^N(t)], \tag{3}$$

where $A^F(t)$ and $A^N(t)$ are the Hicksian neutral technical change terms, $L^F(t)$ and $L^N(t)$ are the labor inputs used in the FIE and non-FIE parts of the economy, and $FDI(t)$ and $K(t)$ are the stocks of accumulated FDI and capital used in the FIE and non-FIE parts of the economy. The strong assumption is made that foreign-supplied capital (FDI) is the only nonlabor input in the FIE portion of the economy.

Taking time derivatives through (2) and (3) yields,

$$\frac{\dot{FIE}}{FIE} = \frac{\dot{A}^F}{A^F} + S_{FDI}^F \frac{\dot{FDI}}{FDI} + S_L^F \frac{\dot{L}^F}{L^F} \tag{4}$$

and

$$\frac{\dot{NFIE}}{NFIE} = \frac{\dot{A}^N}{A^N} + S_K^N \frac{\dot{K}}{K} + S_L^N \frac{\dot{L}^N}{L^N}, \tag{5}$$

where S_L^F and S_{FDI}^F are the shares of labor and FDI in FIE production and S_L^N and S_K^N are the shares of labor and capital in non-FIE production.

The economywide growth accounting equation for this two-stage production structure can thus be expressed as,

$$\frac{\dot{O}}{O} = g^F \left(\frac{\dot{A}^F}{A^F} + S_{FDI}^F \frac{\dot{FDI}}{FDI} + S_L^F \frac{\dot{L}^F}{L^F} \right) + g^N \left(\frac{\dot{A}^N}{A^N} + S_K^N \frac{\dot{K}}{K} + S_L^N \frac{\dot{L}^N}{L^N} \right), \tag{6}$$

where g^f and g^n are shares of FIE and non-FIE output in the GDP function. If (1), (2), and (3) are Cobb Douglas, then the associated share parameters are constant. If (1), (2), and (3) are CES (Constant Elasticity of Substitution), then the share parameters in (6) change over time.

If g^f is the share of FIE output in national income, g^n can then be obtained by residual since the sum of g^f and g^n is one. The labor share parameters, S_L^F and S_L^N, in FIE and non-FIE production functions are calculated using the labor force wage bill divided by value added for the two parts of the economy, and S_{FDI}^F and S_K^N are obtained by residual. The wage bill of FIEs is estimated by multiplying wage rate and labor force data.[22] The wage bill of non-FIEs is China's total labor remuneration minus the FIE wage bill.[23] Data on China's

22. NBSC (2005, pp. 121, 174, and 506).
23. NBSC (2005, p. 62, and various years).

labor force is from NBSC, and the labor force in non-FIEs is taken to be the total labor force minus that in FIEs.[24]

To determine the capital stock and growth variables, we first estimate the Chinese total capital stock along with the FIE capital stock as accumulated FDI net of depreciation. We use the total capital stock minus the FDI stock as our estimate of the non-FIE capital stock.

The Chinese capital stock is obtained by first deflating annual capital formation data using a fixed investment price index.[25] A depreciation rate of 0.04, similar to that used by Chow (1993) and Chow and Lin (2002), is assumed for the depreciation of the annual capital stock after 1985. Before 1985 a depreciation factor of 0.10 is used instead to account for outmoded fixed equipment. Annual capital formation is from the World Bank database in U.S.$.[26]

The resulting growth rates of variables from 1995 to 2004, along with the estimated share parameters, are reported in table 3. These data indicate that while FIEs produce one-fifth of China's total GDP, the FIE subpart of the Chinese economy grew three times faster than the non-FIE portion between 1995 and 2004 and considerably faster than China's economy as a whole. In the two years 2003 and 2004, more than 40 percent of China's economic growth came from FIEs, and in the last decade (from 1995 to 2004), more than 30 percent.

A further striking feature of these data is the high capital share in the non-FIE portion of the economy (declining from 70 percent to only 50 percent in 2004) and the even higher share of FDI in FIE output (more than 80 percent in most years after 1995). The high (and volatile) $\dot{L}^F/L^F$ variable reflects rapid labor growth forces in FIEs from a low base, and the high $\dot{K}/K$ variable reflects high rates of domestic saving in China.

Following Solow's original procedure of specifying no functional form for the production functions (4) and (5), and allowing shares to vary each year, we use data from table 4 and (6) to decompose the growth performance of the FIE and non-FIE parts of China's economy and assess their respective contributions to the total GDP growth. If we instead assume (2) and (3) to be Cobb Douglas, and time invariant, shares are constant over time. If we assume CES, then shares vary over time in ways that reflect the elasticity of substitution, output, and factor input data and need not be the same as observed shares.

The results in table 4 suggest that more than 90 percent of growth in the non-FIE subeconomy in China between 1996 and 2004 has been from growth in the capital stock. In contrast, 20 to 40 percent of FIE growth came from tech-

24. NBSC (2005, p. 118).
25. NBSC (2005, p. 301).
26. WDI (World Development Indicators) database, World Bank, 2005. See http://devdata.world-bank.org/data-query/.

Table 3. Growth Rates of Output and Accumulated FDI, Capital Stock, and Labor Force in FIEs and the Non-FIEs Portion of the Chinese Economy and Share Parameters

Percent

Year	$\dfrac{\dot{FIE}}{FIE}$	$\dfrac{\dot{NFIE}}{NFIE}$	g^F	g^N	S^F_L	S^F_{FDI}	S^N_L	S^N_K	$\dfrac{\dot{L}^F}{I^F}$	$\dfrac{\dot{FDI}}{FDI}$	$\dfrac{\dot{L}^N}{L^N}$	$\dfrac{\dot{K}}{K}$
1995	...	...	10.3	89.7	19.6	80.4	29.9	70.1	41.0	41.8	0.5	14.0
1996	18.9	8.5	11.2	88.8	20.8	79.2	30.2	69.8	26.4	32.6	1.0	14.2
1997	24.8	6.8	12.8	87.2	19.8	80.2	30.3	69.7	5.3	26.6	1.2	13.3
1998	23.5	5.5	14.7	85.3	21.1	78.9	32.8	67.2	7.6	20.7	1.1	12.3
1999	15.9	5.6	15.9	84.1	20.1	79.9	34.9	65.1	2.2	14.2	1.1	11.4
2000	17.4	6.2	17.2	82.8	18.4	81.6	36.9	63.1	7.7	11.9	0.8	10.5
2001	12.5	6.5	18.0	82.0	18.7	81.3	40.4	59.6	10.1	12.4	1.1	11.2
2002	12.3	7.4	18.7	81.3	19.5	80.5	42.7	57.3	12.3	12.5	0.7	11.5
2003	20.4	6.7	20.6	79.4	18.5	81.5	45.2	54.8	19.4	10.6	0.5	13.0
2004	18.8	7.1	22.4	77.6	15.9	84.1	48.8	51.2	14.8	10.4	0.6	13.3

Source: Whalley and Xin (2006).

nological progress and a further 15 percent from growth in the FIE labor force. These decomposition results also suggest that without FDI inflows, growth in China in 2004 would have been lowered by the 1.8 percent attributed to the $\dot{FDI}/FDI$ term. If TFP (Total Factor Productivity) growth of 1.6 percent in the FIE portion of the economy is attributed to technical progress embodied in FDI, this component of growth would also be lost. This yields an estimate of forgone growth were FDI growth to have been interrupted in 2004 of 3.4 percent. The 3 percent labor force growth rate in the FIE portion would remain as a growth contribution through redeployment of labor elsewhere.[27]

While the FIE subeconomy in China is still only 20 percent of the whole economy, it nonetheless accounts for more than 40 percent of China's recent economic growth. Thus, this part of the Chinese economy has substantial implications for the sustainability of China's future economic growth. Whether rapid growth continues into the future, in turn, depends on both continued growth in inward FDI and access to international export markets abroad.

While China's FDI inflow growth rate has averaged more than 10 percent per year since 2002, in the years ahead it seems likely to plateau or slightly decline. Because OECD FDI has been falling in other non-OECD countries (in Brazil to U.S.$10 billion in 2003 and $18 billion in 2004 from U.S.$33 billion in 2000), it seems likely that FDI flows to China will also fall as foreign investment moves increasingly to other low-wage countries such as Vietnam and Indonesia.

27. As Lardy indicates in his comments, Chinese statistical authorities only report data related to industry sector of FIEs. We thus calculate the FIE share in China's total GDP using the key assumption that the marginal revenue of per FDI dollar is equalized across aggregate sectors of the economy (agriculture, manufacturing, and services). The deviation of this assumption from the real situation, as Lardy notes, will certainly affect our decomposition results. However, since no data on the other sectors are available and the real situation is unknown, we must make assumptions. The assumption that the marginal revenue of per FDI dollar is equalized across aggregate sectors of the economy (agriculture, manufacturing, and services) seems plausible from an economics perspective. With this assumption the share of FIEs in China's industrial value added can then be estimated by using value added for FIEs divided by the value added of the industrial sector from NBSC (2005, p. 488). We multiply this share by China's industrial share in total GDP (NBSC, 2005, p. 52), and then divide by the industrial FDI share in total inward FDI (NBSC, 2005, p. 648) to estimate the FIE share in China's total GDP. In 1995 the FIE share was around 10 percent and reached over 20 percent in 2003 and 2004. We then can calculate the growth rates of the two parts of Chinese economy and arrive at the result that China's FIEs may have contributed over 40 percent to China's economic growth in 2003 and 2004. The two-stage decomposition approach we employed in this paper is from top to bottom. This 40 percent thus does not depend on the magnitudes of labor shares in FIE and non-FIE economy. The magnitudes of labor shares do matter for the calculation of the contributions of TFP, labor growth, and capital growth to China's economy growth. However, even when we double the labor share of output in FIEs and correspondingly adjust the labor share of output in the non-FIE sector, the yielding decomposition results are not substantially different from those in table 4.

Table 4. Two-Stage Solow Decomposition of FIE and Non-FIE Growth Rates in China, by Year and Component

Percent

Year	GDP growth rate Total	Growth rate (A) FIE TFP	FIE L	FIE FDI	FIE Total	Non-FIE TFP	Non-FIE L	Non-FIE K	Non-FIE Total	Contribution to GDP growth (B) FIE TFP	FIE L	FIE FDI	FIE Total	Non-FIE TFP	Non-FIE L	Non-FIE K	Non-FIE Total
1996	9.6	-12.4	5.5	25.8	18.9	-1.7	0.3	9.9	8.5	-1.3	0.6	2.7	1.9	-1.5	0.3	8.9	7.7
1997	8.8	2.4	1.0	21.3	24.8	-2.8	0.4	9.3	6.8	0.3	0.1	2.4	2.8	-2.5	0.3	8.2	6.0
1998	7.8	5.5	1.6	16.4	23.5	-3.1	0.3	8.2	5.5	0.7	0.2	2.1	3.0	-2.7	0.3	7.2	4.8
1999	7.1	4.2	0.4	11.3	15.9	-2.2	0.4	7.4	5.6	0.6	0.1	1.7	2.3	-1.8	0.3	6.3	4.8
2000	8.0	6.3	1.4	9.7	17.4	-0.7	0.3	6.6	6.2	1.0	0.2	1.5	2.8	-0.6	0.3	5.6	5.2
2001	7.5	0.5	1.9	10.1	12.5	-0.7	0.5	6.7	6.5	0.1	0.3	1.7	2.2	-0.6	0.4	5.5	5.3
2002	8.3	-0.2	2.4	10.0	12.3	0.5	0.3	6.6	7.4	0.0	0.4	1.8	2.2	0.4	0.3	5.4	6.1
2003	9.3	8.2	3.6	8.6	20.4	-0.6	0.2	7.2	6.7	1.5	0.7	1.6	3.8	-0.5	0.2	5.8	5.5
2004	9.5	7.7	2.4	8.8	18.8	-0.1	0.3	6.8	7.1	1.6	0.5	1.8	3.9	0.0	0.2	5.4	5.6

Year	GDP	Contribution share to total GDP growth (C) FIE TFP	FIE L	FIE FDI	FIE Total	Non-FIE TFP	Non-FIE L	Non-FIE K	Non-FIE Total	Factor contribution share inside (D) FIE TFP	FIE L	FIE FDI	Non-FIE TFP	Non-FIE L	Non-FIE K
1996	100	-13.3	5.9	27.6	20.2	-15.7	2.7	92.7	79.8	-65.8	29.1	136.7	-19.7	3.4	116.2
1997	100	3.0	1.3	27.0	31.4	-28.5	3.7	93.4	68.6	9.7	4.2	86.1	-41.5	5.3	136.2
1998	100	9.0	2.6	26.8	38.5	-34.2	3.9	91.9	61.5	23.5	6.8	69.7	-55.7	6.3	149.3
1999	100	8.5	0.9	23.3	32.7	-25.8	4.4	88.7	67.3	26.1	2.7	71.2	-38.3	6.5	131.8
2000	100	12.5	2.8	19.2	34.5	-7.6	3.3	69.8	65.5	36.3	8.2	55.5	-11.6	5.0	106.6
2001	100	1.2	4.3	23.2	28.8	-7.8	5.0	74.0	71.2	4.2	15.1	80.7	-11.0	7.1	103.9
2002	100	-0.4	5.2	21.8	26.7	5.0	3.1	65.2	73.3	-1.4	19.6	81.8	6.8	4.2	89.0
2003	100	16.5	7.2	17.3	41.1	-5.6	2.0	62.5	58.9	40.3	17.5	42.2	-9.5	3.3	106.1
2004	100	16.6	5.1	19.1	40.8	-0.5	2.6	57.1	59.2	40.8	12.5	46.7	-0.8	4.4	96.4

Source: Whalley and Xin (2006).

With China's accession to the WTO, its WTO commitments imply both capital market liberalization (in banking) and further progress on commitments on rule-based WTO issues, including TRIPs (Trade-Related Aspects of Intellectual Property Rights) and TRIMs (Trade-Related Investment Measures), and these changes may help attract more FDI. China is also continuing to see changes in the legal forms that FIEs take, and this may also help with continued FDI inflows. The share of inward FDI occurring through wholly foreign-owned enterprises at the end of 2000 was 46.9 percent of accumulated FDI, and in recent years, wholly foreign-owned enterprises provided the dominant legal form (more than 66 percent of inward FDI in 2004).[28] This increasing share of wholly owned FIEs may accelerate technology transfer and product upgrading; access to foreign equipment and technology and intermediate goods will improve with trade liberalization, and lower tariffs will apply to imports.

China's rapid export growth that FDI inflows have generated also raises concerns over the continued absorptive capacities of the OECD. China's share of world exports is now around 8 percent and, with a 35 percent growth rate in exports, is doubling every three years. Continued FDI flows thus may also encounter problems here if they are export oriented. China's large trade surplus with the European Union and the United States also fuels protectionist pressure in these countries.

This leaves the issue of whether the non-FIE part of the economy can generate higher growth in the future to compensate for slowing growth in the FIE subeconomy. Chinese reforms for SOEs and labor market and competition-related reforms provide the major hope, but results from these reforms thus far are not conclusive.

Overall then, plateauing or falling FDI, limits to FDI diversification from other non-OECD countries, and continued growth of exports all raise questions about continued high growth in China in the future based on FDI inflows. These negatives are counterbalanced by an ever-improving policy environment for FDI in China, but they seem unlikely to support yet more FDI growth into the country. Whether growth in the non-FIE subeconomy can compensate is the issue.

FDI and Regional Inequality

Growing inequality in the country, and whether FDI plays a central role, is a central policy concern in China and much debated. While absolute poverty in China, measured by headcount ratios (fraction of the population below var-

28. NBSC (2005 and various issues).

ious poverty lines), has been falling sharply, relative inequality has grown quickly. A widely used measure is the ratio of urban to rural incomes, which has increased from around 1.8 in the mid-1980s to around 3.2 today.[29] The national Gini coefficient has increased from under 0.28 in the 1981 to 0.41 today.[30] The geographical nature of China's development—that it has occurred primarily in a relatively small number of western and coastal provinces—is widely thought to be a key determinant in this outcome. That these same provinces are the largest recipients of inward FDI appears to link foreign investment with increased inequality.

In table 5, we report real GDP per capita by province for the years between 1978 and 2004. Provinces are divided by coastal and interior with interior provinces showing GDP per capita well below the national average and coastal provinces well above the national average. The gap between highest and lowest provinces in 2004 is approximately ten times greater, narrowing from approximately fifteen times in 1978. The trend indicates a narrowing over time in the dispersion of provincial GDP per capita both within the two groups of coastal and interior provinces and across the two groups. As national inequality has been increasing in China, this seems to indicate increasing inequality within provinces over time, and especially across the urban-rural divide within provinces.

In table 6 we report FDI inflows by province for individual years from 1978 onward, cumulating them forward after allowing for 4 percent depreciation. The data are in real terms after adjustments by the GDP deflator for the year. They show substantial growth through the 1990s in FDI by province, as well as extreme concentration in Guangdong, Fujian, Jiangsu, Shangdong, and Shanghai, which account for nearly 70 percent of the FDI stock in 2003.

These two tables suggest, however, that while FDI is concentrated by province on both a stock and a flow basis, changes in regional inequality run opposite to FDI trends. Among coastal provinces, more relative income growth is evident in those provinces that receive relatively smaller amounts of FDI. In addition, there is generally a narrowing of income disparities between coastal and noncoastal provinces. This leaves the issue of whether the concentration of FDI inflows into urban areas within provinces is a more critical determinant of growing relative inequality than is revealed here.

For these FDI flows the resulting foreign invested enterprises also employ a relatively small amount of labor, even though FIEs account for a majority of China's exports and imports. Whalley and Xin (2006) report this figure at 3

29. Calculation based on NBSC (2006, table 10-1).
30. See World Bank, China Quick Facts, 2007 (http://web.worldbank.org/WBSITE/EXTER-NAL/COUNTRIES/EASTASIAPACIFICEXT/CHINAEXTN/0,,contentMDK:20680895~pagePK
:1497618~piPK:217854~theSitePK:318950,00.html).

Table 5. Real Provincial-per-Capita GDP in China, Various Years

Area and province	Per capita GDP (in 1978 RMB)				As percent of national average			
	1978	1990	2000	2004	1978	1990	2000	2004
National average, coastal	374.57	888.98	2099.9	2858.14	100	100	100	100
Beijing	1248.2	2558.6	4811.4	6666.8	333.24	287.81	229.13	233.26
Tianjin	1141.6	1951.6	4393.2	6653.4	304.78	219.53	209.21	232.79
Liaoning	675.3	1350.6	2955.4	3787.2	180.29	151.93	140.74	132.51
Shanghai	2484.6	3090.2	7293.1	9938.5	663.32	347.61	347.31	347.73
Jiangsu	427.2	1078.8	3095.4	4849.7	114.05	121.35	147.41	169.68
Zhejiang	329.8	1114.0	3462.2	5535.3	88.05	125.31	164.87	193.67
Fujian	270.6	839.4	2039.6	3954.0	72.24	94.42	144.27	138.34
Shandong	314.9	871.0	2524.0	3921.3	84.07	97.98	120.20	137.20
Guangdong	364.8	1286.8	2999.2	4488.5	97.39	144.75	142.83	157.04
Hainan	310.6	795.1	1767.3	2185.6	82.92	89.44	84.16	76.47
National average, interior								
Hebei	362.0	753.2	2024.2	3015.9	96.64	84.73	96.40	105.52
Shanxi	363.0	765.3	1337.4	2187.1	96.91	86.09	63.69	76.52
Inner Mongolia	318.4	735.5	1581.8	2643.6	85.00	82.74	75.33	92.49
Jilin	381.5	880.3	1790.8	2720.0	101.85	99.02	85.28	95.17
Heilongjiang	558.4	1031.9	2365.5	2985.8	149.08	116.08	112.65	104.47
Anhui	241.8	593.0	1361.5	1731.7	64.55	66.71	64.84	60.59
Jiangxi	273.3	610.9	1297.9	1900.9	72.96	68.72	81.81	66.51
Henan	230.5	574.6	1489.0	2108.1	61.54	64.64	70.91	73.76
Hubei	330.1	807.0	1903.0	2447.1	88.13	90.78	90.62	85.62
Hunan	284.5	636.2	1537.8	1947.1	75.95	71.57	73.23	68.12
Guangxi	223.0	511.1	1225.1	1578.1	59.53	57.54	58.34	55.21
Chongqing			1379.8	2043.4			65.71	71.49
Sichuan	252.2	587.9	1291.6	1746.1	67.33	66.13	61.51	61.09
Guizhou	173.6	432.7	756.1	947.6	46.35	48.67	36.01	33.15
Yunnan	223.3	588.9	1223.1	1557.7	59.62	66.24	58.25	54.50
Xizhang	371.5	611.1	1202.7	1794.1	99.18	68.74	57.27	62.77
Shaanxi	291.6	625.8	1235.9	1808.6	77.85	70.40	58.86	63.28
Gansu	346.1	575.6	1029.6	1383.2	92.40	64.75	49.03	48.40
Qinghai	425.8	821.6	1365.0	2007.9	113.68	92.42	65.00	70.25
Ningxia	365.2	721.3	1267.6	1819.3	97.50	81.14	60.36	63.65
Xinjiang	316.9	914.0	1901.3	2604.5	84.60	102.81	90.54	91.13

Sources: NBSC (various years)

percent of the workforce (including agriculture). If FDI affects inequality through wage rate effects in localized labor markets that are effectively segmented by an absence of labor mobility, the aggregate impact on inequality of 3 percent of the workforce being hired by FIEs would at first sight appear to be small.

Table 6. Cumulative FDI Capital Stock by Province, by Year[a]
U.S.$ millions

Province	1988	1989	1990	1991	1992	1993	1994	1995
Beijing	668.40	983.003	1220.633	1401.953	1654.9	2078.136	2825.8665	3285.968
Tianjin	42.34	70.67025	102.7734	222.9011	309.1879	747.1675	1332.1312	2085.983
Hebei	22.24	50.14094	87.4853	125.6964	220.5618	502.739	799.68934	1057.818
Shanxi	8.67	17.77465	20.46367	23.21735	29.84592	130.4785	144.46224	172.5575
Inner Mongolia	4.48	4.558158	15.01583	15.44927	19.42449	81.23989	102.23989	128.8293
Liaoning	153.21	274.1738	506.9369	814.6281	1238.2	2127.358	2914.6571	3554.092
Jilin	8.24	11.50332	28.64318	44.41857	109.1902	306.8286	441.10332	639.99
Heilongjiang	53.30	75.18416	96.6668	101.6649	161.3466	325.38	522.92438	776.2981
Shanghai	309.98	750.0233	894.0324	994.7586	1390.978	3654.478	5006.4224	6341.235
Jiangsu	136.97	231.793	346.6813	532.408	1962.597	3970.941	6091.7064	8602.737
Zhejiang	39.31	93.27012	137.9693	218.579	421.6352	1161.916	1812.2325	2407.379
Anhui	15.30	19.81286	28.63034	36.45332	83.27676	269.014	482.38829	719.1809
Fujian	173.05	518.5472	787.8254	1194.654	2404.379	4417.603	6490.2311	8376.666
Jiangxi	6.89	12.90258	18.59648	36.17442	122.8108	270.6633	418.35463	554.9252
Shandong	57.28	195.7465	338.7566	493.9474	1360.518	2681.421	4120.3436	5382.536
Henan	85.32	127.6334	183.018	211.3351	249.8383	463.602	679.23729	906.1143
Hubei	29.66	53.07147	79.94861	120.3977	295.008	679.874	1017.2676	1308.83
Hunan	10.25	16.73169	27.22242	47.52933	162.3749	476.9085	658.42683	901.5353
Guangdong	1273.39	2461.97	3823.491	5384.152	8438.003	13645.25	18832.104	23523.72
Guangxi	27.45	75.60513	101.2409	120.9936	276.9246	914.9793	1385.0036	1686.559
Hainan	151.83	247.5512	340.6692	492.6437	872.6786	1356.675	1858.5588	2347.843
Sichuan	31.39	38.71735	53.20866	74.00842	170.1021	582.6255	1117.6828	1360.39
Guizhou	5.85	13.62205	17.75717	23.94694	40.46971	70.36231	106.09295	132.1143
Yunnan	4.12	11.88792	14.0224	16.24409	40.9894	110.5477	145.50079	191.5235
Xizhang	0.04	0.038287	0.036756	0.035285	0.033874	0.032519	0.0312183	0.02997
Shaanxi	148.54	278.805	278.805	297.3493	325.6723	484.5858	609.86019	757.4454
Gansu	2.66	4.442522	4.442522	5.139079	5.242673	13.80244	66.4127	97.67769
Qinghai	3.59	3.308006	3.308006	3.175685	3.649307	5.880999	7.105664	7.691754
Ningxia	0.40	0.617556	0.617556	0.762065	3.840824	12.41997	16.327117	17.74371
Xinjiang	6.70	12.45043	12.45043	12.15923	11.67286	50.09983	77.35452	103.395

At the microlevel, a recent paper by Ma (2006) analyzes in some detail the geographical location of trade flows involving FIEs in an effort to capture regional inequality change resulting from both FDI and transportation costs. Ma notes the dramatic changes in Guangdong with wage rates growing from only 97 percent of the national average in 1978 to 172 percent of the national average by 1997. Reflecting its proximity to Hong Kong, Guangdong, by 1997, accounted for 43 percent of China's total exports, and 88 percent of exports from coastal provinces. Guangdong in 1999 accounted for 58 and 55 percent,

Table 6 (Continued)

U.S.$ millions

Province	1996	1997	1998	1999	2000	2001	2002	2003
Beijing	3925.989	4544.906	5428.39	6189.589	6756.058	7317.344	7825.075	8298.674
Tianjin	3071.991	4172.507	5044.161	5716.093	6051.211	6812.481	7274.183	7674.219
Hebei	1427.947	1908.191	2533.867	2948.621	3159.081	3347.75	3577.104	3868.078
Shanxi	234.2515	355.8898	461.7979	637.1306	720.2966	801.4958	867.6605	929.1307
Inner Mong.	159.3752	188.6837	225.7621	248.708	289.8555	328.5947	397.6033	421.5638
Liaoning	4275.254	5257.004	6123.034	6403.984	7316.313	8034.125	9296.16	10195.85
Jilin	838.7143	1001.13	1162.137	1264.835	1377.184	1480.89	1535.213	1559.616
Helongjiang	1026.879	1343.784	1548.682	1644.378	1724.068	1815.534	1907.723	1976.303
Shanghai	8045.392	9781.946	11160.32	12118.89	13162.05	14653.79	16050.46	17870.59
Jiangsu	10846.93	13060.75	15796.95	18175.27	20554.96	22984.62	26794.34	30478.79
Zhejiang	3066.448	3676.19	4176.772	4620.214	5215.12	6046.581	7232.372	9185.539
Anhui	942.0907	1116.038	1207.372	1288.503	1390.942	1493.44	1612.012	1712.861
Fujian	10070.75	11712.52	13313.71	14774.25	15842.59	17051.44	18150.81	18594.98
Jiangxi	682.3901	889.4267	1082.315	1197.913	1259.866	1395.582	1841.914	2494.04
Shandong	6475.547	7568.629	8348.234	9133.071	10204.31	11451.93	13190.98	15372.08
Henan	1129.967	1421.894	1667.964	1859.468	2057.796	2190.536	2290.708	2441.774
Hubei	1594.194	1943.848	2344.163	2703.534	3051.658	3488.559	4011.141	4557.065
Hunan	1235.729	1633.023	1969.717	2214.724	2454.105	2736.914	3045.24	3381.936
Guangdong	28422.04	33440.23	38008.8	42262.37	46026.15	49796.42	53064.81	54464.45
Guangxi	1948.531	2302.099	2645.429	2854.184	2993.688	3054.601	3126.072	3189.483
Hainan	2645.934	2883.798	3120.828	3235.961	3314.813	3401.796	3503.331	3552.863
Chongqing	0	203.637	407.3044	509.3534	607.1264	703.4617	766.1778	852.9678
Sichuan	1525.008	1585.044	1704.666	1805.38	1944.424	2140.29	2312.645	2405.779
Guizhou	142.4189	160.9674	176.8121	189.9973	194.4896	200.0141	209.7472	221.7219
Yunnan	216.3375	288.3847	348.4314	410.6956	456.2133	468.3303	501.4337	519.1248
Xizhang	0.028771	0.02762	0.026515	0.025455	0.024436	0.023459	0.022521	0.02162
Shaanxi	889.1447	1159.585	1260.66	1330.081	1416.328	1525.088	1631.188	1715.377
Gansu	138.4913	153.139	165.9998	179.6868	202.6453	229.5231	248.7505	249.3452
Qinghai	7.88088	8.768897	8.418141	10.35483	9.940634	26.70328	47.56907	57.02146
Ningxia	19.79113	22.26824	30.49725	54.70589	60.93532	66.3985	73.95301	78.84265
Xinjiang	131.0039	137.806	142.9417	149.1309	152.4053	155.8791	158.8791	159.0259

a. Calculations use 1990 prices and assume a 4 percent depreciation rate.

respectively, of exports and imports used in the processing trade, whereby imported components are added to domestically and then reshipped. These dramatic changes in the Guangdong case seem to suggest a link between FDI and wage inequality despite the small size of the FIE labor force in aggregate.

Ma (2006) uses an economic geography model based on Redding and Venables (2004) to test the two hypotheses: FIEs pay higher wages in provinces where there are lower transportation costs to ship products to foreign markets, and in turn, FIEs with access to low-cost suppliers will also pay higher wages. Ma uses Redding and Venables's structure to generate a wage equation to imply that the maximum wage a representative FIE in any province would pay is a function of two distance-weighted market capability measures on the import and export side. Increased market and supplier access reduces production costs, and immobile labor wage rates in FIEs will rise. Market and supplier access variables are estimated from a gravity model since they are not directly observable and are applied to a dataset of trade between 29 Chinese provinces and 120 export-receiving and import-supplying countries for the ten years between 1990 and 2000. Results suggest that the interaction between transport costs and FDI through FIE behavior explains around one-third to one-fourth of the provincial wage differentials. Ma also finds similar transport-related access impacts affecting processing trade for local firms (state-owned enterprises, communally owned enterprises) and attributes these to competitive effects from FIE wage behavior, even though their involvement in processing trade is small.

Overall then, the links between FDI and relative inequality in China seem hard to support from broad macrodata and the orders of magnitude for the workforce involved, but in more detailed microstudies these effects do seem to emerge. Despite this, it is hard to envisage a policy of limiting FDI flows into China being consciously used by the national government as a way to reduce inequality, given the developmental strategy now so central to China's growth. But the issue highlights the potentially central role that labor market segmentation (due either to policy or other factors) plays in Chinese performance and hence the importance of how this interacts with FDI inflows.

Future Policy Change and Impacts on FDI Inflows

A key issue for the future is whether policy change in China might retard further growth in FDI inflows. Here we discuss two key elements: tax policy change and renmimbi revaluation.

Tax Policy Change

While a central element in China's recent strong growth performance has been large inflows of foreign direct investment, a key factor in attracting foreign investment has been substantial tax preferences. Currently, the government is considering a proposal to establish a single equal-yield tax rate to apply to all enterprises and to remove tax preferences for FIEs. Such a proposal could have negative impacts on future FDI inflows.

The tax preferences currently given to FIEs are both substantial and complex. If they are located in special economic zones, national high-technology industrial zones, and national grade economic and technical development zones, FIEs pay a reduced enterprise tax rate of 15 percent, compared to the general rate of 30 percent. FIEs in coastal regions and all provincial capitals pay 24 percent. FIEs also receive extensive tax holidays with a full exemption for two years, a 50 percent exemption for the next three years, and (if in particular geographical zones) a tax reduction of 15–30 percent for a further three to five years. In addition, local governments frequently exempt them from local surcharges applied to other enterprises of 3 percent of taxable income, and taxable income can again be reduced if income is reinvested. Wages paid to employees between FIEs and other enterprises are also taxed differently. No formal estimates exist for effective tax rates on Chinese enterprises comparable to those for OECD economies; instead, broad consensus within China is that FIEs on average may face tax rates in the 10 to 15 percent range, while non-FIEs face tax rates of between 22 percent and 28 percent.[31]

Converting these tax preferences into effective tax rates by enterprise type is treacherous, as the effective tax rate varies with the time profile of returns to investment (most FIEs make no profit in their first two years, for instance), their location, their financing, and labor costs. There are no estimates of effective tax rates for Chinese enterprises comparable to those of OECD economies (such as in King and Fullerton [1984] and the studies that have followed), but various Chinese sources put the capital tax rates faced by FIEs in the range of 10–14 percent, while for the non-FIEs a range of 22–28 percent is widely used. In 2004, 23 percent of total enterprise taxes were paid by FIEs, and 77 percent were paid by other types of enterprises, even though FIEs accounted for a significantly larger part of the total return to capital.

With more than two decades of reform completed and accession to the WTO accomplished, the government position now is that FDI inflows are mainly attracted by nontax factors. These include China's economic environment, a growing domestic market, low wage rates, well-trained and hard-working labor, a market system, and a stronger judicial system. With tax preferences seen as less important, the government proposal is thus to unify enterprise tax rates and to remove what are seen as distortions associated with the various incentive schemes for FIEs.

31. Whalley and Wang (2007).

The most recent proposal on unified tax reform was discussed by members of the Standing Committee of the National People's Congress at the end of December 2006, which produced a draft of a new corporate income tax law. It includes

—a unified tax rate of 25 percent for both domestic and foreign-funded businesses.

—an income tax for small businesses of 20 percent; depending on what region and what industry they are active in, small businesses now pay either 18 percent or 27 percent.

—allowance for domestic companies to deduct employees' full salaries from taxable income as foreign companies now do.

—transitional measures for FIEs under which the current two-year full tax exemption and three-year partial tax exemption for foreign manufacturers will be removed, and export-oriented foreign-funded businesses will no longer enjoy an additional 50 percent tax reduction; existing FIEs, however, will continue to receive tax preferences for five years after the new law is implemented and will only gradually face increased income taxes.

—extension of some existing tax preferences; for instance, all hi-tech companies will enjoy a 15 percent tax rate to stimulate innovation, while at present only those in state hi-tech zones enjoy this privilege; investments in equipment for environmental protection and water conservancy purposes and for production safety could be used to offset taxes payable.

The new enterprise tax structure will take effect in 2008 as the bill was adopted by the NPC plenary session in March 2007.

How large the impact of these tax changes will be on FDI flows into China is conjectural, but it could be substantial. A relevant consideration would seem to be that China's FDI growth has partly come from reduced FDI flowing elsewhere (such as to Brazil); if the aggregate FDI outflows from the OECD remain largely unchanged, tax-induced intercountry reallocation effects could be key. There are already indications that FDI inflows into India are beginning to grow, and in the textile and apparel area, inflows to Cambodia, Vietnam, Indonesia, and other economies with wage rates lower than those in China are increasing.

The largest yearly increases in FDI in China occurred in 1992 and 1993 immediately after the introduction of tax preferences toward FIEs in 1991. While the more general policy reform package and market orientation of those reforms is usually taken to be the main trigger for these FDI surges, the issue remains as to how important the tax component is. If it were significant, unwinding it now could also have large effects in the other direction, although the high-skilled and reliable low-wage labor force, good infrastructure, and ever-deepening judicial structure—all of which attract FDI to China—remain, along with tax preferences.

Renminbi Revaluation and FDI

A second key policy area that could impact FDI inflows is renminbi (RMB) revaluation. A commonly held view is that China's RMB is undervalued, and a number of studies further indicate that the undervaluation is on the order of 10–30 percent.[32] In response to both international and internal pressures, the People's Bank of China allowed an effective nominal 2.1 percent appreciation of the RMB against the U.S. dollar in July 2005, and the RMB had appreciated by 5.6 percent by the end of 2006. China's rapid export growth and associated trade surplus have brought with it pressure to revalue the RMB to reduce the trade surplus, especially since 2003 and especially from the United States.

Existing literature in general suggests that RMB revaluation may reduce China's inward FDI flows. Both theoretical and empirical studies from other countries imply that the revaluation of a host county's currency can substantially decrease its FDI inflows.[33] The revaluation of an FDI host country's currency increases production costs (measured in foreign currency) and limits inward FDI flows through a relative production-cost effect. For the Chinese case, Xing (2006a) sets up a theoretical model and then empirically tests the model projections of the effects of devaluation of the RMB on FDI inflows from Japan. His results imply that RMB revaluation will significantly reduce China's inward FDI flows from Japan.

The size of such effects will also depend on how heavily China's inward FDI has been involved with China's processing trade, since imports used in processing are denominated in foreign currency and the relative production cost effect will be reduced. Both exports from and imports by FIEs in China are heavily involved in processing trade. MOFCOM (2006) estimates that 78 percent of China's FIE exports are processed exports and 60 percent of FIE imports are processed imports in 2005. FIE-processed exports and imports accounted for 83 percent and 84 percent of China's total processed exports and imports, respectively, in 2005. Moreover, FIEs account for more than 50 percent of China's trade surplus in 2005. These data suggest that China's total trade is composed of distinct parts: processing trade, which involves imports receiv-

32. Chang and Shao (2004); Goldstein (2004); Funke and Rahn (2005).

33. See, for example, Cushman (1985), Froot and Stein (1991), Klein and Rosengren (1994), Blonigen (1997), Goldberg and Klein (1997), Bayoumi and Lipworth (1998), Xing (2006a and 2006b), Xing and Wan (2006).

ing upgrading via added value, and general trade. The impacts of RMB revaluation on these two types of trade differ. This suggests differentiated studies of the impacts of RMB revaluation on FDI since the trade-FDI link reflects the nature of the trade. There is for now little literature on the trade impacts of RMB revaluation other than econometric models that specify no structural form for trade patterns. These models are discussed in Marquez and Schindler (2006). Willenbockel (2006) uses a CGE framework to assess the structural effects on trade and production of a real exchange rate revaluation in China but does not differentiate processing trade and general trade and does not directly evaluate FDI impacts. Quantitative estimates of the effects are thus, for now, missing. But if FDI is heavily trade driven, then the null hypothesis renminbi revaluation of the size speculated in the literature can have significant effects, which will compound tax-related effects.

Concluding Remarks

FDI inflows have grown rapidly in recent years, and China now accounts for nearly 50 percent of OECD outflows. In turn, growth of exports, imports, and GDP increasingly reflect FDI inflows. China's deep integration into the global economy must, therefore, be judged not only by its trade growth, but also by the size of capital flows. These are also now starting to grow on the outward FDI side as well.

In the paper we discuss three issues related to FDI, and primarily FDI inflows. The first is their contribution to growth, which we suggest is substantial, and if any plateauing of FDI growth occurs, then GDP growth may be significantly reduced. We also discuss the links between regional inequality and geographic concentration of FDI. Macrodata suggest limited linkage, while microstudies claim to find it. Finally, we discuss recent proposals to remove tax preferences to FDI and RMB revaluation, suggesting potential negative effects on FDI inflows.

FDI has become so central to Chinese economic performance that what happens on the FDI front in the short term will likely determine the speed of China's development. Many factors influence these flows, including global factors not discussed here. How these all interact and play out remains to be seen.

Comments and Discussion

Nicholas R. Lardy: John Whalley and Xian Xin have provided a very imaginative analysis of the contribution of foreign direct investment to economic growth in China. China is an interesting case since foreign direct investment inflows have been large but China has been a significant and growing net supplier of capital to the rest of the world. China has been the number one recipient of foreign direct investment among emerging markets for fifteen consecutive years, but in the twenty-five years from 1982 through 2006, China absorbed foreign capital on a net basis in only five years. Thus it has long been clear that a principal contribution of foreign investment to China's growth has not been, as is typically the case, through allowing a level of domestic investment that exceeds the level of domestic savings. Rather, the contribution of foreign investment in China must come through other factors that are embodied in foreign investment such as technology, managerial and marketing skills, and so forth.

The authors reach several main conclusions. Of these the most important is that foreign invested firms now produce about a fifth of China's GDP, and these firms account for a disproportionately large share of economic growth, over 40 percent in the most recent years they examine (2003 and 2004). They judge that unless the indigenous portion of the economy becomes more productive, a slowdown in FDI inflows, which they think is likely, will slow China's overall economic growth.

While there is no doubt that inward foreign direct investment has contributed substantially to the transformation of the domestic economy, my view is that the paper has overestimated its contribution.

It is important to recognize explicitly at the outset that the approach of the authors, to estimate separate production functions for the foreign and indigenous components of the economy, is quite challenging. To begin with, there are no data partitioning the output of the Chinese economy into these two components. Only for industry (manufacturing, mining, and utilities) do the Chinese statistical authorities disaggregate value added into the components contributed by foreign invested firms and indigenous firms. In order to partition the entire economy into its foreign and indigenous components, the authors make the strong assumption that the marginal productivity of a dollar of foreign investment in agriculture, construction, and services is the same as that in industry. I don't know of direct evidence of whether or not this is the case, and the issue is not addressed in the paper. Certainly, indirect evidence suggests that the assumption is not warranted.[1] If the productivity of capital is higher (or lower) in manufacturing than in agriculture, construction, and services, then the foreign portion of the economy is overestimated (or underestimated). Similarly, if the capital employed in industry has exhibited a growing positive productivity differential compared to investments in other sectors, then the authors' assumption would result in an overstatement of the overall growth rate of the economy's foreign component.

A second critical building block in the authors' estimation procedures is the labor shares of the foreign and indigenous components of the economy. This calculation seems problematic. The authors estimate the wage bill of the foreign component of the economy as the product of official data on the number employed in the foreign sector and the average wage rate. Then to estimate the labor share of the indigenous component of the economy, this estimate is subtracted from data on employee compensation. Two problems arise. First, what we want is total labor remuneration in each sector as a share of value added. But for the foreign sector the authors' procedure includes only the wage bill in the numerator and appears to make no allowance for non-wage labor costs, such as required social insurance payments to the government. Non-wage labor costs in Chinese manufacturing in 2002 were 55 percent of the wage bill.[2] Thus the authors appear to have substantially understated the labor share of output in the foreign sector. Second, to calculate the labor share of indigenous firms they subtract the foreign wage bill from data on employee compensation. This results in an overstatement of the labor share of output in the indigenous sector for two reasons. First, Chinese data on employee compensation include social insurance payments and other non-wage labor costs. Thus, this procedure incorrectly attributes the non-wage labor compensation of the foreign sector to the indigenous sector. Second, Chinese data on employee compensation come from adding up the provincial entries for the employee compensation component of

1. Dollar and Wei (2007) show that returns to capital vary substantially across regions, forms of ownership, and subsectors of manufacturing in China. But their analysis does not include economic activity outside of manufacturing.

2. Banister (2005, p. 28).

the income side of the gross regional product accounts. But the sum of the provincial regional product accounts from the income side, which are rarely if ever used in Chinese statistical analysis, exceeds the national gross domestic product reported in the GDP production accounts, which are the official data on China's GDP, by a significant amount. For example, in 2003 the sum of the provincial entries for gross regional product in the income accounts exceeds the national gross domestic product in the GDP production accounts by 15 percent.[3] The rest of the authors' analysis is based on the more commonly used GDP production data, suggesting the possibility that the compensation data used in the analysis are not consistent with the other GDP data used. It appears to me, on the one hand, that the authors may have significantly overstated the labor share of output in the indigenous economy, both because they start with a total compensation figure that may be too large and because they then subtract the wage bill of the foreign sector rather than total labor compensation in the foreign sector. On the other hand, the labor share of output in the foreign sector is almost certainly understated by at least half.

What difference could either of these criticisms of the authors' methodology make to the results they present? One striking finding the authors report is that over 30 percent of the growth of China's economy in the decade from 1995 to 2004 was contributed by foreign invested enterprises and that in both 2003 and 2004 foreign invested firms accounted for over 40 percent of China's economic growth. In short, the contribution of foreign capital to China's economic growth is quite high and apparently rising sharply over time.

This seems puzzling. The share of fixed investment in China financed by foreign direct investment fell from a peak of 11–12 percent in 1995–96 to an average of under 5 percent in 2003–04.[4] Could the productivity of foreign firms in China be rising so rapidly relative to that of indigenous firms that they could account for a rising share of overall growth even as their share of investment fell by more than half?

A further check of the plausibility of the estimate that foreign firms account for a high and rising share of China's growth is to analyze the official data, mentioned above, on value added in industry by foreign and indigenous firms. These data show that foreign invested firms accounted for 28.4 percent of the expansion of value added in industry (defined to include manufacturing, mining, and utilities) in 2004. Industry under this definition accounted for 45.9 percent of GDP in 2004.[5] In order for foreign firms across the entire economy

3. NBSC (2005, pp. 52 and 61).
4. NBSC (2005, p. 186).
5. NBSC (2005, p. 488). The data cover value added of all state-owned enterprises and the value added of non-state-owned enterprises with output value above RMB 5 million. On a gross

to account for 40 percent or more of GDP growth in 2004, foreign firms would have had to contribute 50 percent or more of the growth of value added in agriculture, construction, and services, which cumulatively accounted for 54.1 percent of GDP in 2004. How productive must foreign firms have been to contribute 50 percent or more of the growth of value added outside of industry? We know that well over half of China's inbound foreign direct investment has always gone into industry (as just defined), for example, 64 percent in 1998, 67 percent in 1999, 70 percent in 2000, and 74 percent in 2004.[6] That means foreign capital employed outside of industry is half or less the size of that employed in industry. For this foreign capital stock to have contributed 50 percent or more of the growth of value added outside of industry, it would have to be about four times more productive than the foreign capital stock employed in manufacturing, mining, and utilities. This strikes me as unlikely in the extreme. If foreign capital deployed in agriculture, construction, and services was four times more productive than that in manufacturing, mining, and utilities, we would expect the share of foreign capital flowing into the former sectors of the economy to be rising over time. But, as already noted, the actual trend is in the opposite direction.

My conclusion is that the estimate that foreign firms account for an average of 30 percent of the growth of the Chinese economy over the 1995–2004 decade and more than 40 percent in the final two years of that period is likely biased significantly upward. I would speculate, but cannot show, that Whalley and Xin's result is driven by their partitioning procedure. I believe that foreign capital employed in industry has likely exhibited a positive and growing productivity differential compared to that in agriculture, construction, and services and that the procedures Whalley and Xin use thus overstate the growth of the foreign component of the economy.[7]

Similarly, I believe that some of the other findings in the paper do not withstand careful scrutiny. The authors, for example, argue that the share of foreign direct investment in the output of foreign invested enterprises is strikingly high. But since the capital share is a residual, this finding can be attributed in part to

---

value basis the output of the universe of all industrial enterprises exceeds this universe by a little under one-fifth. Data from the *China Statistical Yearbook 2006*, p. 505, can be used to calculate that three-quarters of the gross value of output of the firms excluded from the disaggregation of value added into its indigenous and foreign components is produced by small private and collective indigenous firms, and only one-quarter is produced by foreign invested firms.

6. NBSC (2000, p. 610; 2001, p. 608; 2005, p. 648).

7. One piece of evidence that suggests this possibility is the sharp rise in returns on foreign direct investment in industry. Between 1998 and 2003–04 pre-tax profits as a share of the sum of the depreciated value of fixed assets plus working capital rose from less than 6 percent to an average of 12 percent (NBSC 2005, pp. 505–06).

the 50 percent understatement of the labor share of value added by foreign invested firms. The results from the decomposition of economic growth reported in table 4 presumably also require some modification if the criticisms above are upheld. Overstatement (or understatement) of growth in the foreign (or indigenous) sector of the economy results in an upward (or downward) biased estimate of the pace of growth of total factor productivity in the sector. Similarly, it would seem that the contribution of the growth of the labor force (or capital stock) to the expansion of the foreign sector is understated (or overstated).

Wing Thye Woo: John Whalley and Xian Xin have written a very good paper that provides a wide-ranging discussion on foreign direct investment in China. The important prediction from their paper is that if FDI were to stop flowing into China, Chinese growth would plummet significantly.

I will organize my remarks on their paper in the format of answering the following five questions:

—Why has the flow of FDI into China been so large and sustained?

—What is the relationship between FDI and growth in China?

—What kind of impact is the flow of FDI into China having on the world?

—What is the causal relationship between FDI and regional inequality within China?

—What would happen if the flow of FDI into China were to decline significantly?

Why Has the Flow of FDI into China Been So Large and Sustained?

I find it a little puzzling why the authors did not address this natural question. The answer to it will have a strong bearing on how one would answer the fifth question; and my answer to the last question is more optimistic than the authors' answer.

There are three reasons for this large, sustained FDI flow. The first reason is straightforward: China has a large pool of underemployed agricultural labor. If the same amount of FDI were to have come into Singapore in the mid-1960s, wages in Singapore would have started climbing steeply after three years and halted the FDI flow into Singapore.

The second reason is that there is systematic discrimination against the domestic private sector. Given the high rates of return on investment due to the large cheap labor force, the legal bias in favor of the foreign private sector enables it to expand its presence. Is this legal bias unique to China? No, almost exactly the same situation existed in Malaysia, which also had high, sustained FDI inflows until 2002. In Malaysia, the indigenous ethnic Chinese entrepreneurs face a wealth tax of 30 percent if they were to list on the Malaysian stock markets so as to expand the size of their operations. The result is that the bulk of Chinese Malaysian enterprises do not grow despite the high rate of return on investments, and because FDI is exempted from this 30 percent wealth tax, foreign investors have been rushing in to reap these high rates of return. In short, the high flow of FDI into China and Malaysia was partly created by the legal discrimination against the domestic private business.

Of course, the legal discrimination in China against the domestic private sector has been declining over time. This outcome is partly the result of the triumph of rationality over ideology and partly the result of the entry of the children of the Communist Party elite into independent businesses.

The third reason for why the flow of FDI into China has been so big is that 25 to 33 percent of FDI (according to Hong Kong–based observers) is actually from mainland capital in origin; that is, private Chinese capital is round-tripping (for example, mainland capital enters Hong Kong surreptitiously and then returns to the mainland as foreign capital) so as to receive the legal protection and preferential tax treatment extended to foreign private capital. It is likely that a large part of the illegal capital flight is from the massive embezzlement of Chinese state assets that has been, and still is, occurring. So even if the legal discrimination against domestic private capital were to end, capital round-tripping would continue as long as the theft of state assets cannot be stopped.

What Is the Relationship between FDI and Growth in China?

The authors' answer is that FDI is becoming more and more important to Chinese economic growth, see table 4. The GDP growth rate in 1996 and 2004 are about the same (9.6 percent and 9.5 percent, respectively), but the contribution of Foreign Invested Enterprises (FIEs) to the GDP growth rate jumped from 1.9 percentage points in 1996 to 3.9 percentage points in 2004.

In my opinion, the fragility of the authors' answer is indicated by some purported Chinese economic characteristics in table 3 that are highly unusual by international experience; for example, the capital share of income in the FIE sector is much larger than the usual range of estimates. These unusual characteristics in table 3 produce two trends that are puzzling. First, the proportion of GDP originating in the FIE sector has increased greatly over time, going from 10.3 percent in 1995 to 22.4 percent in 2004. Second, there is a large and growing gap between the capital income shares in the FIE sector and those in the non-FIE sector, a gap $(S^F_{FDI}-S^N_K)$ that went from 10.3 percentage points in 1995 to 32.9 percentage points in 2004.

These two trends are puzzling because the following three developments would have led me to expect the opposite trends:

—Between 1995 and 2005, the ratio of total investment (INV) to GDP (INV/GDP) increased, and the ratio of FDI to total investment (FDI/INV) decreased, falling from 36.5 percent in 1995 to 19.5 percent in 2004. This development should lead to a fall in the FIE share of output unless there is increasing inefficiency in the non-FIE sector.

—The agricultural sector (the least efficient sector) shrank during the period 1995–2004, and this ought to have increased efficiency in the non-FIE sector.

—The legal discrimination against the domestic private sector also decreased during this period (for example, allowing large-scale privatization of small and medium state enterprises, lowering the barriers for the establishment of new private enterprises, and permitting capitalists to join the Communist Party), and the displacement of the state-owned sector by the private sector ought to have increased efficiency in the non-FIE sector.

One way to reconcile these three developments with the authors' two trends is to recognize that the authors have measured the size of the capital stock in the FIE sector and the capital share of income in the FIE sector incorrectly.

The fact is that most of China's FIEs are not funded entirely by FDI, as assumed by the authors. Most FIEs are actually joint ventures. Since the FDI-to-INV ratio has been falling, it means that the domestic financing component in FIEs could have gotten larger, which is to say that the FDI growth rate is an understatement of the actual growth rate of the FIE capital stock.[1] Since the capital input growth rate in FIEs is understated, the Total Factor Productivity (TFP) growth rate of FIEs is overstated. (Conversely, the capital input growth rate in non-FIEs is overstated, and the TFP growth rate of non-FIEs is understated.) Another implication of the growing share of China-originated capital in FIEs is that a growing part of output growth in the FIE sector should not be attributed to the infusion of foreign capital.

The authors' estimate of capital income share in FIEs is an overstatement because the wage bill used by the authors did not include various benefits. The overall result of these two mismeasurements is that the contribution of FDI to

1. The authors cited Fung (2004) as saying that an increasing share of FDI in recent years has gone into wholly foreign-owned enterprises. This finding, therefore, deserves more investigation.

GDP growth is exaggerated, yielding the surprising conclusion in table 4 that China's economic growth has come to rest increasingly on the FIE sector.

My comments on mismeasurements should not be misinterpreted as saying that FDI does not have a big role for FIE in China's growth. I am only saying that the authors have overstated its contribution. I want to mention that there is a view especially held in South Korea, Taiwan, and Japan that FDI is not important because these three countries grew very fast with very little FDI. This is why the Northeast Asians have always browbeat the Southeast Asians in various academic forums for selling their countries by allowing FDI to come in. This superior Northeast Asian attitude misses the point that Southeast Asia welcomes FDI not because it needs the capital. The savings rate is more than 30 percent in many cases. The reason is that Southeast Asia does not have the indigenous technical expertise to be able to just buy the technology from abroad and then use it. The Southeast Asians need the FDI to not only bring the technology but also to put the technology into operation. The case of China is between the two cases of the expertise-rich Northeast Asians and the expertise-poor Southeast Asians, which means that FDI is needed to play a big role in powering China's economic growth. But China has given too big a role to FDI (and, hence, has come to resemble the Southeast Asians on its dependency on FDI) because of its discrimination against its own domestic private sector, a good example being that while foreign private banks are allowed to operate in China, there are no truly domestic private banks.

What Kind of Impact is the Flow of
FDI into China Having on the World?

The authors have limited themselves to suggesting that if FDI continues to be export oriented, then the "large trade surplus with the European Union and the United States [could fuel] protectionist measures in these countries."

Although I think that protectionist sentiments are currently very strong (as of February 2008), I do not think that FDI-fueled trade surpluses are the causes. The question is whether trade with China is the primary cause of reallocation of resources in countries within the Organization for Economic Cooperation and Development. My answer is no, and I see two much more important factors forcing structural adjustment within the OECD.

The first factor is economic globalization of which the emergence of China is only a part. The integration of China's labor force into the international division of labor occurs at the same time as the integration of the large labor forces from the former Soviet bloc and India. Specifically, at most, only half of the increase in the amount of labor in the international division of labor can be attributed to China.

The second factor causing massive structural adjustment within the OECD is the accelerated rate of technological innovation since the mid-1980s.[2] The reality is that the faster rate of technological innovation has caused more structural adjustment than economic globalization (particularly, the FDI-fueled exports from China).[3] This is because economic globalization and technological innovation have opposite effects on blue-collar labor compensation in the United States; the former lowers it and the latter raises it.[4] The evidence is that blue-collar labor compensation has been rising, not falling, in the last two decades, and it actually started rising faster in 2001 when the U.S. trade deficits started ballooning.

The important aspect about the impact from the FDI flow into China on the rest of the world is the impact on Southeast Asia. The authors cited the finding by Barry Eichengreen and Hui Tong that the flow of FDI into China has not hurt the flow of FDI into Southeast Asia because they both have gone up.[5] The authors should not have accepted this finding so uncritically because the Eichengreen and Tong paper analyzed the 1988–2002 period, which is before China joined the World Trade Organization (WTO).[6]

The fact is that the moment China joined the WTO at the end of 2001, there was a sharp a drop in FDI into Southeast Asia and an acceleration of FDI into China.[7] The reason is quite simple. Until China joined the WTO, China needed approval as a most favored nation (MFN) from Congress every year, and so when a foreign company established one firm in China, it also invested one in Southeast Asia to hedge against the possibility that China might not get MFN approval the next year. So as long as China was not a WTO member, FDI into China and FDI into Southeast Asia were seemingly complementary because of risk management by the multinational corporations.

However, the moment China joined WTO, the threat of MFN nonapproval was removed, and foreign firms began to consolidate their production in China

2. For example, the difference between working in Brookings twenty years ago and today is that there were three Xerox operators in 1985 and there are none today, and typists are in short supply today. This acceleration is emphasized by Alan Greenspan in his recent autobiography.

3. Woo (forthcoming).

4. I am assuming that the technological change is not of the capital-bias type. Otherwise, there would not have been the observed rise in the compensation of blue-collar labor.

5. Eichengreen and Tong (2005).

6. The period of analysis in Eichengreen and Tong (2005) was stated to be 1988–2002 in table 1 but 1990–2002 in footnote 24 in their paper.

7. McKibbin and Woo (2003).

(as the lowest-cost location) to lower management costs. The result was a diversion of FDI from Southeast Asia to China.

What is the Causal Relationship between FDI and Regional Inequality within China?

Well, if one were participating in a TV show and were asked to name which country was richer, one should, in general, guess that a coastal country was richer than an inland country, because the coastal economy has the ability to participate in international trade and thus reap the gains from the division of labor. By this logic, we see that FDI has flowed mostly to the coastal provinces, because their potential income level is higher than the potential income of the inland provinces. FDI is not the cause of the regional income inequality; the cause is the transportation costs associated with locating a production plant inland.

In the case of China, there is one more reason, a policy-created reason, for regional income inequality. Empirical studies of the United States have found absolute convergence of income in the fifty states; that is, income in North Dakota is catching up with income in California. This catching-up is driven to a large extent by the poorest people in North Dakota moving to California, thereby raising the average income of the remaining North Dakotans.[8] In China, however, the household registration system prevents the movement of labor and, hence, prevents the natural income catch-up mechanism from operating.

What Would Happen if the Flow of FDI into China Were to Decline Significantly?

The authors' answer, based on table 4, is that China's growth would decline significantly. My prediction is less bleak, however. The political legitimacy of the present Chinese government rests on its ability to generate a sustained high growth rate, and so if FDI were to decline drastically, the government then would have to terminate legal discrimination against the domestic private sector to enable it to be the new growth engine.

8. In an economy that is growing secularly, the movement of low-income people from North Dakota to California would increase the original growth rate of per capita income in North Dakota and decrease the original growth rate of per capita income in California. The *original growth rate* refers to the counterfactual growth rate if there were no relocation of poor people from North Dakota to California.

What else China would do depends on the reason why the FDI stopped coming to China. If it were protectionism against Chinese exports that discouraged FDI coming into China, then perhaps we might see China taking a more serious role in the support of global economic institutions, like the WTO.

China, which has benefited so much from the multilateral free trade system, has done very little to defend it. With China so far playing a very passive role in pushing forward the Doha Round, by default, Brazil and India have assumed the leadership of the developing economies camp in the trade negotiations. According to Susan Schwab, the U.S. trade representative at the G-4 (the United States, European Union, Brazil, and India) meeting in Potsdam in June 2007, Brazil and India retreated from their earlier offers to reduce their manufacturing tariffs in return for cuts in agricultural subsides by the developed economies because of "their fear of growing Chinese imports."[9] The Brazilian-Indian action caused the Potsdam talks to fail, which hurt the many developing economies that are agricultural exporters. The reality is that Brazil is now attempting to bypass multilateral trade liberalization by entering into free trade agreement (FTA) negotiations with the European Union.

A growing number of nations like Brazil "are increasingly wary of a multilateral deal because it would mandate tariff cuts, exposing them more deeply to low-cost competition from China. Instead, they are seeking bilateral deals with rich countries that are tailored to the two parties' needs."[10] Furthermore, because the present international atmosphere is ripe for protectionism (because of the structural adjustments in OECD forced by heightened economic globalization and because of accelerated technological innovation), China could now be motivated to work with the United States to provide the leadership to prevent the unraveling of multilateral free trade.[11]

So the slowdown of FDI into China could mean a slowdown of growth in the short run, but the long-run outcome could be a China that has a more dynamic domestic private sector and a China that has become a more-engaged global citizen.

---

9. "Schwab surprised by stance of India and Brazil," *Financial Times*, June 22, 2007; "China's shadow looms over Doha failure," *Financial Times*, June 22, 2007.

10. "Brazil, Others Push Outside Doha For Trade Pacts," *Wall Street Journal*, July 5, 2007.

11. We realize, of course, that although it is desirable for Chinese economic growth that China become more active in supplying global public goods, it might not be allowed to do so because of the usual reluctance of the existing dominant powers to share the commanding heights of the world political leadership. The sad experience of Japan being denied permanent membership on the Security Council of the United Nations is a case in point.

Discussion: Shang-Jin Wei began the general discussion by offering a contrary perspective of FDI in China. He argued that perhaps the strength of FDI in recent years is a reflection of the weak financial system in China. Therefore, as China gradually improves its financial sector efficiency, it is likely that a drop in FDI would be accompanied by offsetting benefits for the domestic sector, which may not result in overall slower economic growth. Shang-Jin Wei offered two reasons for this to be a plausible alternative. First, he highlighted recent research that shows that the Chinese banking system is biased against the private sector. Because of the shortage of credit in the private sector, many domestic firms and entrepreneurs look for foreign partners as a source of capital. Second, pointing to his own work, Wei noted that the typical developed country tends to be a net exporter of FDI and a net importer of financial capital, whereas an emerging country tends to have the opposite balance. The theory behind this is that a country with a low capital-to-labor ratio should have a very high return to capital. Therefore, if the financial system is bad, then the returns on household savings may be very low, so much so that the household wants to take the savings out of the country and invest in a foreign country.

Mihir Desai raised two questions related to the data used in the paper. First, it is likely that there are significant inconsistencies in the reporting of FDI between the source and destination countries. Research by Bosworth and others with respect to software exports in India has shown that the differences can indeed be quite substantial. Is there any evidence of inconsistencies in FDI reporting? In addition, Desai agreed with Wing Thye Woo that there may be some problems related to the measurement of capital across FIEs and non-FIEs. Specifically, recent research has shown tax avoidance behavior in non-FIE firms, while the FIEs are less prone to manipulate financial records with their joint venture partners. So, in effect, part of the distinction offered by the paper may be a result of different profit-reporting practices.

Some participants raised questions related to the paper's growth accounting calculations. Barry Bosworth was concerned about the low share of labor in the reported calculations. He noted that if employment and capital are both growing very rapidly over a time period, then the shares associated with capital and labor are relatively unimportant, as the weighted average would be invariant to the shares. This is not the case, however, with the residual growth. In many countries, the problem comes from the allocation of "mixed income," or self-employment income. Since this is neither compensation in a labor sense nor is it a form of profits, one has to find some way to allocate it. Bosworth remarked that this could be a particularly problematic in services and agriculture, two sectors with large numbers of self-employed. The treatment of mixed income may be one cause of differences between the results of this paper and those found by Bosworth and Collins in a study released earlier that year. Margaret McMillan identified a concern in the microliterature of the presence of a selection bias, where the foreign investors are picking the fastest growing firms with which to set up joint ventures. Because of this, McMillan questioned how the authors could calculate the performance of domestic firms in the absence of foreign investment.

Assaf Razin followed up on the comments made by Wing Thye Woo and Shang-Jin Wei to discuss FDI in terms of the growth in capital flows. The net international capital flows, like the trade balance, must be explainable in terms of the balance between saving and investment. Razin suggested that perhaps weak saving institutions give rise to precautionary and ample saving, yet the low technology in domestic investment projects accounts for low investments relative to saving. Thus the new technology offered by FDI, coupled with the relatively cheap labor, would explain why FDI is the dominant flow back in this two-way capital flow relationship.

Nicholas Lardy raised a number of points related to previous comments. First, he offered a reminder that FDI is still less than 4 percent of all investment in China. This is a very big economy that invests 40 percent of GDP, and although FDI is large in absolute terms, it is still a small fraction of total domestic investment. Regarding the inconsistencies between FDI data, he argued that the difference may arise out of U.S. firms failing to include accurate accounts of the investments from their foreign affiliates. Finally, Lardy questioned the counterfactual raised by Shang-Jin Wei on the weakness of the Chinese financial system, specifically on the biases against the private sector. He pointed to evidence in the data that the composition of bank lending has changed dramatically in recent years, from more than 80 percent of bank credit going to state-owned companies in the mid 1990s to less than 40 percent today. Therefore, it may no longer be accurate to say that the private sector does not have sufficient access to capital.

The session concluded with brief responses from John Whalley. First, he remarked that if the additional component to be applied to the nonwage measure is 55 percent, then this could relate to the growth in labor and considerably affect the mechanics of the growth accounting calculations. In addition, he suggested that a more detailed exercise of growth accounting is needed for the Chinese case, especially when various studies from the Chinese government are reporting 40 percent of growth coming from technical change. Regarding the data, Whalley emphasized that the structure of the calculations can dramatically affect the conclusions. So although the concerns about the quality of the data are important, obtaining the correct functional form of growth accounting can potentially make an even bigger difference.

He offered a more radical approach to the growth accounting framework. According to this reasoning, the driving mechanism for intergenerational transfer is a pension, which is in the form of a child. If the Chinese social structure is one characterized by collective commitment to family, and one combines this with a demographic transition from three children to one, the impacts on effort and investment are phenomenal. So, a consideration of the social structure would yield considerably different results.

Whalley made several other brief responses to other comments made by the participants. As to the inquiry on differences in FDI measures across countries, he noted that these differences could be as much as 30 to 40 percent. The counterfactual in these growth accounting exercises was a simple plateauing of FDI growth; however, he stressed that the Solow model is very simple, and more complicated models would suffer from reduced transparency.

As a final point, Whalley emphasized that the contribution of this paper is to offer a few simplifying frameworks for how to look at FDI in China. Because every economy is encased in a unique social structure, he argued that the explanation of the growth process in China must have different elements than those used for analysis of OECD countries.

References

Antkiewicz, Agata, and John Whalley. 2006. "Recent Chinese Buyout Activity and the Implications for Global Architecture." Working Paper 12072. Cambridge, Mass.: National Bureau of Economic Research.

Banister, Judith, 2005. "Manufacturing Earnings and Compensation in China." *Monthly Labor Review* 128, no. 8 (August): 22–40.

Bayoumi, Tamim, and Gabrielle Lipworth. 1998. "Japanese Foreign Direct Investment and Regional Trade." *Journal of Asian Economics* 9, no. 4: 581–607.

Blonigen, Bruce A. 1997. "Firm-Specific Assets and the Link between Exchange Rates and Foreign Direct Investment." *American Economic Review* 87, no. 3: 447–65.

CAITEC (Chinese Academy of International Trade and Economic Cooperation) and Welsh Development Agency. 2005. "Chinese Enterprises' Expansion into European and North American Markets." Beijing.

Chang, Gene Hsin, and Qin Shao. 2004. "How Much Is the Chinese Currency Undervalued? A Quantitative Estimation." *China Economic Review* 15, no. 3: 366–71.

Chow, Gregory C. 1993. "Capital Formation and Economic Growth in China." *Quarterly Journal of Economics* 108, no. 3: 809–42.

Chow, Gregory C., and An-Loh Lin. 2002. "Accounting for Economic Growth in Taiwan and Mainland China: A Comparative Analysis." *Journal of Comparative Economics* 30, no. 3: 507–30.

Cushman, David O. 1985. "Real Exchange Rate Risk, Expectation, and the Level of Direct Investment." *Review of Economics and Statistics* 67, no. 2: 297–308.

Dennison, Edward F. 1967. *Why Growth Rates Differ: Post War Experiences in Nine Western Countries.* Brookings.

Dollar, David, and Shang-Jin Wei. 2007. "Das (Wasted) Kapital: Firm Ownership and Investment Efficiency in China." Working Paper 07/9. Washington: International Monetary Fund (January).

Eichengreen, Barry, and Hui Tong. 2005. "Is China's FDI Coming at the Expense of Other Countries?" Working Paper 11335. Cambridge, Mass.: National Bureau of Economic Research.

Feenstra, Robert C., and Gordon H. Hanson. 2005. "Ownership and Control in Outsourcing to China: Estimating the Property-Rights Theory of the Firm." *Quarterly Journal of Economics* 120, no. 2: 729–61.

Froot, Kenneth A., and Jeremy C. Stein. 1991. "Exchange Rates and Foreign Direct Investment: An Imperfect Capital Markets Approach." *Quarterly Journal of Economics* 106, no. 4: 1191–217.

Fung, K. C. 2004. "China as an Emerging Regional and Technological Power: Implications for U.S. Economic and Security Interests." Hearing before U.S.-China Economic and Security Review Commission 108 Cong. 2 sess., February 12–13. Government Printing Office.

Funke, Michael, and Jörg Rahn. 2005. "Just How Undervalued Is the Chinese Renminbi?" *World Economy* 28, no. 4: 465–89.

Goldberg, Linda S., and Michael W. Klein. 1997. "Foreign Direct Investment, Trade and Real Exchange Rate Linkages in Developing Countries." Working Paper 6344. Cambridge, Mass.: National Bureau of Economic Research.

Goldstein, Morris. 2004. "Adjusting China's Exchange Rate Policies." Working Paper 04-1. Washington: Peterson Institute for International Economics.

Jorgensen, Dale W., and Zvi Griliches. 1967. "The Explanation of Productivity Change." *Review of Economic Studies* 34, no. 3: 249–83.

King, Mervyn A., and Don Fullerton. 1984. *The Taxation of Income from Capital.* University of Chicago Press.

Klein, Michael W., and Eric Rosengren. 1994. "The Real Exchange Rate and Foreign Direct Investment in the United States: Relative Wealth vs. Relative Wage Effects." *Journal of International Economics* 36, no. 3-4: 373–89.

Kohli, Ulrich. 2003a. "Growth Accounting in the Open Economy: International Comparisons." *International Review of Economics and Finance* 12, no. 4: 417–35.

_____. 2003b. "GDP Growth Accounting: A National Income Function Approach." *Review of Income and Wealth* 49, no. 1: 23–34.

Lemoine, Francoise. 2000. "FDI and the Opening Up of China's Economy." Working Paper 2000-11. Paris: CEPII (June).

Ma, Alyson C. 2006. "Geographical Location of Foreign Direct Investment and Wage Inequality in China." *World Economy* 29, no. 8: 1031–55.

Marquez, Jaime, and John W. Schindler. 2006. "Exchange-Rate Effects on China's Trade: An Interim Report." Working Paper 2006-41. Federal Reserve Bank of San Francisco.

McKibbin, Warwick J., and Wing Thye Woo. 2003. "The Consequences of China's WTO Accession on its Neighbours." *Asian Economic Papers* 2, no. 2 (Spring–Summer): 1–38.

MOFCOM (Ministry of Commerce of the People's Republic of China). 2004. *Foreign Direct Investment Report.* Beijing.

_____. 2006. *Foreign Direct Investment Report.* Beijing.

_____. 2007. "Statistics about Utilization of Foreign Investment in China from Jan to Dec" 2006 (www.fdi.gov.cn/pub/FDI/wztj/wstztj/lywztj/t20070116_72412.htm).

NBSC (National Bureau of Statistics of China). 2000, 2001, 2005, 2006 and various issues. *China Statistical Yearbook.* Beijing: China Statistics Press.

Rauch, James E. 2001. "Business and Social Networks in International Trade." *Journal of Economic Literature* 39, no. 4: 1177–203.

Redding, Stephen, and Anthony J. Venables. 2004. "Economic Geography and International Inequality." *Journal of International Economics* 62, no. 1: 53–82.

Roach, Stephen S. 2003. *Getting China Right.* Special Economic Study. Washington: Morgan Stanley (September 23).

Solow, Robert M. 1957. "Technical Change and the Aggregate Production Function." *Review of Economics and Statistics* 39, no. 3: 312–20.

Tomiura, Eiichi. 2005. "Foreign Outsourcing and Firm-level Characteristics: Evidence from Japanese Manufacturers." *Journal of the Japanese and International Economies* 19, no. 2: 255–71.

United Nations. 2006. *World Investment Report*. New York: UNCTAD.

Whalley, John. 2006. "The Post MFA Performance of Developing Asia." Working Paper 12178. Cambridge, Mass.: National Bureau of Economic Research.

Whalley, John, and Li Wang. 2007. "The Unified Enterprise Tax and SOEs in China." Working Paper 12899. Cambridge, Mass.: National Bureau of Economic Research.

Whalley, John, and Xian Xin. 2006. "China's FDI and Non-FDI Economies and the Sustainability of Future High Chinese Growth." Working Paper 12249. Cambridge, Mass.: National Bureau of Economic Research.

Willenbockel, Dirk. 2006. "Structural Effects of a Real Exchange Rate Revaluation in China: A CGE Assessment." MPRA Paper 920. Munich Personal RePEc Archive (MPRA). Munich: Munich University Library.

Woo, Wing Thye. Forthcoming. "Dealing Sensibly with the Threat of Disruption in Trade with China: The Analytics of Increased Economic Interdependence and Accelerated Technological Innovation." *Economic Change and Restructuring*.

Xing, Yuqing. 2006a. "Exchange Rate Policy and the Relative Distribution of FDI among Host Countries." Discussion Paper 15/2006. Helsinki: Bank of Finland Institute for Economic Transition.

_____. 2006b. "Why Is China So Attractive for FDI? The Role of Exchange Rates." *China Economic Review* 17, no. 2: 198–209.

_____. 2006c. "Japanese FDI in China: Trend, Structure, and the Role of Exchange Rates." In *China as a World Factory*, edited by Kevin Honglin Zhang. New York: Routledge.

Xing, Yuqing, and Guanghua Wan. 2006. "Exchange Rates and Competition for FDI in Asia." *World Economy* 29, no. 4: 419–34.

Young, Alwyn. 1995. "The Tyranny of Numbers: Confronting the Statistical Realities of the East Asian Growth Experience." *Quarterly Journal of Economics* 110, no. 3: 641–80.

ASSAF RAZIN
Tel Aviv University, Cornell University, CEPR, NBER, CESifo, and IZA

EFRAIM SADKA
Tel Aviv University, CESifo, and IZA

Productivity and Taxes as Drivers of Foreign Direct Investment

Foreign direct investment (FDI) is a form of international capital flows. It plays an important role in the general allocation of world capital across countries. It is often portrayed, together with other forms of capital flows, as shifting capital from rich, capital-abundant economies to poor, capital-scarce economies, as a means to close the gap between the rates of return to capital and enhance the efficiency of the worldwide stock of capital. This general portrayal of international capital flows may indeed pertain to FDI flows from developed countries to developing countries, which are almost all net recipients of FDI. However, this portrayal of international capital flows is hardly reminiscent of the FDI flows among developed countries, which are much larger than those from developed to developing countries. Although *net* aggregate FDI flows from, or to, a developed country are typically small, the *gross* flows are quite large.

In this paper we indeed focus on bilateral FDI flows among member countries of the Organization for Economic Cooperation and Development (OECD). We study the effects of two sets of driving forces that affect FDI: productivity and taxation. Specifically, we attempt to shed some light on some key mechanisms through which these sets affect FDI flows.[1] An important feature of our FDI model (which distinguishes FDI flows from portfolio flows) is fixed setup costs of new investments. This introduces two margins of FDI decisions: an intensive margin of determining the magnitude of the flows of FDI, according

Thanks are due to Hui Tong and Thiess Buttner for providing us with some of the data and to Alon Cohen for competent research assistance.

1. Some macroeconomic studies emphasize the effect of FDI on long-run economic growth and cyclical fluctuations. A comprehensive study by Bosworth and Collins (1999) studied a somewhat related effect: that of FDI on growth. They provided evidence on the effect of capital inflows on domestic investment for fifty-eight developed countries during the period 1978 to 1995.

to standard marginal productivity conditions, and also an extensive margin of determining whether to make a new investment at all. Productivity and taxes may affect these two margins in different, possibly conflicting, and crucial ways. The magnitude of the setup costs can well be industry-specific, thereby giving rise to two-way rich-rich, as well as rich-poor, FDI flows.

Also, threshold barriers play an important role in determining the extent of trade-based foreign direct investment.[2] The trade-based literature typically focuses on issues such as the interdependence of FDI and trade in goods and the ensuing industrial structure. For instance, studies have attempted to explain how a source country can export both FDI and goods to the same host country. The explanation essentially rests on productivity heterogeneity within the source country and on differences in setup costs associated with FDI and export of goods. The trade-based literature on FDI is based on a framework of heterogeneous firms.[3] Thus the empirical approach in this trade-based literature focuses on firm-level decisions on exports and FDI in the source country, using microdatasets. Our approach is to analyze aggregate bilateral FDI using countrywide datasets. Note that micro–cross-country panel datasets are not available, so that micro-based empirical studies typically have to be confined to a single source or host country and to extremely short time spans. In contrast, we have data for nineteen OECD countries over a large interval of time (1987–2003).

We first study the role of source country and host country productivities on the twofold FDI decisions. Specifically, we develop a framework in which the host productivity has a positive effect on the *intensive margin* (the size of FDI flows), but an ambiguous effect on the *extensive margin* (the likelihood of FDI flows to occur). The source productivity has a negative effect on the extensive margin. These predictions are tested in the data. We then study the effects of corporate taxation on FDI. Earlier studies have suggested that FDI is sensitive to tax rate differences.[4] Our contribution to this discussion is that the tax rates of the host and source countries may have differential effects on the two margins of FDI decisions. Therefore, the sensitivity of FDI to tax rate differentials may be blurred.[5]

The organization of the paper is as follows. The next section presents an analytical framework with productivity as a driving force of FDI. The third sec-

2. See, for instance, Zhang and Markusen (1999); Carr, Markusen, and Maskus (2001); Helpman, Melitz, and Yeaple (2004).

3. See Melitz (2003).

4. See, for example, Gropp and Kostial (2000); Bénassy-Quéré, Fontagné, and Lahrèche-Révil (2000).

5. See Devereux and Griffith (2003) on the different effects of marginal and average taxes on the investment decisions about location and magnitudes.

tion extends this framework to include corporate taxation as an additional driving force. The fourth section describes our econometric approach. The fifth section describes the data, followed by the presentation of the results of the estimations. The last section concludes.

A Stripped-Down Model of Foreign Direct Investment

Datasets of source-to-host FDI flows typically include many observations with zero flows. This may indicate the existence of fixed setup costs of establishing new FDI, thereby generating two margins for FDI decisions—an extensive margin about whether to invest at all and an intensive margin about how much to invest.

We present in this section a simple, stripped-down model of FDI with fixed setup costs. Consider a pair of countries, *host* and *source*, in a world of free capital mobility that fixes the world rate of interest, denoted by r. We will now describe the host country, whose economic variables will be subscripted by H, and the source country, described by subscript S. Variables with either subscript are not identical for the two countries. There is a representative industry whose product serves for both consumption and investment. Firms last for two periods. In the first period, there is a continuum of N_H firms that differ from each other by an idiosyncratic productivity factor ε. The number (N_H) of firms (or entrepreneurs) is fixed. We refer to a firm that has a productivity factor of ε as an ε-*firm*. The cumulative distribution function of ε is denoted by $G(\cdot)$ with a density function $g(\cdot)$. That is, the number of ε-*firms is* $N_H g(\varepsilon)$.

We assume for simplicity that the initial net capital stock of each firm is the same and denote it by K_H^0. If an ε-*firm* invests I in the first period, it augments its capital stock to $K = K_H^0 + 1$, and its gross output in the second period will be $A_H F(K, L)(1 + \varepsilon)$, where L is the labor input, $F(\cdot)$ is the production function, and A_H is a country(H)-specific aggregate productivity parameter. Note that ε is firm specific, whereas A_H is country specific.

We assume that there is a fixed setup cost of investment, C_H, which is the same for all firms (that is, it is independent of ε). We assume that the fixed cost has two components. One component (denoted by C_{SH}) is borne by the FDI investor in her or his source country. This may involve, for instance, management time and other expenses at the home headquarters of a multinational. The second component is a standard adjustment cost carried out in the host country. We assume that this cost involves labor input L_H^C (as a proxy for all nontraded inputs) only. Thus,

$$C_H = C_{SH} + w_H L_H^C, \tag{1}$$

where w_H is the host country wage rate. We assume that, due to some (suppressed) fixed factor, F is strictly concave, exhibiting diminishing returns to scale and diminishing marginal products of labor and capital. Note that the average cost curve of the firm is U-shaped so that perfect competition, which we assume, can prevail.[6] Consider an ε-firm that invests in the first period an amount $I = K - K_H^0$ to augment its stock of capital to K. Its present value becomes $V^+(A_H, K_H^0, \varepsilon, w_H) - C_H$, where

$$V^+(A_H, K_H^0, \varepsilon, w_H) = \max_{(K,L)} \left\{ \frac{A_H F(K,L)(1+\varepsilon) - wL + (1-\delta)K}{1+r} - K - K_H^0 \right\}, \tag{2}$$

where δ is the rate of physical depreciation and r is the world (fixed) rate of interest.

The demands of such a firm for K and L are denoted by $K^+(A_H, \varepsilon, w_H)$ and $L^+(A_H, \varepsilon, w_H)$. They are given by the marginal productivity conditions

$$A_H F_K(K,L)(1+\varepsilon) = r + \delta \tag{3}$$

and

$$A_H F_L(K,L)(1+\varepsilon) = w_H, \tag{4}$$

where F_K and F_L denote the partial derivatives of F with respect to K and L, respectively. Naturally, ε is bounded from below by -1, so that output is always nonnegative. We denote the upper bound of the productivity factor by $\bar{\varepsilon}$, that is, $G(\bar{\varepsilon}) = 1$. Note, however, that an ε-firm may choose not to invest at all (that is, it may choose to stick to its existing stock of capital, K_H^0) and avoid the lumpy setup cost C_H. Naturally, a firm with a low ε may not find it worthwhile to incur the setup cost C_H. In this case, its present value is

$$V^-(A_H, K_H^0, \varepsilon, w_H) = \max_L \left\{ \frac{A_H F(K_H^0, L)(1+\varepsilon) - w_H L + (1-\delta)K_H^0}{1+r} \right\}. \tag{5}$$

The labor demand of such a firm, denoted by $L^-(A_H, K_H^0, \varepsilon, w_H)$, is defined by

---

6. With constant returns to scale, the fixed cost will entail a diminishing average cost curve, in which case perfect competition cannot be sustained. Were we to assume that entry is free, one could have constant returns to scale at the industry level.

$$A_H F_L(K_H^0, L)(1+\varepsilon) = w_H. \tag{6}$$

A firm will choose to make a new investment if its present value with the investment exceeds its present value without the investment. Naturally, a higher productivity firm (namely, a firm with a higher ε) benefits more from investment; that is, the gap between V^+ and V^- increases with ε.[7]

Therefore, a cutoff level of ε exists, denoted by ε_0, such that an ε-firm will make a new investment if and only if $\varepsilon > \varepsilon_0$. This cutoff level of ε depends on A_H, C_H, K_H^0, and w_H. We write the cutoff of ε as $\varepsilon_0(A_H, C_H, K_H^0, w_H)$. It is defined implicitly by

$$V^+(A_H, K_H^0, \varepsilon_0, w_H) - C_H = V^-(A_H, K_H^0, \varepsilon_0, w_H). \tag{7}$$

That is, the cutoff productivity level is the level at which the firm is just indifferent between making a new investment and incurring the setup cost and sticking to its existing capital stock, thereby avoiding the setup cost.

The wage rate (w_H) is determined in equilibrium by a clearance in the labor market. We assume that labor is confined within national borders. Denoting the country's endowment of labor by $\bar{L}_H^0$, we have the following labor market–clearing equation:

$$N_H \int_{-1}^{\varepsilon_0(A_H, C_H, K_H^0, w_H)} L^-(A_H, K_H^0, \varepsilon, w_H) g(\varepsilon) d\varepsilon$$

$$+ N_H \left\{ 1 - G\left[\varepsilon_0(A_H, C_H, K_H^0, w_H) \right] \right\} L_H^C \tag{8}$$

$$+ N_H \int_{\varepsilon_0(A_H, C_H, K_H^0, w_H)}^{\bar{\varepsilon}} L^+(A_H, \varepsilon, w_H) g(\varepsilon) d\varepsilon = \bar{L}_H^0.$$

Dividing the latter equation through by N_H yields

$$\int_{-1}^{\varepsilon_0(A_H, C_H, K_H^0, w_H)} L^-(A_H, K_H^0, \varepsilon, w_H) g(\varepsilon) d\varepsilon$$

$$+ \left\{ 1 - G\left[\varepsilon_0(A_H, C_H, K_H^0, w_H) \right] \right\} L_H^C \tag{9}$$

$$+ \int_{\varepsilon_0(A_H, C_H, K_H^0, w_H)}^{\bar{\varepsilon}} L^+(A_H, \varepsilon, w_H) g(\varepsilon) d\varepsilon = L_H^0,$$

7. A formal proof is available in Razin and Sadka (2007).

where $L_H^0 \equiv \bar{L}_H^0/N_H$ is the amount of labor per firm. (Note that there are N_H [1 − $G(\varepsilon_0)$] firms that make new investments, employing an extra fixed input of L_H^C.) Note also that no similar market-clearing equation is specified for capital, because we assume that capital is freely mobile internationally and its rate of return (r) is equalized internationally. The same description with the subscript S replacing H holds for the source country.

Differences in labor abundance between the two countries are manifested in the wage differences. To see this, suppose that the two countries are identical, except that effective labor per firm is more abundant in the host country than it is in the source country, that is, $L_H^0 > L_S^0$. In addition, the number of firms in the economy is also a measure of the abundance of entrepreneurship. Thus the abundance (or, respectively, scarcity) of labor is also relative to the scarcity (respectively, abundance) of entrepreneurship. If wages were equal in the two countries, then labor demand per firm would be equal and the market-clearing condition (equation 8) could not hold for both countries. Because of the diminishing marginal product of labor, it follows that wages in the relatively labor-abundant country are lower than those in the relatively labor-scarce country, that is, $w_H < w_S$.[8] Therefore, equal returns to capital (through capital mobility) coexist with unequal wages.[9]

Mergers and Acquisitions FDI

One may think of FDI as the investment of source country entrepreneurs in the acquisition of host country existing firms (whose number is fixed, N_H). We indeed deal initially with this kind of FDI through mergers and acquisitions (M&A). Suppose that the source country entrepreneurs are endowed with some intangible capital, or know-how, stemming from their specialization or expertise in the industry at hand. We model this comparative advantage by assuming that the setup cost of investment in the host country, when investment is done by source country entrepreneurs (that is, FDI investors), is only $C_H^* = C_{SH}^* + w_H L_H^{C*}$, which is less than C_H (the setup cost of investment when carried out by the host country direct investors). This cost advantage implies that the foreign investors can bid up the direct investors of the host country in the purchase of the investing firms in the host country. Each such firm (that is, each firm whose

8. The equilibrium wage gap implies that the host country employs more workers per firm than does the source country. Thus, even though the productivity distribution across firms is assumed equal, the source country is effectively more productive in equilibrium.

9. See also Amiti (2005), who studies the effect of agglomeration on cross-regional wage differences, and Melitz (2003) for the role of fixed costs in intra-industry reallocations in reaction to industry-specific productivity shocks.

ε is above $\varepsilon_0(A_H, C_H^*, K_H^0, w_H)$) is purchased at its market value, which is $V^+(A_H, K_H^0, \varepsilon, w_H) - C_H^*$. This essentially assumes that competition among the foreign direct investors shifts all the gains from their lower setup cost to the host country original owners of the firm. The new owners also invest an amount, $K^+(A_H, \varepsilon, w_H) - K_H^0$, in the firm.

Thus, the amount of foreign direct investment made in an ε-firm (where $\varepsilon > \varepsilon_0$) is

$$FDI(A_H, C_{SH}^*, K_H^0, \varepsilon, w_H) = V^+(A_H, K_H^0, \varepsilon, w_H) - C_{SH}^* + K^+(A_H, \varepsilon, w_H) - K_H^0 . \quad (10)$$

Note that the acquisition price is $V^+ - C_{SH}^* - w_H L_H^C$, but $w_H L_H^C$ constitutes part of FDI; therefore only C_{SH}^* is subtracted in equation 10.

Aggregate notional FDI is given by

$$FDI_N(A_H, C_H^*, C_{SH}^*, K_H^0, w_H) = N_H \int_{\varepsilon_0(A_H, C_H^*, K_H^0, w_H)}^{\bar{\varepsilon}} FDI(A_H, C_{SH}^*, K_H^0, w_H, \bar{\varepsilon}) g(\varepsilon) d\varepsilon . \quad (11)$$

Note that FDI_N, as defined in equation 11, would be the actual flow of FDI, when $\varepsilon_0(A_H, C_H^*, K_H^0, w_H)$ is below $\bar{\varepsilon}$. That is, FDI_N is the actual FDI only if

$$\varepsilon_0(A_H, C_H^*, K_H^0, w_H) \leq \bar{\varepsilon}. \quad (12)$$

Otherwise, the actual FDI would be zero. For this reason, we refer to FDI_N as the *notional* FDI. The *actual* FDI, denoted by FDI_A, is defined by:

$$FDI_A(A_H, C_H^*, C_{SH}^*, K_H^0, w_H) = \begin{cases} FDI_N(A_H, C_H^*, C_{SH}^*, K_H^0, w_H) & \text{if (12) holds,} \\ 0 & \text{otherwise.} \end{cases} \quad (13)$$

We refer to equation 12 as the selection-condition equation. It specifies when there will by any FDI flow to the host country. Equation 11, referred to as the flow equation, describes the actual FDI flow only if the selection-condition equation is satisfied.

Aggregate Productivity Shock: Flow and Selection

As described earlier, the parameter A_H is a host country–specific productivity factor that applies to all firms in this country. We examine how a shock to this factor affects the aggregate level of FDI flowing to the host country. Suppose first that the domestic wage rate (w_H) is fixed. A positive productivity shock has three positive effects on the notional FDI (namely, FDI_N), as specified in equation 11. First, it raises the marginal productivity of capital, thereby increasing the amount of investment that is made by each investing firm (which is acquired by FDI investors). Second, it raises the value of such firms and, consequently, their acquisition price, which constitutes a part of the notional FDI flows. Third, it increases the number of firms purchased by FDI investors (by lowering the threshold productivity level ε_0).[10]

Turning to the selection-condition equation 13, we see that a positive aggregate productivity shock (while still maintaining the wage rate [w_H] constant) increases the profitability of investments and, consequently, reduces the likelihood that no firm will make any investment. Formally, a rise in A_H reduces the likelihood that the threshold idiosyncratic productivity ε_0 exceeds the upper bound on the idiosyncratic productivity $\bar{\varepsilon}$. That is, a positive aggregate productivity shock raises the likelihood of satisfying the selection condition, so that the notional FDI turns out to be realized. Thus a positive aggregate productivity shock, keeping w_H fixed, raises the actual FDI (both through the flow and selection-condition equations).

Now, we drop the supposition that the wage rate (w_H) is fixed. When wages are not fixed (but rather are determined by the labor market–clearing equation 9), then the increase in the demand for labor raises the wage rate (w_H) in the host country (and the fixed setup cost, $w_H L_H^C$), thereby countering the above three effects on the notional FDI. With a unique equilibrium, the initial effects of the increase in A_H are likely to dominate the subsequent counter-effects of the rise in w_H, so that the notional FDI still rises. Thus an increase in the host country's aggregate productivity factor (A_H) raises the volume of the notional FDI flows from country S to country H, which is governed by the flow equation.

Next, consider the effect of an aggregate productivity shock on the selection-condition equation. A rise in A_H increases the value of the domestic component of the setup cost, $w_H L_H^C$. This effect by itself weakens the advantage of carrying out positive FDI flows at all from country S to country H. In other words, as w_H rises, ε_0 rises, thereby reducing the likelihood of satisfying the selection-condition equation. The follow-up effect that is triggered by a positive aggregate productivity shock works in the opposite direction of the initial effect (when holding w_H constant) and may dominate it.

10. For a formal derivation of the results, see Razin and Sadka (2007). We assume plausibly that the third effect, which represents the marginal investing firm, is rather small relative to the margin of investment of all investing firms (the first effect). We ignore the third effect in the empirical investigation.

To sum up, a positive aggregate productivity shock in the host country raises the observed notional FDI flows in the flow equation and, at the same time, may lower the likelihood of observing positive FDI flows at all. Indeed, this possibility is demonstrated in a recent paper by Razin and Sadka.[11] Also, the source country aggregate productivity factor (A_S) does not affect the flows of M&A FDI from country S to country H. This is because we assumed free international mobility of portfolio capital, which set a common rate of interest (r) worldwide.

Greenfield FDI

So far, FDI has taken the form of mergers or acquisitions of the N_H existing firms. Consider now the possibility of establishing a new firm (that is, a greenfield FDI, where $K_H^0 = 0$). Suppose that the newcomer entrepreneur does not know in advance the productivity factor (ε) of the potential firm. The entrepreneur therefore takes $G(\cdot)$ as the cumulative probability distribution of the idiosyncratic productivity factor of the new firm. However, we assume that ε is revealed to the entrepreneur, before she or he decides whether or not to make a new investment. The expected value of the new firm is therefore:

$$V(A, C_{nH}^*, w) = \int_{-1}^{\bar{\varepsilon}} \max\{V^+(A_H, 0, \varepsilon, w_H) - C_{nH}, 0\} g(\varepsilon) d\varepsilon, \qquad (14)$$

where C_{nH} is the setup cost of a greenfield investment. When K_H^0 is equal to zero, only the firms with ε high enough to justify a greenfield investment have a positive value. This explains the max operator in equation 14.

Suppose that greenfield entrepreneurship is in limited capacity. Thus an entrepreneur in a source country (and there are a limited number of them) may have to decide whether to establish a new firm at home (the source country) or abroad (the host country), but not in both. The entrepreneur's decision is naturally determined by which country will produce the higher $V(\cdot)$, as defined in equation 14. The entrepreneur will invest in the host country rather than in the source country if and only if

$$V(A_H, C_{nH}^*, w_H) > V(A_S, C_{nS}^*, w_S). \qquad (15)$$

(We continue to maintain the assumption that the source country entrepreneurs have a cutting-edge advantage over their counterparts in the host country in estab-

11. Razin and Sadka (2007).

lishing greenfield investments.) This is a selection-condition equation for greenfield FDI. In contrast to the M&A case, the aggregate productivity factor plays a role in the source country (A_S) in greenfield FDI. A positive shock to A_S increases the likelihood that source country entrepreneurs will stay at home and in turn reduces the likelihood of greenfield FDI flows from country S to H.

In an example wherein an entrepreneur is deciding in which country among many to invest, an entrepreneur from source country S chooses to invest in host country H if the latter offers the most profitable investment. Also, the entrepreneur may need to outbid competitors from other source countries (for instance, in the case of acquiring a concession from the host country government to operate something). In this case, $V(A_H', C_{nH}^*{}', w_H')$ in the selection-condition equation 15 must be the maximum over all $V(A_H, C_{nH}^*, w_H)$ for potential other host countries:

$$V(A_H, C_{nH}^*, w_H) = \arg\max_{H' \in D} V(A_H', C_{nH}^*{}', w_H') > V(A_S, C_S^*, w_S), \qquad (15')$$

where D is the set of potential host countries in which the entrepreneurs of source country S can outbid all competing entrepreneurs from other potential source countries.[12] Each entrepreneur in the source country who decides to actually make a greenfield FDI in host country H invests according to the marginal productivity conditions. Aggregation over these entrepreneurs from source country S provides a flow equation of greenfield FDI from S to H.

As we have seen, the host country aggregate productivity factor (A_H) affects positively the notional FDI flows from source countries in the case of M&A flows, whereas the source country aggregate productivity factor (A_S) has no effect on these flows. At the same time, a positive shock to A_H may reduce the likelihood of having M&A FDI flows to the host country H (because of general equilibrium effects on wages in the host country). Again, A_S has no effects on these flows. In the case of greenfield FDI, a positive shock to A_H has positive effects both on the notional FDI flows to host country H and on the likelihood of these flows to actually materialize. A positive shock to A_S does not affect the notional flows to host country H, but it reduces the likelihood of such flows to occur at all. Also, the likelihood of having greenfield FDI flows from country S to country H is negatively affected by positive productivity shocks in all other potential host countries (A_H').[13]

---

12. Eaton and Kortum (2002) applied the probability theory of extremes to provide a tractable form for a selection-condition equation in a similar context.

13. A comprehensive study of the latter effects (A_H') is not available. We ignore these effects in the empirical investigation.

Source Country and Host Country Corporate Taxation

The economic literature has dealt extensively with the effects of taxation on investment, going back to the well-known works of Harberger and Hall and Jorgenson.[14] Of particular interest are the effects of international differences in tax rates on foreign direct investment.[15]

In this section we attempt to provide a new look at the mechanisms through which corporate tax rates influence aggregate FDI flows in the setup adopted here of twofold investment decisions in the presence of threshold barriers. In this context, the tax rates of the source country and host country may have different effects on these two decisions (the flow and selection-condition equations).

Consider, for the sake of concreteness, the case of a parent firm that weighs the development of a new product line. We can think of the fixed setup cost as the outlays of developing this product line. The firm may choose to develop the line at home and then produce it at a subsidiary abroad. This choice may be determined by some genuine economic considerations, such as source and host aggregate productivity factors (as discussed in the preceding section) and by tax considerations.

In this context, the issue of double taxation arises. The income of a foreign affiliate is typically taxed by the host country. If the source country taxes this income too, then the combined (double) tax rate may be very high and even could exceed 100 percent.[16] This double taxation is typically relieved at the source country level by either exempting foreign source income altogether or granting tax credits.[17] In the former case, foreign source income is subject to the tax levied by the host country only. When the source country taxes its residents on their worldwide income and grants full credit for foreign taxes (residence taxation), then in principle the foreign source income is taxed at the source country tax rate, so that the host country tax rate becomes irrelevant for investment decisions by the source country residents. But, in practice, foreign source income is far from being taxed at the source country rate. First, there are various reduced tax rates for foreign source income. Second, foreign source income is usually taxed only upon repatriation, thereby effectively reducing the present value of the tax. Thus, in practice, the host country tax rate is very much relevant for

14. Harberger (1962); Hall and Jorgenson (1967).

15. See, for instance, Auerbach and Hassett (1993); Hines (1999); Desai, Foley, and Hines (2004); de Mooij and Ederveen (2001); Devereux and Hubbard (2003).

16. For a succinct review of this issue, see, for example, Hines (2004).

17. This is also the recommendation of the OECD model tax treaty; see OECD (1997). A similar recommendation is made also by the United Nations model tax treaty; see UN (1980).

investment decisions by the parent firm at the source country. The relevance of the host country tax rate intensifies through transfer pricing.[18]

One of the major elements through which corporate taxation affects an investment decision is the treatment of depreciation.[19] We denote the true rate of depreciation in host country H by δ_H and the rate allowed for tax purposes by δ'_H. Concentrating for simplicity on M&A FDI, equation 2 becomes in this case

$$V^+(A_H, K_H^0, \tau_H, \varepsilon, w_H) =$$
$$\max_{(K,L)} \left\{ \frac{[A_H F(K,L)(1+\varepsilon) - w_H L](1-\tau_H) + \tau_H \delta'_H K + (1-\delta_H)K}{1+(1-\tau_H)r} - \left(K - K_H^0\right) \right\}, \quad (16)$$

where τ_H is the host country corporate tax rate. Note that in the presence of taxation, the discount rate is the after-tax rate $(1 - \tau_H)r$. (This specification assumes that the subsidiary uses debt in the host country to finance the new investment.) Employing the envelope theorem, it follows from equation 16 that $\partial V^+/\partial\tau_H < 0$. That is, the present value of the cash flow falls when the corporate tax rate in the host country rises, as it is indeed expected to do. Furthermore, the amount of new investment depends negatively on τ_H. The first-order condition for the stock of capital (equation 3) now becomes

$$A_H F_K(K,L)(1+\varepsilon) = r + \frac{\delta_H - \delta'_H \tau_H}{1 - \tau_H} . \quad (17)$$

This latter equation defines (implicitly) an equation for the flow of FDI. As δ'_H is typically smaller than δ_H, it follows that the flow of FDI declines in τ_H.

The source country parent firm will undertake the project if and only if

$$w_H L_H^{C^*}(1-\tau_H) + C_{SH}^*(1-\tau_S) < V^+(A_H, K_H^0, \tau_H, \varepsilon, w_H) , \quad (18)$$

where τ_S is the corporate tax rate in the source country. Recall that $w_H L_H^{C^*}$ and C_{SH}^* are, respectively, the host country and source country components of the fixed cost C_H^*.

To sum up, as is evident from selection-condition equation 18, the tax rate in the source country, τ_S, affects positively the decision by a parent firm in country S about whether to carry out a foreign direct investment in country H; under plausible assumptions, the tax rate in the host country, τ_H, has a negative effect on this decision. The tax rate in the source country, τ_S, is irrelevant for the determination of the magnitude of FDI flows, which are negatively affected by τ_H.

18. The U.S. Jobs Creation Act of 2005 allows U.S. companies to pay a tax of merely 5.25 percent on their foreign source income.
19. See, for instance, Auerbach (1983).

As before, there is a cutoff productivity level, denoted by $\varepsilon_0(A_H, C_H, L_H^{C^*}, C_{SH}^*, K_H^0, \tau_H, \tau_S, w_H)$, such that all firms with a firm-specific productivity level above ε_0 will make new investments and will be acquired by FDI investors. All other firms will make no new investments and will remain under domestic ownership. The cutoff level of ε_0 is defined implicitly by equation 18 with the inequality sign being replaced by an equality sign. It follows from equation 18 that an increase in the source country corporate tax rate (τ_S) reduces ε_0, so that more firms are purchased by FDI investors. The reason for this is that a rise in τ_S reduces the after-tax source country component of the fixed cost. Note that V^+ declines in τ_H. But a rise in τ_H reduces the after-tax host country component of the fixed cost (namely, $w_H L_H^{C^*}(1 - \tau_H)$). However, if the first effect dominates the second, which is plausible, then an increase in τ_H raises ε_0; that is, an increase in the host country corporate tax rate reduces the number of investing firms (which are purchased by FDI investors).

Similarly, as before, aggregate notional FDI is given by

$$FDI_N(A_H, w_H L_H^{C^*}, C_{SH}^*, K_H^0, \tau_H, \tau_S, w_H) =$$
$$\int_{\varepsilon_0(A_H, w_H L_H^{C^*}, C_{SH}^*, K_H^0, \tau_H, \tau_S, w_H)}^{\bar{\varepsilon}} FDI(A_H, C_{SH}^*, w_H L_H^{C^*}, K_H^0, \tau_H, \tau_S, \varepsilon, w_H) g(\varepsilon) d\varepsilon, \quad (19)$$

where, as before,

$$FDI(A_H, C_{SH}^*, w_H L_H^{C^*}, K_H^0, \tau_H, \tau_S, \varepsilon, w_H) =$$
$$V^+(A_H, K_H^0, \tau_H, \varepsilon, w_H) - C_{SH}^*(1 - \tau_S) + K^+(A_H, \tau_H, \varepsilon, w_H) - K_H^0 , \quad (20)$$

and where K^+ is implicitly defined by equation 17.

The *actual* FDI will be equal to the notional FDI only when ε_0 is below $\bar{\varepsilon}$:

$$\varepsilon_0(A_H, w_H L_H^{C^*}, C_{SH}^*, K_H^0, \tau_H, \tau_S, w_H) \leq \bar{\varepsilon}, \quad (21)$$

which is the selection-condition equation. The actual flow of FDI (FDI_H) is thus

$$FDI_A(A_H, w_H L_H^{C^*}, C_{SH}^*, K_H^0, \tau_H, \tau_S, w_H) =$$
$$= \begin{cases} FDI_N(A_H, w_H L_H^{C^*}, C_{SH}^*, K_H^0, \tau_H, \tau_S, w_H) & \text{if condition (21) holds,} \\ 0 & \text{otherwise.} \end{cases} \quad (22)$$

Note that an increase in the host country corporate tax rate (τ_H) reduces the actual FDI flows from S to H and the likelihood that such flows will occur. An increase in the source country corporate tax rate (τ_S) increases the likelihood that FDI flows from S to H will occur.[20]

Econometric Approach

The twofold nature of FDI decisions gives rise to many cases of zero actual FDI flows. With n countries in a sample, there are potentially $n(n-1)$ pairs of source and host (s,h) countries. In fact, the actual number of (s,h) pairs with observed flows is typically much smaller. Therefore, the selection of the actual number of (s,h) pairs, which is naturally endogenous, cannot be ignored; that is, this selection cannot be taken as exogenous. This feature of FDI decisions lends itself naturally to the application of the Heckman selection model.[21] This selection bias method is adopted to jointly estimate the likelihood of surpassing a certain threshold (the selection-condition equation) and the magnitude of the FDI flow (the flow equation), provided that the threshold is indeed surpassed.

Failing to take into account the selection-condition equation, either by dropping out observations with zero flows or by treating such observations as actually indicating zero flows, results in biased estimates of the coefficients of the flow equation. In addition, the selection-condition equation per se provides meaningful economic information about the determinants of FDI flows through the likelihood of having such flows at all.[22]

Figure 1 explains the intuition for the cause of the bias. Suppose, for instance, that x_{ijt} is an explanatory variable that measures the productivity differential between the i-th source country and the potential j-th host country in period t, holding all other explanatory variables constant. Our theory predicts that the parameter β_x is positive. This is shown by the upward sloping line AB. Note that the slope is an estimate of the "true" marginal effect of x_{ijt} on Y^*_{ijt}, the latent variable denoting the flow of notional FDI from the source country i to host country j in period t. But recall that flows could also be equal to zero, if the setup costs are sufficiently high. A threshold, which is derived from the setup costs, is shown as the curve TT' in figure 1. However, if we discard observations with actual zero FDI flows, the remaining subsample is no longer random.

---

20. As before, we ignore the extensive margin effect of τ_S in the flow equation.
21. Heckman (1974, 1979).
22. For a more detailed analysis, see Razin and Sadka (2007, chapter 7).

Figure 1. Biased OLS Estimates of the Flow Equation

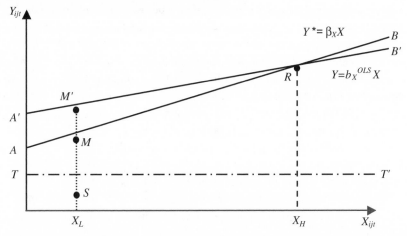

To illustrate in figure 1, suppose that for high values of x_{ijt} (say, X_H), (i,j) pair-wise FDI flows are all positive. That is, for all pairs of countries in the sub-sample, the threshold is surpassed and the observed average of notional FDI flows for $x_{ijt} = X^H$ is also equal to the conditional population average for FDI flows, which is point R on line AB. However, suppose that this does not hold for low values of x_{ijt} (say, X_L). For these (i,j) pairs, we observe positive values of Y_{ijt}, the observed actual flow of FDI, only for a subset of country pairs in the population.[23] Point S is, for instance, excluded from the subsample of positive FDI flows. Consequently, for low values of x_{ijt}, we observe only flows between country pairs with low setup costs. As a result, the observed average of the FDI flows is at point M', whereas the "true" average is at point M. As seen in fig-ure 1, the ordinary least squares (OLS) regression line for the subsample is therefore the $A'B'$ line, which underestimates the effect of productivity differ-entials on bilateral FDI flows. If we do not discard the zero FDI flow observations, the OLS estimates of β are still biased, because they are based on observations on Y, the actual FDI, rather than on Y^*, the notional FDI.

Data and Descriptive Statistics

We consider several potential explanatory variables of the twofold decisions on FDI flows. As in another paper by Razin and Sadka, these variables include

---

23. This indeed will be the case when the residuals in the flow and selection-condition equa-tions are positively correlated. An opposite bias occurs in the case of a negative correlation.

standard *mass* variables (the population sizes of the source country and host country), *distance* variables (physical distance between the source and the host countries and whether or not the two countries share a common language), and *economic* variables (source country and host country real GDP per capita, differences in average years of schooling between the source and the host countries, and source and host financial risk ratings).[24] We also control for country and time fixed effects. The dependent variable in the flow equation is the log of the FDI flows. (The flow equation is also known as the *gravity* equation.)

The main variables are grouped as follows:

—Standard country characteristics, such as real GDP per capita, population size, educational attainment (as measured by average years of schooling), and financial soundness rating (the inverse of financial risk rating)

—Source and host (s,h) characteristics, such as (s,h) FDI flows, geographical distance, and common language (variable with a value of either zero or one)

—Productivity

—Corporate tax rates

Productivity is approximated by labor productivity, that is, output per worker, as measured by purchasing power parity–adjusted real GDP per worker. This variable is at times instrumented by the capital-to-labor ratio and years of schooling. Corporate taxes are measured by the statutory rates or by the effective average rates, as compiled by Devereux, Griffith, and Klemm.[25] The effective rates are at times instrumented by the statutory corporate tax rates and GDP per capita.

Table 1 summarizes the data sources. Table A-1 describes the list of the countries in the sample and indicates for each source-host pair the (time) average of FDI flows as percentages of the source and host GDPs. Some source countries interact with only a few host countries. We do not smooth the data by taking multiyear averages but rather employ unfiltered annual data. This enables us to investigate the effects of the explanatory variables over the business cycle. We present in table 2 some aggregate statistics of the detailed country-pair data of table A-2. Specifically, we consider all the EU countries, except the United Kingdom and Ireland, as one block of countries. We then present (time) average flows among this block, the United Kingdom, the United States, Ireland, Australia, and Japan as percentages of the GDP of the source and host countries or the block of countries. This underscores the prominence of the United States as a source of FDI and the United Kingdom, Ireland, and Japan as recip-

24. Razin and Sadka (2007).
25. Devereux, Griffith, and Klemm (2002).

Table 1. Data Sources

Variable	Source
FDI flows	International Direct Investment Database (OECD)
GDP	World Economic Indicators
Population	World Economic Indicators
Number of workers	World Economic Indicators
Distance	Andrew Rose website: www.haas.berkeley.edu/~arose
Common language	Andrew Rose website: www.haas.berkeley.edu/~arose
Educational attainment	Barro-Lee dataset: www.nber.org/pub/barro.lee/
International Country Risk Guide (ICRG) index of financial soundness rating (the inverse of financial risk rating)	Political Risk Services (PRS) Group
Capital stock	Francesco Caselli website: http://personal.lse.ac.uk/casellif
Effective tax rates	Devereux, Griffith, and Klemm (2002)

ients of FDI. Note that the EU block (which excludes the United Kingdom and Ireland) plays a relatively small role either as a source or as a host of FDI.

Data on FDI flows are drawn from the International Direct Investment (IDI) database, covering the bilateral FDI flows among eighteen OECD countries during the period 1987 to 2003.[26] The dataset reports FDI flows from OECD countries to OECD and non-OECD countries, as well as FDI flows from non-OECD countries to OECD countries. However, it does not report FDI flows from non-OECD to non-OECD countries. This is why we employ in our sample OECD countries only. The IDI dataset provides data on FDI flows in U.S. dollars, and we deflate the dollars by the U.S. consumer price index for urban consumers.

Empirical Evidence

As was mentioned before, productivity is taken as one of the drivers of FDI, which in our study is measured by labor productivity. However, because labor productivity and FDI flows are both affected by other variables that are not controlled for in the regression, such as business cycle variables (for example, interest rates and unemployment rates), we present alternatives in our results. In the first regression we simply employ labor productivity. In the second

---

26. The International Direct Investment database is available through OECD's website, SourceOECD (www.sourceoecd.org). Razin and Sadka (2007) use also samples containing both OECD and non-OECD countries.

Table 2. Time Average of FDI Flows[a]

Host country	11 EU members[b]		United States		Source country United Kingdom		Japan		Ireland		Australia	
	Source	Host	Source	Host	Source	Host	Source	Host	Source	Host	Source	Host
11 EU members[b]			0.313	0.179	2.377	0.213	0.145	0.043	3.054	0.017	0.134	0.004
United States	0.256	0.448			2.113	0.331	0.436	0.228	2.288	0.022	0.627	0.029
United Kingdom	0.159	1.776	0.228	1.457			0.136	0.453	0.801	0.049	0.429	0.128
Japan	0.016	0.053	0.046	0.087	0.061	0.018			0.189	0.003	0.016	0.001
Ireland	0.033	5.963	0.042	4.397	0.130	2.125	0.007	0.387			0.019	0.091
Australia	0.013	0.470	0.034	0.721	0.134	0.449	0.044	0.495	0.066	0.013		

Source: Authors' calculations.

a. As a percentage of the source and host countries' GDP

b. Austria, Belgium, Finland, France, Germany, Greece, Italy, Netherlands, Spain, Sweden, and Portugal.

Table 3. Predicted Effect of Shocks on FDI

	M&A		Greenfield	
	Flow	*Selection*	*Flow*	*Selection*
Productivity increase, fixed host wages				
Host	+	+	+	+
Source	0	0	0	–
Productivity increase, flexible host wages				
Host	+	amb.	+	+
Source	0	0	0	–
Tax increase				
Host	–	–		
Source	0	+		

Source: Author's calculations.

FDI = foreign direct investment; M&A = mergers and acquisitions; + = positive effect; – = negative effect; amb = ambiguous effect; 0 = no effect.

regression we instrument the labor productivity variable by the capital-to-labor ratio, years of schooling, and country fixed effects.

As for the tax variables, we employ first the statutory tax rates. Another alternative is the effective tax rates as compiled by Devereux, Griffith, and Klemm.[27] Their rates measure the gap between the cost of capital in the corporate sector (that is, the required rate of return on an investment) and the tax-free interest rate. For the same reasons as in the case of productivity, we also use the statutory corporate tax rates, GDP per capita, and country fixed effects as instruments to generate fitted values for the effective tax rates. Table 3 summarizes the predicted effects generated by our theoretical framework.

Table A-2 presents the instrumented productivity and tax equations. As expected, the coefficients of the capital-to-labor ratio and years of schooling are positive and significant in the instrumented productivity equation. Similarly, the statutory tax rate and GDP per capita are positive and significant in the instrumented tax equation. R^2 is very high, close to one, in both equations.

Consider, first, productivity as a driver of FDI flows. The estimation results are described in table 4. Column 1 refers to the uninstrumented productivities, whereas column 2 considers fitted productivities. The first four variables are for productivity or instrumented productivity for the source and the host countries, followed by the coefficients of the other variables. Source GDP per capita has a positive and significant effect on the flows of FDI in both columns. Host GDP per capita has a positive and significant effect on the flow of FDI in column 2 only. Neither source nor host GDP per capita is significant in the selection

27. Devereux, Griffith, and Klemm (2002).

Table 4. Bilateral FDI Flows and Selection Equations: Productivity Effect[a]

Variable	Uninstrumented productivities		Fitted productivities	
	Flow	Selection	Flow	Selection
Productivity–source	–0.066	–0.059		
	(0.018)**	(0.024)*		
Productivity–host	0.042	0.014		
	(0.018)*	(0.028)		
Instrumented productivity–source			–0.080	–0.136
			(0.033)*	(0.052)**
Instrumented productivity–host			–0.012	0.047
			(0.036)	(0.046)
ln GDP per capita–source	5.812	2.150	3.515	0.996
	(0.837)**	(1.124)	(0.621)**	(0.667)
ln GDP per capita–host	1.437	–1.532	3.955	–1.452
	(0.853)	(1.204)	(0.607)**	(0.797)
Schooling difference	0.093	–0.053	0.002	0.022
	(0.063)	(0.069)	(0.070)	(0.081)
Common language	0.516	–0.179	0.497	–0.089
	(0.090)**	(0.118)	(0.106)**	(0.148)
ln Distance	–1.013	–0.305	–1.081	–0.388
	(0.044)**	(0.074)**	(0.048)**	(0.088)**
ln Population–source	0.754	–3.889	–1.363	–7.880
	(1.739)	(2.554)	(2.081)	(2.972)**
ln Population–host	–2.764	–5.529	–0.217	–9.043
	(1.463)	(2.597)*	(1.683)	(3.040)**
Financial risk–source	–0.03	0.023	–0.017	0.009
	(0.012)*	(0.019)	(0.014)	(0.025)
Financial risk–host	–0.015	–0.029	–0.019	–0.016
	(0.011)	(0.017)	(0.013)	(0.020)
Previous FDI dummy (1 if yes)		1.538		1.5
		(0.085)**		(0.093)**
Observations	4,702	4,702	3,833	3,833

Source: Authors' calculations.
*Significant at the 5 percent level; **significant at the 1 percent level.
a. Country and time fixed effects are accounted for; robust standard errors are in parentheses.

equation. In contrast, the host population size has a negative and significant effect in the selection equation only, for both columns. The source population follows a similar pattern but is significant only in column 2. As expected, the physical distance variable has a negative and significant effect in both equations and in both columns. Common language has a positive and significant effect in both columns, but only in the flow equation. Turning to the financial soundness rating variable, it is only the source variable that has a negative (as expected) and significant effect and only in the flow equation of column 1. The source-host schooling gap is not significant throughout. The existence of previous FDI (a dummy variable) may be indicative of low setup costs. We therefore employ it as an exclusion restriction variable in the selection equation. Indeed, its coefficient is found to be significant and positive.

We turn now to the first four variables, which are at the focus of the investigation: the source and host productivity factors, as approximated by outputs per worker. In column 1 of table 4, the host country output per worker has a positive effect in both the flow and selection equations, but it is significant only in the flow equation. Source country output per worker has a negative and significant effect on the selection mechanism. This result is consistent with the analytical framework developed earlier. Noteworthy, the source country output per worker has also a negative and significant effect on the flow of FDI. In column 2 of table 4, with the productivity variables instrumented by capital per worker and educational attainment, the host productivity coefficient is negative in the flow equation yet positive in the selection equation; however, neither displays significance. The source instrumented productivity has a negative and significant effect in the flow and selection equations. All in all, the estimation results are consistent with the prediction of our theory that the source productivity has a negative effect on the likelihood of the occurrence of FDI, but that the host productivity has an ambiguous effect on this likelihood.

The effect of productivity on the flow and selection of FDI are depicted in figures 2 and 3. Figure 2 depicts the effect of productivity in five host countries (the United Kingdom, Ireland, France, Germany, and Japan) on the flow of FDI from the United States. Throughout, all the explanatory variables, except the productivities in these host countries, are held constant at their sample averages. The estimated coefficient of the host productivity (which is positive) is used to draw the graphs. The shaded areas describe the frequencies of the productivities in all of these five host countries in the sample. The United Kingdom exhibits a high sensitivity of the FDI flows from the United States to its productivity, relative to the other countries in the relevant range (where the sample observations are concentrated). In figure 3, we depict the effect of U.S. productivity on the likelihood of generating FDI from the United States to each one of the aforementioned five host countries. This effect is negative, but relatively weak in the relevant range.

We next consider the tax variables. The estimation results are presented in the first three columns of table 5. The first column refers to the statutory tax rates, the second to the effective tax rates, and the third to the fitted effective tax rates. As expected, and also as predicted by our theory, the host tax rate has a negative and significant effect on the flow of FDI in the flow equation in all three columns. This negative effect rises in magnitude when moving from the

Figure 2. The Flow Equation: The Effect of Host Country Productivity

Source Country: United States
Host Countries: France, Germany, Ireland, Japan, United Kingdom
FDI flows in 1982–84 US dollars (billions)

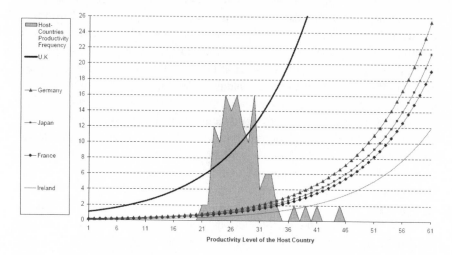

Figure 3. The Selection Equation: The Effect of Source Country Productivity

Source Country: United States
Host Countries: France, Germany, Ireland, Japan, United Kingdom

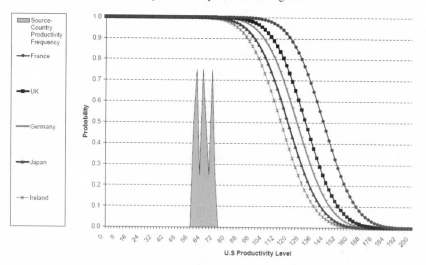

statutory to the effective and to the fitted effective tax rates. Noteworthy, the source tax rate follows exactly the same pattern of the magnitude of the effect rising when moving from the statutory to the effective and to the fitted effective rate; however, it has a positive and significant effect in the flow equation in all three columns. This result may allude to the existence of source residence taxation in the source countries: as the source country taxes its residents on their income in the host country, the source country tax has a positive effect on their investment abroad. The source tax rate has a positive and significant effect on the selection mechanism, as predicted by our theory, but only in column 1. However, this effect intensifies and becomes even more significant when we consider in column 4 a larger set of countries (for which we had data on the statutory rates only).

The effect of the statutory tax rates on the flow and selection of FDI are depicted in figures 4 and 5. Figure 4 depicts the effect of corporate taxes in the aforementioned five host countries on the flow of FDI from the United States. Throughout, all the explanatory variables, except the tax rates in these host countries, are held constant at their sample averages. The estimated coefficient of the host tax (which is negative) is used to draw the graphs. As before, the shaded areas describe the frequencies of the productivities in all of these five host countries in the sample. The United Kingdom exhibits a high sensitivity of the FDI flows from the United States to its tax rate, relative to the other countries in the relevant range (where the sample observations are concentrated). In figure 5, we depict the effect of the U.S. tax rate on the likelihood of generating FDI from the United States to each one of the aforementioned host countries. This effect is positive and relatively strong for Ireland and Japan.

Apparently, when we look at the two sets of drivers (productivity and taxation) together, some multicolinearity problems arise. As a result, the estimated results do not change much in sign, but their statistical significance weakens. We present these results in table A-3.

Conclusion

We study the role of productivity and corporate taxation as driving forces of FDI among OECD countries in the presence of threshold barriers, which generate two margins for FDI decisions. An important feature of our FDI model (which distinguishes FDI flows from portfolio flows) is fixed setup costs of new investments. As usual, FDI flows come in two main forms: M&A and greenfield flows. In our setup, the key difference between these two forms is that the

Table 5. Bilateral FDI Flows and Selection Equations: Tax Effect[a]

	Statutory tax rates		Effective tax rates		Fitted effective tax rates		Corporate tax rate[b]	
	Flow	Selection	Flow	Selection	Flow	Selection	Flow	Selection
Tax rate–source	1.795 (0.579)**	1.656 (0.759)*					-0.131 (0.652)	2.418 (0.904)**
Tax rate–host	-2.955 (0.621)**	-0.504 (0.694)					-1.963 (0.734)**	-1.063 (0.900)
Effective tax rate–source			2.383 (0.790)**	1.331 (1.051)				
Effective tax rate–host			-3.096 (0.841)**	0.124 (1.031)				
Instrumented effective tax rate–source					2.400 (0.912)**	2.047 (1.193)		
Instrumented effective tax rate–host					-4.536 (0.974)**	-0.778 (1.093)		
ln GDP per capita–source	2.961 (0.490)**	-0.498 (0.505)	2.928 (0.494)**	-0.443 (0.511)	2.841 (0.507)**	-0.581 (0.524)	1.867 (0.519)**	-0.053 (0.543)
ln GDP per capita–host	3.235 (0.460)**	-0.798 (0.580)	3.186 (0.460)**	-0.860 (0.588)	3.493 (0.470)**	-0.747 (0.595)	1.814 (0.495)**	-0.701 (0.603)
Schooling difference	0.197 (0.065)**	-0.045 (0.070)	0.1740 (0.065)**	-0.075 (0.069)	0.185 (0.065)**	-0.054 (0.069)	-0.068 (0.070)	-0.151 (0.078)
Common language	0.516 (0.087)**	-0.192 (0.114)	0.518 (0.087)**	-0.189 (0.114)	0.517 (0.087)**	-0.192 (0.114)	0.609 (0.103)**	0.088 (0.130)
ln Distance	-1.005 (0.043)**	-0.248 (0.070)**	-1.003 (0.043)**	-0.246 (0.070)**	-1.004 (0.043)**	-0.248 (0.070)**	-0.97 (0.046)**	-0.457 (0.071)**

	(1)	(2)	(3)	(4)	(5)	(6)	(7)	(8)
ln Population–source	-0.114	-4.395	-0.563	-5.064	-0.06	-4.433	-1.364	-1.312
	(1.588)	(2.220)*	(1.604)	(2.276)*	(1.594)	(2.223)*	(1.599)	(1.813)
ln Population–host	-2.032	-2.845	-1.662	-2.922	-1.906	-2.822	-1.94	-0.466
	(1.315)	(2.323)	(1.348)	(2.366)	(1.320)	(2.324)	(1.232)	(1.721)
Financial risk–source	-0.022	0.023	-0.023	0.025	-0.023	0.023	0.002	0.019
	(0.011)*	(0.018)	(0.011)*	(0.018)	(0.011)*	(0.018)	(0.013)	(0.014)
Financial risk–host	-0.015	-0.031	-0.017	-0.032	-0.015	-0.032	-0.008	-0.021
	(0.011)	(0.016)	(0.011)	(0.016)*	(0.011)	(0.016)*	(0.011)	(0.015)
Previous FDI dummy (1 if yes)		1.622		1.626		1.624		0.86
		(0.083)**		(0.083)**		(0.083)**		(0.108)**
Observations	4,974	4,974	4,974	4,974	4,974	4,974	3,210	3,210

Source: Authors' calculations.
*Significant at the 5 percent level; **significant at the 1 percent level.
a. Country and time fixed effects are accounted for; robust standard errors are in parentheses.
b. This column relates to a corporate tax rate (without local taxes) for an additional five OECD countries: Denmark, Korea, Mexico, New Zealand, and Turkey. Observations are smoothed over a two- to three-year period.

Figure 4. The Flow Equation: The Effect of Host Country Tax Rate

Source Country: United States
Host Countries: France, Germany, Ireland, Japan, United Kingdom
FDI flows in 1982–84 US dollars (billions)

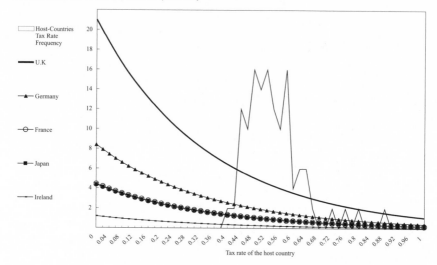

Figure 5. The Selection Equation: The Effect of Source Country Tax Rate

Source Country: United States
Host Countries: France, Germany, Ireland, Japan, United Kingdom

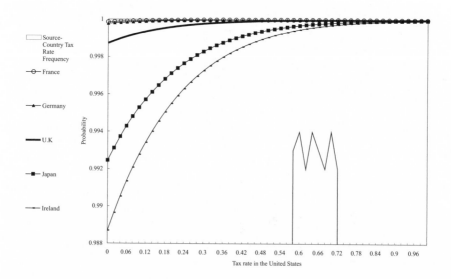

former is not restricted by the limited supply of entrepreneurial capacity in source countries. Thus the alternative investment opportunities in the source countries do not affect the flow of M&A FDI into a host country, as long as the world capital market can offer unlimited investment funds to this country. In contrast, greenfield FDI in a host country must compete with greenfield investment in the source countries for the limited supply of entrepreneurs in these countries.

We considered first the effect of aggregate productivity shocks on M&A FDI. Suppose initially that the host country wage rate is fixed. A positive productivity shock has three positive effects on the notional flow of FDI, which is the flow of FDI that would have occurred in the absence of fixed costs. First, it raises the marginal productivity of capital, thereby increasing the amount of investment that is made by each investing firm (which is acquired by FDI investors). Second, it raises the value of such firms and, consequently, their acquisition price. Third, it increases the number of firms purchased by FDI investors. Turning to the selection-condition equation, which governs the decision on whether to make an FDI at all, a positive aggregate productivity shock (while still maintaining the wage rate constant) increases the profitability of investments, so that the notional FDI turns out to be realized.

Then, we dropped the supposition that the wage rate is fixed. When wages are not fixed, then the increase in the demand for labor raises the wage rate in the host country and, consequently, the domestic component of the fixed costs, thereby mitigating, but not eliminating, the above three effects on the notional FDI. But with respect to the selection-condition equation, a positive aggregate productivity shock in the host country equation may raise the domestic component of the setup cost to such an extent so as to reduce the likelihood of positive FDI flows to occur. Note, however, that a source country aggregate productivity shock does not affect the flows of M&A FDI.

Next we considered the effect of aggregate productivity shocks on greenfield FDI. On the one hand, a positive host country productivity shock has positive effects both on the notional FDI flows and on the likelihood of these flows to actually materialize. On the other hand, a positive source country productivity shock does not affect the notional flows of FDI, but it reduces the likelihood of such flows to occur at all.

The main empirical findings concerning productivity and taxes as drivers of FDI show that the host output per worker has a positive effect in both the flow and selection equations, but it is significant only in the flow equation. Source country output per worker has a negative and significant effect on the selection mechanism. These results are fairly robust.

The host tax rate has a negative and significant effect on the flow of FDI in the flow equation. This negative effect rises in magnitude when moving from the statutory rate to the effective rate and the instrumented effective tax rate. Noteworthy, the source tax rate follows exactly the same pattern: it has a positive and significant effect in the flow equation, with the magnitude of the effect rising when moving from the statutory to the effective rate and to the fitted effective rate. (This result may allude to the existence of source residence taxation in the source countries: as the source country taxes its residents on their income in the host country, the source country tax has a depressing effect on their investment abroad.) These results are fairly robust. The source tax rate has a positive and significant effect on the selection mechanism. This effect intensifies and becomes even more significant for a larger set of countries (for which we had data on the statutory rates only).

Some simulations, based on the estimation results, suggest that there are marked differences in the sensitivity of FDI flows from the United States to productivity and taxes in OECD countries. The sensitivity of these flows to productivity in the United Kingdom is positive and high, relative to other EU countries and Japan. Similarly, the sensitivity of these flows to taxes in the United Kingdom is negative and high, relative to the other countries.

Table A-1. Time Average of FDI Flows[a]

| | *Source country* | | | | | | | |
| | *United States* | | *United Kingdom* | | *Austria* | | *Belgium* | |
Host country	Source	Host	Source	Host	Source	Host	Source	Host
United States			2.1131	0.3307	0.0503	0.0013	0.1445	0.0043
United Kingdom	0.2281	1.4574			0.0927	0.0147		
Austria	0.0055	0.2196	0.0220	0.1385				
Belgium	0.0239	0.8078						
France	0.0338	0.1940	0.2495	0.2242	0.0268	0.0038		
Germany	0.0520	0.2055	1.0118	0.6259	0.1957	0.0192		
Italy	0.0257	0.1779	0.0494	0.0535	0.0415	0.0071		
Netherlands	0.1082	11.3238	0.5877	9.6242	0.0610	0.1589		
Norway	0.0089	0.4769	0.0504	0.4230	0.0023	0.0030	0.3661	0.5807
Sweden	0.0361	0.0361	0.2852	0.0446	0.0286	0.0007		
Switzerland	0.0615	1.8512	0.2500	1.1770	0.0554	0.0415	0.2872	0.2558
Canada	0.1084	1.3516	0.1219	0.2378	0.0122	0.0038	0.1877	0.0693
Japan	0.0455	0.0870	0.0605	0.0181	0.0018	0.0001	0.1545	0.0087
Finland	0.0020	0.1291	0.0158	0.1573	0.0032	0.0050		
Greece	0.0008	0.0571	0.0252	0.2841	0.0023	0.0040		
Ireland	0.0420	4.3968	0.1297	2.1247	0.0237	0.0616		
Portugal	0.0032	0.2551	0.0281	0.3522	0.0084	0.0167		
Spain	0.0217	0.3015	0.1019	0.2216	0.0192	0.0067		
Australia	0.0338	0.7209	0.1344	0.4491	0.0266	0.0141	0.0737	0.0466

| | *France* | | *Germany* | | *Italy* | | *Netherlands* | |
	Source	Host	Source	Host	Source	Host	Source	Host
United States	0.6661	0.1160	0.6503	0.1645	0.0721	0.0104	10.5764	0.1011
United Kingdom	0.5726	0.6370	0.3348	0.5412	0.0892	0.0824	4.3388	0.2649
Austria	0.0133	0.0931	0.0830	0.8442	0.0069	0.0400	0.4940	0.1898
Belgium								
France			0.1645	0.2390	0.0850	0.0706	2.3512	0.1291
Germany	0.3326	0.2289			0.0397	0.0227	2.8226	0.1066
Italy	0.1155	0.1391	0.0617	0.1081			0.8949	0.0592
Netherlands	0.2632	4.7957	0.1077	2.8523	0.1717	2.5967		
Norway	0.0196	0.1824	0.0056	0.0757	0.0007	0.0055	0.1956	0.1001
Sweden	0.0378	0.0066	0.0581	0.0147	0.0046	0.0007	0.7326	0.0070
Switzerland	0.1070	0.5603	0.0572	0.4354	0.0231	0.1004	1.7004	0.4889
Canada	0.1582	0.3433	0.0236	0.0743	0.0041	0.0073	0.6300	0.0751
Japan	0.0537	0.0179	0.0288	0.0139	0.0084	0.0023	0.2918	0.0053
Finland	0.0041	0.0455	0.0091	0.1457	0.0012	0.0112	0.2061	0.1250
Greece	0.0058	0.0722	0.0077	0.1395	0.0036	0.0373	0.3343	0.2297
Ireland	0.0588	1.0710	0.0669	1.7706	0.0266	0.4026	1.3414	1.3414
Portugal	0.0174	0.2429	0.0143	0.2889	0.0082	0.0943	0.2017	0.1542
Spain	0.1129	0.2731	0.0563	0.1978	0.0339	0.0681	1.3620	0.1809
Australia	0.0225	0.0836	0.0196	0.1056	0.0046	0.0142	0.7249	0.1479

Table A-1. Time Average of FDI Flows[a] (*continued*)

| | Source country | | | | | | | |
| | Norway | | Sweden | | Switzerland | | Canada | |
Host country	Source	Host	Source	Host	Source	Host	Source	Host
United States	0.2470	0.0046	0.0226	0.0226	1.8723	0.0622	1.2120	0.0972
United Kingdom	0.3060	0.0365	0.0184	0.1177	0.8926	0.1896	0.2792	0.1431
Austria	0.0304	0.0228	0.0004	0.0162	0.0988	0.1320	0.0034	0.0108
Belgium	0.4630	0.2918			0.3193	0.3584		
France	0.0928	0.0100	0.0089	0.0512	0.2122	0.0405	0.0837	0.0386
Germany	0.3041	0.0224	0.0137	0.0543	0.5071	0.0666	0.0289	0.0092
Italy	0.0237	0.0031	0.0052	0.0359	0.3404	0.0783	0.0083	0.0046
Netherlands	0.1770	0.3457	0.0158	1.6565	0.3684	1.2814	0.2184	1.8333
Norway			0.0128	0.6853	0.0980	0.1746	0.0016	0.0070
Sweden	0.4273	0.0080			0.1303	0.0043	0.0287	0.0023
Switzerland	0.0111	0.0062	0.0035	0.1050			0.0867	0.2093
Canada	0.0939	0.0218	0.0012	0.0153	0.1250	0.0518		
Japan	0.0019	0.0001	0.0004	0.0007	0.0876	0.0056	0.1048	0.0161
Finland	0.0725	0.0859	0.0308	1.9554	0.0305	0.0644	0.0024	0.0122
Greece	0.0027	0.0036		0.0022	0.0439	0.1050	0.0024	0.0138
Ireland	0.1090	0.2128	0.0086	0.8952	0.1486	0.5169	0.0086	0.0723
Portugal	0.0058	0.0087	0.0005	0.0366	0.0654	0.1738	0.0218	0.1401
Spain	0.0594	0.0154	0.0017	0.0237	0.1786	0.0825	0.0239	0.0266
Australia	0.0102	0.0040	0.0005	0.0108	0.1026	0.0728	0.0783	0.1341

| | Japan | | Finland | | Greece | | Ireland | |
Host country	Source	Host	Source	Host	Source	Host	Source	Host
United States	0.4363	0.2283	0.7384	0.0116	0.0517	0.0007	2.2877	0.0219
United Kingdom	0.1355	0.4533	0.2971	0.0299	0.0912	0.0081	0.8013	0.0489
Austria	0.0009	0.0197	0.0273	0.0173	0.0009	0.0005	0.0022	0.0008
Belgium	0.0115	0.2039						
France	0.0246	0.0739	0.2059	0.0186	0.0063	0.0005	0.4087	0.0224
Germany	0.0168	0.0348	0.6342	0.0395	0.0153	0.0008	0.5556	0.021
Italy	0.0038	0.0136	0.0683	0.0074	0.0023	0.0002	0.1225	0.0081
Netherlands	0.0775	4.2425	0.8166	1.347	0.0071	0.0104	1.3921	1.3921
Norway	0.0024	0.0663	0.4541	0.3836	0.0004	0.0003	0.0083	0.0042
Sweden	0.0018	0.001	1.6341	0.0258	0.0015	0.0000	0.0285	0.0003
Switzerland	0.0049	0.0765	0.5742	0.2723	0.0040	0.0017		
Canada	0.018	0.1174	0.0888	0.0175	0.0048	0.0008		
Japan			0.0384	0.0012	0.0006	0.0000	0.1893	0.0035
Finland	0.0013	0.0424			0.0004	0.0004	0.057	0.0346
Greece	0.0000	0.0012	0.0045	0.0051			0.0035	0.0024
Ireland	0.0071	0.3873	0.0765	0.1262	0.01	0.0145		
Portugal	0.0006	0.0242	0.019	0.0239	0.0043	0.0048	0.0906	0.0693
Spain	0.0058	0.0422	0.0457	0.0100	0.0044	0.0009	0.3936	0.0523
Australia	0.0443	0.4954	0.0376	0.0127	0.0008	0.0002	0.0657	0.0134

Table A-1. Time Average of FDI Flows[a] (*continued*)

Host country	Portugal Source	Portugal Host	Spain Source	Spain Host	Australia Source	Australia Host
United States	0.0387	0.0005	0.2079	0.015	0.6272	0.0294
United Kingdom	0.0714	0.0057	0.1613	0.0742	0.4286	0.1283
Austria	0.0210	0.0106	0.0133	0.0385	0.0003	0.0006
Belgium					0.0144	0.0228
France	0.0497	0.0036	0.0977	0.0404	0.01	0.0027
Germany	0.0150	0.0007	0.2154	0.0613	0.0168	0.0031
Italy	0.0321	0.0028	0.0896	0.0446	0.0128	0.0041
Netherlands	0.5102	0.6675	0.1753	1.3203	0.0747	0.366
Norway	0.0001	0.0001	0.0035	0.0135	0.0004	0.001
Sweden	0.0003	0.0000	0.0101	0.0007	0.0023	0.0001
Switzerland	0.0092	0.0035	0.1071	0.2319	0.0048	0.0067
Canada	0.0038	0.0006	0.0135	0.0121	0.0524	0.0306
Japan	0.0000	0.0000	0.0208	0.0029	0.0164	0.0015
Finland	0.0000	0.0000	0.0046	0.0211	0.0003	0.0008
Greece	0.0059	0.0053	0.0087	0.0448	0.0000	0.0000
Ireland	0.0653	0.0854	0.0259	0.1947	0.0186	0.0911
Portugal			0.1373	0.7905	0.0001	0.0002
Spain	0.653	0.1135			0.0025	0.0016
Australia	0.0007	0.0002	0.0220	0.0339		

Source: Authors' calculations.
a. As a percentage of the source and host countries' GDP.

Table A-2. Instrumented Equations for Productivity and Effective Tax Rates[a]

Variable	Productivity	Effective tax rate
Capital-labor ratio	0.0001808 (6.09e-06)**	
Years of schooling	1.262 (0.092)**	
Tax rate		0.642 (0.005)**
GDP per capita		0.00000319 (1.5e-07)**
Observations	4,279	5,414
R^2	0.958	0.962

Source: Authors' calculations.
a. Standard errors are in parentheses.
**Significant at the 1 percent level.

Table A-3. Bilateral FDI Flows and Selection Equations: Productivity and Tax Effects[a]

Variable	Productivity effect		Tax effect	
	Flow	Selection	Flow	Selection
Productivity–source	–0.06	–0.051		
	(0.020)**	(0.026)		
Productivity–host	0.018	0.006		
	(0.018)	(0.031)		
Instrumented productivity–source			–0.089	–0.135
			(0.033)**	(0.054)*
Instrumented productivity–host			–0.039	0.040
			(0.036)	(0.046)
Tax rate–source	1.036	1.212		
	(0.652)	(0.826)		
Tax rate–host	–2.747	–0.612		
	(0.655)**	(0.787)		
Instrumented effective tax rate–source			1.473	0.924
			(1.036)	(1.375)
Instrumented effective tax rate–host			–5.388	–1.489
			(1.115)**	(1.244)
ln GDP per capita–source	5.419	1.666	3.383	0.895
	(0.949)**	(1.222)	(0.657)**	(0.725)
ln GDP per capita–host	2.766	–1.152	4.890	–1.192
	(0.878)**	(1.342)	(0.624)**	(0.834)
Schooling difference	0.174	–0.019	0.104	0.053
	(0.066)**	(0.073)	(0.074)	(0.083)
Common language	0.513	–0.182	0.495	–0.094
	(0.090)**	(0.118)	(0.106)**	(0.148)
ln Distance	–1.015	–0.306	–1.082	–0.393
	(0.044)**	(0.074)**	(0.048)**	(0.089)**
ln Population–source	0.712	–3.860	–1.006	–7.596
	(1.788)	(2.556)	(2.058)	(2.986)*
ln Population–host	–1.738	–5.398	–0.081	–8.931
	(1.493)	(2.633)*	(1.689)	(3.023)**
Financial risk–source	–0.026	0.023	–0.012	0.011
	(0.012)*	(0.019)	(0.014)	(0.025)
Financial risk–host	–0.02	-0.027	–0.029	–0.015
	(0.011)	(0.017)	(0.013)*	(0.02)
Previous FDI dummy (1 if yes)		1.534		1.501
		(0.085)**		(0.093)**
Observations	4,702	4,702	3,833	3,833

Source: Authors' calculations.
*Significant at the 5 percent level; **significant at the 1 percent level.
a. Country and time fixed effects are accounted for; robust standard errors are in parentheses.

Comments and Discussion

Mihir A. Desai: Assaf Razin and Efram Sadka have synthesized some of their recent work on productivity, taxes, and foreign direct investment (FDI) in this welcome contribution. Their theoretical work emphasizes how setup costs at home and in the host country can drive a wedge between marginal and total profit conditions. This insight combines with a description of FDI decisionmaking that separates the decisionmaking process into two parts: whether to invest and how much to invest. Their theory leads to some intriguing results on the relationship between productivity, taxes, and FDI, and their empirical work provides some support for their theoretical results.

In the Razin and Sadka setup, setup costs at home (the source country) and in the host country are critical and lead to the curious results they present. For example, they argue that a positive productivity shock in the host country can deter entry of multinational firms. The productivity shock bids up wages and, because host country setup costs are entirely based on wage costs, the total profit conditions that dictate entry now are tilted toward not entering. Setup costs, and their deductible nature, also influence the role of taxes. In particular, tax rate increases at home can lead to increased outbound FDI because the value of the deductions for setup costs borne at home goes up.

Setup costs are surely important to the spread of multinational firms. But such counterintuitive results demand some motivation for the underlying mechanism. For example, what are these sizable wage-driven setup costs that are so critical to the model? Little motivation is provided for these costs, and while the results are all derived nicely, it is hard to know what to make of their importance without such motivation. I confess to having a hard time deriving any intuition or examples for such costs other than the fees paid to investment bankers and consultants upon entry in a country. I find it hard to believe that such costs are meaningful relative to the scale of the projects under consideration.

It is also not clear that such setup costs in the host country, and particularly at home, are the same every time a multinational enters a new country. When General Electric sets up operations in the nth country that it operates in, are we to believe that it bears considerable setup costs at home or, even for that matter, that the costs it bears in the nth country are the same as the costs borne when it first became a multinational firm? These costs would also seem to bear some relationship to market size that are not developed in the model. Similarly, it is also not clear why firms are choosing among projects in an exclusive manner, which presumably reflects some hidden financing constraints. Finally, the treatment of taxes, particularly home country taxes, is somewhat primitive since the rich interactions of home country and host country regimes that have been shown to be so important to patterns of multinational firm activity are neglected in the model.

The paper takes these intuitions from the authors' theory and attempts to apply them to bilateral FDI flows within the Organization for Economic Cooperation and Development (OECD). Given the interest in the separability of the decision into whether to invest and how much to invest, it would seem that it would be useful to look for data sources outside of the OECD in which "zeros" (that is, bilateral pairs where there is no FDI) are more likely to be prevalent. I was also puzzled by the treatment of Europe in some of the tables, as the authors appear to not examine any FDI flows within Europe. Nonetheless, the authors report results on productivity shocks at home and taxes at home that conform to the theory's predictions.

Of course, it is always possible to come up with alternative explanations for such results. For example, the result that increases in the source country tax rate lead to more outbound FDI because of the increased value of the deductions of the setup costs could have a simpler interpretation. The more naïve interpretation of that result is that when the source country tax rate goes up, the multinational has an incentive to go abroad with real activity to facilitate profit relocations. This alternative explanation and others like it are hard to disentangle in this empirical setting. It would be nice for the authors to attempt to take their intuitions to microdata on multinational firms as this is where their predictions would seem to have the most purchase and where the focus of most of the recent literature on multinational firms is now.

This fine paper pushes the scholarly community to take setup costs seriously in its consideration of FDI. This is surely a welcome direction for scholarship as the recent work on firm heterogeneity and patterns of trade and FDI has suggested. I look forward to further work by these scholars as they elaborate on these mechanisms and provide more empirical evidence of their relevance.

Deborah Swenson: Recent work on foreign direct investment (FDI) has shifted focus from a framework in which an anonymous river of capital flows internationally to a framework in which trade and investment are conducted by a diverse group of traders. Naturally, recognition of traders brings with it an enriched setting in which heterogeneous traders make a wide range of decisions as they balance their individual opportunities against transaction costs. In adopting this new approach, Razin and Sadka highlight how productivity and tax factors influence foreign investment in a world that is populated by heterogeneous firms distinguished by their differing levels of productivity.

A key insight of this approach is the recognition that investment decision-making includes an extensive margin, for which firms decide whether or not to invest in foreign markets, and for firms that do invest, the intensive margin, which involves the choice of investment volume. This recognition of firm heterogeneity enables Razin and Sadka to bring forward a number of interesting insights. First, unlike a homogenous world in which profit maximization implies that all firms should make the same decision, recognition of heterogeneity explains the coexistence of firms' differing strategies in the organization of their resources and, with it, the potential for firms' heterogeneous responses to changes in the tax environment. In addition, firm heterogeneity brings with it the implication that changes in underlying conditions may have unexpected effects, as these changes will influence the selection into investment as well as the desired level of investment by those firms that do invest. In this regard, I think Razin and Sadka's paper does an excellent job of describing these issues in a way that clarifies the effects of productivity and taxes on the levels of foreign investment via greenfield or acquisition investment.

Nonetheless, I think there are still a number of avenues that remain to be analyzed as this line of research moves forward. First is the question of how to characterize productivity at a national level. Do firms experience productivity that is based on the national location of their headquarters, or does engagement in international markets change their productivity opportunities? This question is potentially most salient in the case of foreign investment via acquisition. For example, when the Chinese company Lenovo purchases IBM's ThinkPad laptop assets, does Lenovo continue to experience productivity tied to its base in China, or is its productivity altered by its purchase of U.S. assets? The second practical question is how we can apply models such as those of Razin and Sadka to the data. Since their work has different predictions regarding greenfield versus acquisition FDI, we have to wonder what the aggregate prediction is for a world where both are relevant and large. The *World Investment Report* reported that 18.8 percent of FDI value in 2005 was due to mergers and acquisitions (M&A) activities, and in many developed countries within the Organization for Economic Cooperation and Development (OECD), the percentage was much larger![1] A third practical question is whether one should think of investment choices as a choice of home or foreign investment, or whether one should consider instead the alternative problem facing multinationals that have decided to move abroad but have yet to decide on the country or countries where they will place their overseas operations. Such interdependencies seem particularly relevant, given the empirical findings by Blonigen and others (2007) or Swenson (1998, 2006) that show how conditions in neighboring or competitor locations affect foreign investment or foreign assembly decisions, while noting that the attractiveness of one country or state jurisdiction often appears to be affected by conditions in neighboring locations.[2] Nonetheless, while these topics remain to be explored in future research, Razin and Sadka's paper discusses the important implication that tax policy may influence aggregate levels of economic activity, since changes in policy may influence the scale and population of investing firms.

Razin and Sadka follow their theoretical discussion with an empirical exercise that examines data on foreign investment flows among OECD countries. Since Razin and Sadka's theoretical model involves foreign investment changes on the extensive and the intensive margins, identification of the model's predictions is based on the pattern of investment and noninvestment in the data and on the levels of foreign investment in the cases in which investment occurs. Although this exercise is straightforward in concept, I am concerned that the OECD data on aggregate investment flows between bilateral country pairs are not well suited to the task.

First, although the model is straightforward and makes compelling arguments for the effects on the extensive and intensive margins, it is difficult to know how these aspects will play out when foreign investment data combine greenfield and acquisition investments, since the predicted effects of productivity or taxes on the incentive to undertake foreign greenfield or merger investment differ. My second and bigger concern is that this dataset offers too little variation to identify the extensive margin. Ideally, for example, one could identify extensive margin effects of taxes on investment if a country's tax reform caused an investment transition from no investment to positive investment. However, while the population of investing firms changes from year to year, there will be far fewer transitions between zero and positive investment

1. See the United Nations Conference on Trade and Development website to view this series and the database (www.unctad.org/wir).
2. Blonigen and others (2007); Swenson (1998, 2006).

at a national level for most OECD country pairs. This is because large investor countries such as the United States, the United Kingdom, or the Netherlands have positive investment in almost all OECD countries in every year of the panel, even if the number of investing firms changes from year to year. Similarly, Razin and Sadka's dataset includes some country pairs that experience no investment during the sample period. Although it is easy to imagine reasons for the complete absence of investment by Australian firms in Greece or Portuguese firms in Japan or Finland, the omnipresence of zero investment for these country pairs means that they fail to provide any information on selection. Thus identification of the selection equation in this project relies on the limited set of country-pairs that experienced transitions between years of investment and no investment. Although the paper does not provide enough information to determine which country pairs experienced transitions in the empirical exercise, or to determine the frequency of transitions, it is my sense that transitions at this aggregate level were few and far between in aggregate OECD investment relations. For this reason, aggregate investment by OECD nations can only provide minimal information on the extensive margin, even though changes in taxes or productivity conditions are likely to change the number of investing companies from year to year. Although the influence of the extensive margin is important and interesting, I look forward to future quantification of these effects based on industry- or firm-level data that track the foreign investment decisions of multinational firms.

Even if the OECD data provide limited information on selection, as I believe, Razin and Sadka are right in arguing that the extensive margin plays an important role in shaping the frequency and size of foreign investments between countries. To begin, the relevance of the extensive margin is apparent in Muendler and Becker's discovery that German firms' investment involves adjustment on the extensive and intensive margins.[3] Similarly, when Mutti and Grubert studied microdata on U.S. firms, they found that the likelihood of a firm locating in a given host country is influenced by taxes and that investment geared toward export markets is particularly sensitive to host country taxation.[4] In addition, Mutti and Grubert found that tax sensitivity appears to be greater in developing countries than in developed countries and that tax sensitivity is growing over time.

The subtle question raised by this paper is that if firm heterogeneity influences how firms respond to international tax differentials, should tax policy be modified to reflect this element of the international economy? While the answer

3. Muendler and Becker (2006).
4. Mutti and Grubert (2004).

may ultimately be yes, the practical answer is: not yet. To effectively bring this issue to policy, policymakers must have a better sense of the margins on which firms operate, since multinational firms make decisions along many different dimensions, many of which are influenced by tax policy. These decisions include whether to export or conduct FDI as noted in Devereux and Griffith, the decision to undertake merger or greenfield FDI as shown in Scholes and Wolfson and in Swenson, as well as the apparent differences between the effects on vertical and horizontal foreign investment found in Mutti and Grubert.[5] Thus the large number of margins for multinational decisionmaking leaves me skeptical that tax policy can be easily designed to encompass issues related to heterogeneity. Nonetheless, Razin and Sadka's work makes apparent a deeper point: since tax policy has the potential to influence which firms decide to do foreign investment, policymakers need to be aware that tax policy may influence average firm productivity at the national level.

The more direct policy question is whether international tax differentials exert a large influence on the level of foreign investment a country ultimately receives. While tax differentials create clear investment incentives in a stripped-down model of foreign investment, many practical considerations may blunt their ultimate influence. To begin, as Altshuler and Grubert showed, firms have many tax planning avenues, such as the creation of financial structures that may enable firms to reduce their repatriation taxes.[6] In fact, they provided evidence that these financial choices are a salient feature of U.S. multinational activity. Along related lines, Koncz and Yorgason noted the dramatic increase in the use of foreign holding companies.[7] In particular, the share of U.S. foreign affiliate activity conducted through holding companies rose from 9 percent in 1982 to 30 percent in 2005. Although holding companies may be formed for reasons other than tax planning, the dramatic change in the organization of multinational activity suggests that multinational firms may be able to blunt the effects of international tax differentials, thus obviating the real investment incentives that are noted in most models of foreign investment.

Nonetheless, there is still anecdotal evidence that taxes influence firm investment decisions. One striking example was the Jobs Creation Act of 2004 that enabled U.S. firms to repatriate their foreign earnings in 2005 at a *temporarily* lowered tax rate. Since Koncz and Yorgason showed that the percentage increase in U.S. direct investment abroad in 2005 was smaller than it had been in any year since 1982, while financial repatriations were large, it appears that

5. Devereux and Griffith (1998); Scholes and Wolfson (1990); Swenson (1994); Mutti and Grubert (2004).

6. Altshuler and Grubert (2003).

7. Koncz and Yorgason (2006).

tax incentives, at least in some cases, influence firm decisions regarding foreign investment.[8] For this reason, while governments may be concerned about the revenue implications of multinational firm activity, it appears that international tax differentials still shape the incentives of multinational firms in the fashion suggested by the theory.[9]

The income and jobs brought to host countries by foreign affiliates of multinational firms ensure that countries will continue to be concerned about the effects of their tax policy environment on foreign firms.[10] This concern is apparent as tax policies enacted in neighboring or competitor countries are consciously noted during policy debates and have been influential in convincing many countries to lower their corporate tax rates. Nonetheless, Altshuler and Grubert offered the intriguing hypothesis that the race to the bottom may be stemmed in part because of the avenues for financial planning that governments make available to multinational firms.[11] In particular, by reducing the effects of international tax differentials on multinational firms, countries may retain the substantial benefits conferred by the economic activities of their growing multinational firms.

Discussion: Barry Bosworth opened the general discussion with a question on the data used in the paper. He remarked that the effective tax rate measure is actually extremely difficult to measure. It seems that most people use University of Michigan data; however, if one compares these data with data from the Bureau of Economic Analysis, the correlation is essentially zero. Bosworth went on to note that the differences are particularly large for oil-producing countries, because the large taxes they charge can be interpreted by foreign companies as either a corporate profit tax or an excise tax. Therefore, the differences between the institutional and effective tax rates, as well as what the data actually report for these measures, can have a fairly dramatic effect on your results.

On a similar note, John Whalley commented that the system of bilateral tax systems may play a large role in the tax effects on FDI. He noted that the literature seems to agree that bilateral treaties in some cases are a primary

8. Koncz and Yorgason (2006).

9. Even when tax planning techniques reduce the effects of taxes on real investment, it is important to remember that such avenues are not costless, since planning techniques require firms to expend resources that might otherwise be used in productive activities.

10. For example, Mataloni and Yorgason (2006) noted that in 2004 the value added generated by the foreign affiliates of U.S. multinational firms contributed on average 2.8 percent of all GDP in the fifty-one countries that hosted the largest U.S. foreign affiliate activity, as measured by foreign affiliate value added at the national level.

11. Altshuler and Grubert (2005).

determinant of bilateral investment flows. Therefore, Whalley argued that unless there was a more sophisticated discussion of the institutional realities of the tax systems, the empirical results are not as clear.

Deborah Swenson reflected on what policymakers are trying to achieve when they set tax rates. In the past, tax rates were set with sole regard to the domestic economy. To the extent that rates have been coming down in recent years, Swenson argued that this is an implicit acknowledgment that the base is somewhat flexible and thus a response to the elasticity of foreign activities across countries. So now there is a discussion in Europe about the potential need to harmonize their base, but unfortunately these are areas that cannot be put into models.

Susan Collins began by agreeing with Deborah Swenson's earlier comment that the regression analysis including both productivity and tax effects was the most interesting part of the paper. She went on to note that a lot of the empirical analyses of firm-level FDI have focused on the extent to which those investments tend to be "lumpy." Rather, she argued that there are different types of investments. Some investment is bunched together, often spread out over one to three years, which may be related more closely to the specification offered in the model. Other investments are the FDI flows between a firm and its affiliates that are more in the form of regular maintenance. Therefore, particularly for smaller countries with small numbers of firms engaged in FDI, the flow equation could be picking up a shift from a major investment spread over several years to an extended period of investment maintenance.

Assaf Razin concluded by offering a few brief responses to the questions and comments raised by the participants. Regarding the setup costs specified in the model, Razin discussed how these costs are associated with things that have to "breathe" between the different institutions of the source and host countries, different legal systems as well as language barriers. Of course, this is just a partial list of the determinants of selection, because there are simply no variables for predicting all of the parameters, such as different legal systems.

Responding to concerns about the lack of zeros in the observations, Razin commented that even with a 20 or 30 percent rate of zeros, it is still remarkable that there is a significant selection equation. Moreover, every regression is controlled by country fixed effects, so the effect shown is on top of the country effects.

Razin noted that although some participants identified a potentially large difference between effective and institutional tax rates, the results in the paper were similar for both measures. In addition, the macronature of the data has many advantages over microdata, yet there are still some elements that cannot be captured. For instance, Razin revealed that they could not capture whether a firm would make an investment or not, which could bias the selection equation. However, he argued that this would not translate into a significant bias in the flow equation.

Last, Razin discussed potential policy implications of the results. Specifically, these estimates could be useful in simulating a model of tax competition and tax coordination. For countries undergoing greater integration, such as the European Union, this simulation would be useful in analyzing whether a "race to the bottom" would ensue for corporate taxes. According to their framework, the result could potentially be a two-tier situation, in which the established countries would maintain higher tax rates but provide much better welfare systems and public good and infrastructure, whereas the newcomer countries would provide lower taxes but be a bit poorer in terms of infrastructure and welfare.

References

Altshuler, Rosanne, and Harry Grubert. 2003. "Repatriation Taxes, Repatriation Strategies and Multinational Financial Policy." *Journal of Public Economics* 87, no. 1: 73–107.

———. 2005. "The Three Parties in the Race to the Bottom: Host Governments, Home Governments and Multinational Companies." CESifo Working Paper 1613. Munich: CESifo Group.

Amiti, Mary. 2005. "Location of Vertically Linked Industries: Agglomeration versus Comparative Advantage." *European Economic Review* 49, no. 4: 809–32.

Auerbach, Alan. 1983. "Corporate Taxation in the U.S." *BPEA* no. 2: 451–513.

Auerbach, Alan J., and Kevin Hassett. 1993. "Taxation and Foreign Direct Investment in the United States: A Reconsideration of the Evidence." In *Studies in International Taxation*, edited by Alberto Giovannini, R. Glenn Hubbard, and Joel Slemrod, pp. 119–44. University of Chicago Press.

Bénassy-Quéré, Agnès, Lionel Fontagné, and Amina Lahrèche-Révil. 2000. "Foreign Direct Investment and the Prospects for Tax Co-Ordination in Europe." CEPII Working Paper 2000-06. Paris: Centre d'Études Prospectives et d'Informations Internationales.

Blonigen, Bruce A., and others. 2007. "FDI in Space: Spatial Autoregressive Relationships in Foreign Direct Investment." *European Economic Journal* 51, no. 5 (July): 1303–325.

Bosworth, Barry, and Susan Collins. 1999. "Capital Flows to Developing Economies: Implications for Saving and Investment." BPEA no. 1: 143–69.

Carr, David L., James R. Markusen, and Keith E. Maskus. 2001. "Estimating the Knowledge-Capital Model of the Multinational Enterprise." *American Economic Review* 91, no. 3: 693–708.

de Mooij, Ruud A., and Sjef Ederveen. 2001. "Taxation and Foreign Direct Investment: A Synthesis of Empirical Research." CESifo Working Paper 588.

Desai, Mihir A., Fritz Foley, and James R. Hines. 2004. "Foreign Direct Investment in a World of Multiple Taxes." *Journal of Public Economics* 88, no. 12: 2727–744.

Devereux, Michael P., and Rachel Griffith. 1998. "Taxes and the Location of Production: Evidence from a Panel of US Multinationals." *Journal of Public Economics* 68, no. 3: 335–67.

———. 2003. "Evaluating Tax Policy for Location Decisions." *International Tax and Public Finance* 10, no. 2: 107–26.

Devereux, Michael, Rachel Griffith, and Alexander Klemm. 2002. "Corporate Income Tax Reforms and International Tax Competition." *Economic Policy* 17, no. 35: 449–95.

Devereux, Michael P., and R. Glenn Hubbard. 2003. "Taxing Multinationals." *International Tax and Public Finance* 10, no. 4: 469–88.

Eaton, Jonathan, and Samuel Kortum. 2002. "Technology, Geography, and Trade." *Econometrica* 70, no. 5: 1741–779.

Gropp, Reint, and Kristina Kostial. 2000. "The Disappearing Tax Base: Is Foreign Direct Investment Eroding Corporate Income Taxes?" Working Paper 31. Frankfurt: European Central Bank.

Hall, Robert, and Dale Jorgenson. 1967. "Tax Policy and Investment Behavior." *American Economic Review* 57, no. 3: 391–414.

Harberger, Arnold. 1962. "The Incidence of the Corporation Income Tax." *Journal of Political Economy* 70, no. 3: 215–40.

Heckman, James J. 1974. "Shadow Prices, Market Wages and Labor Supply." *Econometrica* 42, no. 4: 679–94.

———. 1979. "Sample Selection Bias as a Specification Error." *Econometrica* 47, no. 1: 153–61.

Helpman, Elhanan, Marc Melitz, and Stephen Yeaple. 2004. "Exports versus FDI with Heterogeneous Firms." *American Economic Review* 94, no. 1: 300–16.

Hines, James R., Jr. 1999. "Lessons from Behavioral Responses to International Taxation." *National Tax Journal* 52, no. 2 (June): 305–22.

———. 2004. "Corporate Taxation." In *International Encyclopedia of the Social and Behavioral Sciences*, edited by Neil J. Smelser and Paul B. Balts, pp. 2810–812. Amsterdam: Elsevier.

Koncz, Jennifer L., and Daniel R. Yorgason. 2006. "Direct Investment Positions for 2005: Country and Industry Detail." *Survey of Current Business* (July): 20–35.

Mataloni, Raymond J., Jr., and Daniel R. Yorgason. 2006. "Operations of U.S. Multinational Companies: Preliminary Results from the 2004 Benchmark Survey." *Survey of Current Business* 86, no. 11 (November): 37–68.

Melitz, Marc J. 2003. "The Impact of Trade on Intra-Industry Reallocations and Aggregate Industry Productivity." *Econometrica* 71, no. 6: 1695–725.

Muendler, Marc-Andreas, and Sascha O. Becker. 2006. "Margins of Multinational Labor Substitution." CESifo Working Paper 1713. Munich: CESifo Group.

Mutti, John, and Harry Grubert. 2004. "Empirical Asymmetries in Foreign Direct Investment and Taxation." *Journal of International Economics* 62, no. 2: 337–58.

[OECD] Organization for Economic Cooperation and Development. 1997. *Model Tax Convention on Income and on Capital*. Paris: OECD, Centre for Tax Policy and Administration.

Razin, Assaf, and Efraim Sadka. 2007. *Foreign Direct Investment: Analysis of Aggregate Flows*. Princeton University Press.

Scholes, Myron S., and Mark A. Wolfson. 1990. "The Effects of Changes in Tax Laws on Corporate Reorganization Activity." *Journal of Business* 63, no. 1: S141–S164.

Swenson, Deborah L. 1994. "The Impact of U.S. Tax Reform on Foreign Direct Investment in the U.S." *Journal of Public Economics* 54, no. 2: 243–66.

———. 1998. "The Effect of U.S. State Tax and Investment Promotion Policy on the Distribution of Inward Direct Investment." In *Geography and Ownership as Bases for Economic Accounting*, edited by Robert E. Baldwin, Robert E. Lipsey, and J. Davis Richardson, pp. 285–310. University of Chicago Press.

————. 2006. "Country Competition and U.S. Overseas Assembly." *World Economy* 29, no. 7: 917–37.

[UN] United Nations. 1980. *Articles of the United Nations Model Double Taxation Convention between Developed and Developing Countries.* Document ST/ESA/102, Sales No. E.80.XVI.3. New York.

Zhang, Kevin H., and James R. Markusen. 1999. "Vertical Multinationals and Host-Country Characteristics." *Journal of Development Economics* 59, no. 2: 233–52.

MARGARET MCMILLAN
Tufts University

ANDREW R. WAXMAN
World Bank

Profit Sharing between Governments and Multinationals in Natural Resource Extraction: Evidence from a Firm-Level Panel

At the beginning of the last century, Venezuela, with its rudimentary agricultural economy, had the reputation as being one of the most backward nations in the Western Hemisphere. The country was run by Juan Vicente Gómez, who was put into power in 1908 by a U.S.-backed coup d'état and the first in a line of *caudillos*, or military-style dictators. Seven years after the coup, the Mene Grande oil field was discovered, and in 1917 Venezuela began exporting petroleum. The "understanding" that Gómez had with the U.S. oil companies and the U.S. government allowed him to use revenues to equip the first national army and expand the bureaucracy and his repressive regime in exchange for cheap oil concessions and accommodating legislation.[1]

Yet, from the beginning, the Venezuelan authorities and the oil companies were engaged in a tug-of-war over the terms of profit sharing. By the 1950s, Venezuela enjoyed greater bargaining power than did its Middle Eastern competitors.[2] In 1958 the government increased the tax rate on oil extraction 10 percentage points over the initial rate agreed with U.S. companies, shattering its amiable business relationship with the United States. This break in relations between Venezuela and the United States began a period of greater assertion of bargaining power over government take of oil rents by the government of Venezuela—culminating

The statistical analysis of firm-level data on U.S. multinational companies was conducted at the International Investment Division, Bureau of Economic Analysis, U.S. Department of Commerce under arrangements that maintain legal confidentiality requirements. The views expressed in this paper are those of the authors and do not reflect the views or official positions of the U.S. Department of Commerce or the World Bank.

1. Karl (1987).
2. Mommer (1998).

in its major role in the formation of the Organization of the Petroleum Exporting Countries (OPEC) in 1960, which through the cartelization of oil resources afforded member countries an organization to coordinate production to influence international prices. With the uptick in oil prices during the mid-1970s, the Venezuelans were again able to increase their share of economic rents through contract renegotiation. On the tails of OPEC came the establishment of the national Venezuelan oil company (la Corporación Venezolana del Petróleo). By developing technical ability and expertise in oil extraction, the Venezuelans were able to play a bigger role in upstream negotiations and put extra leverage on negotiations.[3] In 1973 the Acción Democrática government of Carlos Andrés Pérez nationalized the petroleum sector after taking power.

Chad has not been as successful as Venezuela at protecting the rents associated with natural resource extraction. It is a landlocked Saharan country with one of the lowest per capita income levels in Africa. It suffers major security problems from incursions on its borders with Sudan and Libya and substantial refugee influxes from the Darfur region. The country is universally considered a failed state with consistently some of the highest levels of corruption in the world. Nevertheless, the World Bank undertook an effort with a petroleum consortium in 1995 to begin to take advantage of the country's oil resources in an effort to reduce the drastic levels of poverty in the country.

Construction of the Chad-Cameroon pipeline to transport extracted oil from the Doba fields in Chad began in 2000, with oil flows beginning in 2004. The revenues accruing to the government were set up in such a way as to promote transparency and poverty reduction.[4] According to a *Guardian* article, the government's original take was 28 percent of the total value of oil, far smaller than that of other oil-producing countries in the region with comparably low scores on governance such as Equatorial Guinea, Angola, the Republic of the Congo (Congo-Brazzaville), and Gabon.[5] In addition, the consortium of foreign petroleum companies seems to have been able to negotiate contracts such that when national laws conflicted with any contracts, the contracts would supersede. In an attempt to renegotiate its contracts, the Chadian government spent $1.6 mil-

---

3. This was later followed by the 1967 Hydrocarbon Law, which also allowed the government to get improved concessions; see Mommer (1998).

4. The issue of how and to what extent these petrodollars will promote development of Chad is an interesting issue, but one beyond the scope of this paper. Here, we will be concerned with the question of how bargaining over economic rents proceeded.

5. For various measures of "governance," see Kaufmann, Kraay, and Zoido-Lobatón (1999); Political Risk Services (PRS) Group's International Country Risk Guide (www.prsgroup.com); Transparency International's Corruption Perception Index (www.transparency.org/); World Bank's Country Policy and Institutional Assessment (http://info.worldbank.org/governance/kkz2002/notes.html). Xan Rice, "Fuels to Ourselves," *Guardian Unlimited*, September 1, 2006.

lion on lawyers and consultants with the result being a mere 2 percent increase in the terms of the second contract.[6]

As of late, Chad has not been the only case of extremely generous extraction concessions. A recent op-ed piece in the *Boston Globe* notes that "for a minimal return, [the Democratic Republic of the Congo] has signed away millions—if not billions–of dollars' worth of copper and cobalt for 35 years."[7] Even a leaked World Bank document cited in the article admits that "to allow the contracts to proceed without comment would put us in the difficult position of perceived complicity and/or tacit approval of them."[8]

The evidence presented in this paper suggests that the terms of profit sharing vary widely across countries and over time. Between 1982 and 1999, the share of rents going to host country governments in the natural resource extraction industries fell from 52.1 percent to 28.1 percent (see table 1, panels b and c). This decline is driven by a reduction in tax collections and is consistent with the reforms in the mining sector reported by James Otto and others in a World Bank report.[9] According to the World Bank, competition to attract exploration and mining investment has intensified, which has resulted in more generous terms for investors. However, the share of rents paid to developed country governments averaged 40.1 percent while the share of rents paid to developing country governments averaged 31.9 percent. This differential is unlikely to be entirely explained by country risk. According to industry analysts, international financial institutions and the involvement of bilateral donors lessen the likelihood of expropriation and have significantly reduced the importance of country risk.[10] Anecdotal evidence suggests that some of the cross-country variation in the distribution of rents is also likely to be a function of the host country's bargaining power vis-à-vis the multinational corporation.

To quantify the importance of bargaining strength on rent sharing, we develop an empirical framework based on Nash bargaining. Our economic measures of bargaining power include sunk costs, technical expertise of the host country,

6. Christina Katsouris, "Chad: Growing Oil Revenues, Growing Instability," *Energy Compass*, June 11, 2004.

7. John le Carré and Jason Stearns, "Getting Congo's Wealth to Its People," *Boston Globe*, December 22, 2006.

8. le Carré and Stearns, "Getting Congo's Wealth to Its People." This is also not to imply that developed countries do not, sometimes, offer consortiums concessions that are perceived to be inequitable. As a recent *New York Times* article explains, "The United States offers some of the most lucrative incentives in the world to companies that drill for oil in publicly owned coastal waters." Furthermore, "a newly released study suggests that the government is getting very little for its money." Edmond L. Andrews, "Incentives on Oil Barely Help U.S., Study Suggests," *New York Times*, December 22, 2006, p. A1.

9. Otto and others (2006).

10. Boulos (2003).

number of competitors, and oil prices. We also seek to understand how the quality of governance, as measured by a number of governance indexes (see Data section for further discussion), and the development of institutions impact the negotiation process and, in turn, the outcome. Conventional wisdom holds that good governance produces desirable economic outcomes. For example, numerous studies document the link between the amount of foreign direct investment received by a country and the quality of governance infrastructure.[11] However, in the case of natural resource extraction, it may be that poor governance leads to higher corporate profitability and a smaller share of rents for the host country. For this we draw on the large literature on institutions from the past several decades using country-level governance measures to assess their impact on economic outcomes.

We find that the bargaining power of host governments and extraction companies does impact the relative distribution of rents. Moreover, our evidence indicates that the higher the quality of host country government institutions and the more democratic a government is, the better the government's deal ends up being. Although this may not seem like a highly surprising result, and anecdotal evidence has indicated this for some time, it is—to our knowledge—the first econometric attempt to investigate this relationship.

The importance of political and economic considerations for the outcome of the bargaining process is widely recognized but has not been systematically studied in this context.[12] Examining profit sharing between producing countries and oil companies in the Middle East, Edith Penrose noted that "the superior economic power of the oil companies arising from their ability to inflict a disastrous economic loss on the producing country does give them a bargaining position which holds down the share of the profits the producing country can obtain in the oil agreement."[13] However, she argued that reducing the monopoly power of oil companies would not likely be welfare improving, even for oil-exporting countries, given the increasing returns of the market.

More theoretical work has explored the structure and determinants of *government take*—sometimes referred to as the share of economic rent from extraction that goes to the government of the country in which the resource is located. Pedro van Meurs's text on petroleum economics lays some theory for defining government take, which is developed further by Morris Adelman who sought to model investment and returns along with risks over long-term oil investments.[14] David Newbery's work on industrial organization within the petroleum

11. Globerman and Shapiro (2002).
12. An exception would be Theodore Moran's 1974 study of bargaining over rents between copper companies and the Chilean government.
13. Penrose (1959, 1960).
14. van Meurs (1981); Adelman (1991).

industry was, in part, motivated by a desire to understand the dynamics behind cartelization, but his work also sketched out some ideas for understanding the nature of government take within this imperfectly competitive market.[15]

Shang-Jin Wei has done considerable work looking at the "corruption premium" that firms pay to do business in countries with poor governance.[16] Using a matrix of data on foreign direct investment (FDI) that links fifteen source countries to roughly forty host countries, Wei demonstrated the taxing effect of corruption on FDI flows (as compared with taxes themselves).[17] The implication of this finding is that corruption will, in a sense, offset revenue collection as FDI flows adapt to corruption in much the same way as they would to a distortionary tax. In two follow-up papers, Wei (using the same dataset) and Beata Javorcik and Wei (using firm-level data) demonstrated how corruption changes the composition and volume of FDI flows entering countries with poor governance.[18] This research presents a relatively strong case for a negative correlation between government take and corruption, but there is no clear focus on what the relationship may be in natural resource extracting industries (nor is it evident whether these industries are included in the FDI or firm-level data). Given the more extensive (over time) and intensive nature of rent sharing negotiations in resource extraction, the nature of the trade-off between corruption and revenues warrants further investigation.

The outline of this paper is as follows. The next section formalizes Penrose's ideas into an empirical strategy based on a Nash bargaining framework. The third section describes the data from the Bureau of Economic Analysis and our measures of rents and bargaining power. The fourth section provides the cross-section and time series evidence. The fifth section discusses some of the limitations of the analysis and directions for further research. The final section provides concluding remarks. Our appendix describes our data sources and construction in greater detail.

Bargaining over Rents

We formalize the bargaining process between multinationals and host country governments using a Nash bargaining framework. Total rents are given by:

$$\pi = P^{oil}Q^{oil} - C(Q), \qquad (1)$$

---

15. Newbery (1981, 1992).
16. Wei (2002).
17. Wei (2000b).
18. Wei (2000a); Javorcik and Wei (2000).

where Q^{oil} is the quantity of oil produced, P^{oil} is the world price of oil, and $C(Q)$ is the cost of producing a given quantity of oil. In our empirical work, we make the distinction between operating costs and *sunk costs*, which consist primarily of research and development expenditures. Let the outside options for a multinational (multinational corporation or MNC) and host country government be given by π^*_{MNC} and π^*_G, respectively.[19] The outside options for the multinational are defined by the opportunities that are available in other countries while the outside options for the government are defined by what the government could earn if it were to operate the company itself. The bargaining strengths of the two parties are denoted by α and $(1 - \alpha)$ for the government and the multinational, respectively. While the two parties' respective bargaining strengths are partially determined by outside options, they may also be influenced by institutional factors not specific to the particular project at hand. For example, Penrose talked about the importance of popular opinion in shaping a government's ultimate bargaining position.[20]

The outcome of this bargaining process is determined as the solution to maximizing—over π_G and π_{MNC}—the following:

$$[(\pi_G - \pi^*_G)^\alpha x (\pi_{MNC} - \pi^*_{MNC})^{1-\alpha}], \text{ such that } \pi_G + \pi_{MNC} = \pi. \qquad (2)$$

This yields the following solution for government rents:

$$\pi_G = \alpha(\pi - \pi^*_{MNC}) + (1-\alpha)\pi^*_G, \qquad (3)$$

which, for the purposes of the empirical work, we rewrite in the following way:

$$\frac{\pi_G}{\pi} = \alpha \left[1 - \frac{\pi^*_{MNC}}{\pi} \right] + (1-\alpha)\frac{\pi^*_G}{\pi}. \qquad (4)$$

Three factors influence the share of rents going to the host country: the relative bargaining strength of the government π, the outside options available to the government π^*_G, and the outside options available to the multinational π^*_{MNC}.

Our empirical investigation is guided by the solution to the bargaining game. In particular, we estimate the following equation:

$$R_{Git} = \beta_0 + \beta_1\alpha_{it} + \beta_2 R_{MNC*it} + \beta_3 R_{G*it} + \varepsilon_{it}. \qquad (5)$$

---

19. We adopt the subscript *MNC* for variables describing the multinational corporation and *G* for those pertaining to the host country government.
20. Penrose (1959, 1960).

The dependent variable, R_{Git}, is government take, the share of rents going to the government. We are able to measure this variable directly as the ratio of taxes, royalties, and government profits to total profits generated by the project. The impact of the government's bargaining strength relative to that of the multinational on the share of rents going to the government is measured by β_1, which we expect to be positive. The measure of the impact of the multinational's outside options is β_2, and its expected sign is negative. And the measure of the impact of the government's outside options on the share of rents going to the government is β_3, and its expected sign is positive.

We turn now to a description of the data and our proxies for bargaining power and outside options.

The BEA Data

We analyze firm-level surveys on U.S. direct investment abroad, which are collected each year by the Bureau of Economic Analysis of the U.S. Department of Commerce. The BEA requires that U.S.-based multinationals disclose on a confidential basis balance sheet–type data about their overseas activities. In our analysis, a *U.S.-based multinational* is defined as the combination of a single U.S. entity that has made the direct investment, called "the parent," and at least one foreign business enterprise, called the "foreign affiliate." We use the data collected on majority-owned, nonbank foreign affiliates and nonbank U.S. parents for the benchmark years between 1982 and 1999, which are 1982, 1989, 1994, and 1999 and include more comprehensive information than the annual surveys.

While our choice of benchmark years has been dependent on the availability of BEA's survey data, it seems important to note that the beginning of our panel data series follows five years after the enactment of the U.S. Foreign Corrupt Practices Act (FCPA) in 1977, which requires any company that has publicly traded stock to "maintain records that accurately and fairly represent its transactions" and which make it "unlawful for a U.S. person to make payment to a foreign official for the purpose of obtaining or retaining business for or with any person."[21] In effect, our data are, therefore, coming from the era of FCPA enactment and may reflect less corruption than a sample taken from the period before (or shortly after) 1977.

---

21. For more information on the act, see the U.S. Department of Justice FCPA website (www.usdoj.gov/criminal/fraud/fcpa/).

Creating a panel using the benchmark years of the BEA survey data requires a number of adjustments. First, not all firms are required to report to the BEA, and reporting requirements vary across years. Second, because we are interested in understanding what is happening at the industry level, we must consider the implications of the changes to the Standard Industrial Classification (SIC) codes in 1972 and 1987 and the switch from SIC codes to the North American Industrial Classification System (NAICS) codes in 1999. And finally, the fact that parents are allowed to consolidate information for several affiliates in one country on a single form calls for special care in the aggregation and interpretation of affiliate-level data.

All foreign affiliates with sales, assets, or net income in excess of a certain amount in absolute value must report to the BEA. This amount was $3 million in 1982, 1989, and 1994, and it jumped to $7 million in 1999. In addition, a new reporting requirement was imposed on parents in 1999. Parents whose sales, assets, or net income exceeded $100 million (in absolute value) were required to provide more extensive information than were parents whose sales, assets, or net income fell below $100 million. To determine whether the changes in reporting requirements biased our sample toward small firms in the early years, we imposed a double filter on the data based on the 1999 requirements, using a constant dollar cutoff for affiliates of $5.59 million and $79.87 million for parents, both in 1982 U.S. dollars.[22] As it turns out, the reporting requirements were large enough that imposing the filter on the data made little difference.

To focus our analysis on the subset of resource-extracting foreign affiliates, our sample only includes affiliates classified before 1999 as "Mining or Oil and Gas Extraction" (SIC87 codes 10–14) and in 1999 as "Oil and Gas Extraction" (NAICS97 code 211) and "Mining" (NAICS97 code 212).

Key Variables

Our analysis looks at several variables that include government share of rents, bargaining power of the government and of the multinational, and the outside options of the government and of the multinational.

Government Share of Rents

We define this variable as the sum of all direct payments to the government as a result of the project, divided by income net of operating costs. In practice,

22. See Bureau of Economic Analysis for its dataset on U.S. direct investment abroad.

government take on extraction projects can take a number of different forms. Very generally, the systems of government take can be divided into royalty payment, taxation, and profit sharing. Any given investment may be subject to one or more of these transfers as stipulated by contract, and the government's revenue profile and share of risk will certainly depend on the type of system that is in place.

For our purposes, we define payments to the government as taxes (income and other), royalty payments, and profits earned by the government as a result of profit sharing agreements. The dataset does not make a clear distinction between payments to the national government (versus payments to regional or local governments), but given the national importance that most oil investments have, in addition to the scale of revenues that are realized, it seems reasonable to assume that these payments accrue solely to the national government. Our measurement of profit sharing is an admittedly imperfect one, but profit sharing is often a major share of government take in extraction contracts, so it is important to include even an imperfect control. The BEA's survey of U.S. direct investment abroad provides information on what share of a foreign affiliate's equity is held by a foreign owner. Assuming that this foreign owner is, at least in most instances, the host country government, we then multiply this percentage by the affiliate's net income to get a rough estimate of profits accruing to the host country.

Table 1 reports the trends in the government share of rents across regions and over time. We also report separately the share of rents earned from taxes, royalty payments, and profit sharing. A number of things stand out: for all regions and as a whole, the share of total rents going to the host country has decreased from 1982 to 1999. The decline has been most dramatic in Europe and Central Asia and sub-Saharan Africa. This fact poses an intriguing entry point for our discussion: Why did government take fall so dramatically during this period from 1982 to 1999 in two of the world's most politically tumultuous regions (excluding Europe itself, that is)? Also, why in 1999 was government take in developed countries almost twice that in sub-Saharan Africa? Finally, looking at the breakdown of the different types of transfers, we can see that taxes make up the largest chunk of government take but that the relative size of profit sharing and royalty payments compared with taxes varies from region to region.

Bargaining Power

The bargaining power of the government is affected by a host of country-specific institutional factors. One factor is the government's accountability to

Table 1. Means of Key Variables, by Region[a]

Region	Host country share of total benefits	Host country share of benefits from		
		Taxes	*Royalties*	*Profits*
A. Means over all years				
Developed economies	0.409	0.258	0.070	0.033
EAP	0.335	0.212	0.059	0.036
ECA	0.173	0.091	0.011	0.069
LAC	0.382	0.252	0.023	0.058
MENA	0.349	0.236	0.053	0.029
SSA	0.354	0.229	0.062	0.038
Total	0.378	0.242	0.056	0.039
B. Means in 1982				
Developed economies	0.528	0.394	0.066	0.041
EAP	0.481	0.376	0.053	0.038
ECA	0.442	0.441	0.001	0.000
LAC	0.494	0.415	0.013	0.063
MENA	0.502	0.367	0.047	0.043
SSA	0.590	0.395	0.087	0.086
Total	0.521	0.394	0.056	0.049
C. Means in 1999				
Developed economies	0.333	0.202	0.064	0.028
EAP	0.316	0.196	0.057	0.046
ECA	0.100	0.062	0.011	0.037
LAC	0.270	0.154	0.036	0.068
MENA	0.264	0.187	0.034	0.039
SSA	0.162	0.090	0.068	0.009
Total	0.281	0.169	0.052	0.039

Source: Authors' calculations.

ECA = Europe and Central Asia, EAP = East Asia and Pacific Islands, MENA = Middle East and North Africa, SSA = sub-Saharan Africa, LAC = Latin America and Caribbean, OECD = Organization for Economic Cooperation and Development, developed economies = high-income OECD and high-income non-OECD countries.

a. South Asia is included in the totals but is not listed separately since it was not part of the sample in 1982 and currently represents only 0.28 percent of the observations.

its people, which is likely to influence its bargaining power. In a country in which the outcome of negotiations is more transparent, the government will feel more pressure to push for a better deal. In an extreme case, the government's threat point under high transparency is determined by the possibility of civil unrest and subsequent plant closure. Thus the country must balance the revenue it stands to lose if it takes too tough a stance with the possibility of political upheaval. We measure the level of accountability to the people using two subjective measures: democracy and voice and accountability. A second factor is political risk, that is, the risk of political factors resulting in loss or diminished return on investment. High political risk increases the likelihood of disruption of a project, thereby increasing political risk and decreasing the government's bargaining power. Therefore it should not be surprising that firms require a higher share of a project's total benefits in developing countries, where political risks are greater. We measure political risk using the *International Country Risk Guide* (ICRG) composite index since it is the only measure available that dates back to 1982.

Our measure of government accountability to the people is determined by using a rating of the country's level of democracy, which is based on two categories taken from the annual survey conducted by Freedom House. Freedom House publishes information on civil liberties and political rights separately. Since these two variables are highly correlated, we follow Helliwell and combine the two ratings into a single index, democracy, that ranges from 0 to 1 with higher values indicating greater democracy.[23] In the Freedom House survey, ratings of civil liberties (civlib) and political rights (prights) can range between 1 and 7; we transform these into a single variable that ranges between 0 and 1 (with higher values indicating greater democracy) using the transformation (14 − civlib − prights) / 12. Data for these two categories and thus for this composite variable of democracy have been collected since 1970. As a check for robustness of our measure of democracy, we also use the subcomponent of the ICRG political risk index that measures democratic accountability. We expect that the level of corruption will influence the outcome of the bargaining process—in more corrupt environments, multinationals may be able to strike a better deal. A third factor is corruption. Our measure of corruption is based on ICRG's corruption component of political risk. And finally, the government's bargaining power is directly a function of the technical expertise of its bureaucrats in operating natural resource extraction independently without the help of a private company; our measurement of the quality of the bureaucracy in the regions studied is based on ICRG's the bureaucratic quality component of political risk.

We measure the bargaining power of the multinational vis-à-vis the host government in two ways. We assume that the amount of competition from similar firms in that same market reduces a given multinational's bargaining power. If there are more firms in the consortium, the host government would be in a better position to bid up its own take, despite any collusion among the competing firms that may occur. Therefore, we set the bargaining power of the multinational as *n*, the number of U.S. multinationals in the market in a given country and year. An increase in *n* weakens the bargaining power of any given multinational in the country. Following Raymond Vernon's obsolescing bargaining

23. Helliwell (1994).

model, we also include in our measurement of the multinational's bargaining power the ratio of sunk costs to total costs of production.[24] The greater the share of sunk costs a firm has paid, the more it is "stuck" with its investment, the more costly expropriation would be, and the more likely it is for the firm to concede to terms that are less profitable for itself. We define *sunk costs* as the firm's expenditure on exploration and development—namely, how much it has spent in a country's oil fields to find oil plus the cost of investment in property for constructing a plant and equipment, and we normalize this variable by dividing by total costs of production to obtain the ratio of sunk costs to total costs. Both an increased share of sunk costs and a greater *n* are associated with lower bargaining power for MNCs.

OUTSIDE OPTIONS. The host country's alternative to agreeing to a deal with the consortium of extraction firms is largely determined by the government's capacity to run the oil company without the multinational. This in turn is a function of the technical knowledge of its labor force. We establish a proxy for this aspect of bargaining power by using the share of employees working in the foreign affiliate that are local citizens. We justify the proxy with the following logic: the ultimate threat point for a national government in negotiations with a consortium of extraction firms is nationalization, that is, seizure of the means of production and therefore the entire investment. In so doing, the country must balance the increased revenues it gains from complete ownership (of production and assets) with the decrease in revenues from being a less efficient operator of the extraction process than the private companies. In extremely underdeveloped countries, it may be the case that almost all of the skilled employees of the operation are foreign, in which case the national government will not be able to run the operation at all, and therefore it has a relatively low threat point and limited outside options.[25]

For the multinational, the alternative to investing in a particular country is what the firm could make if it shut down operations and relocated to another country. The costs associated with doing this are—to some extent—already captured in the ratio of sunk costs to total costs of production. The potential benefits of relocating to another country are the profits the multinational could make in another country relative to the profits it stands to make if it stays put. To measure this, we first compute the firm's profit margin as the ratio of net income to costs of production. The profit margin is then normalized by the average profit margin across all firms operating in the same sector in a given year

24. Vernon (1971).
25. Granted not all of the foreign skilled employees running the operations of a U.S. multinational abroad may be U.S. citizens—they could be skilled citizens of other nations—but we believe, nonetheless, that it is a reasonable estimate that most are U.S. citizens.

by subtracting from the firm's profit margin the industry average. Increases in this variable can be interpreted as lowering the multinational's threat point in a bargaining situation.

THE PRICE OF OIL. We include as a regressor the real price of crude oil, which is meant to capture the fact that tax and royalty payments are often tied to prices. For example, following the first oil shock in the 1970s, the government of Alberta in Canada refined its royalty formula to make it sensitive to price changes.[26] This type of provision is also common in the mining industry.[27] For the sake of completeness, we should also include in our regressions the prices of all other minerals. However, with the exception of oil, data limitations make it impossible for us to know exactly which mineral is being extracted by the firms in our sample. Nonetheless, to the extent that oil prices are demand driven, movements in the price of oil will capture movements in other minerals prices.

Results

Table 2 presents summary statistics of the variables used in our analysis. As discussed earlier, the first four variables are measures of government take (the dependent variable) and vary between 0 and 1. The standard deviations for all four of these variables are large (and the variation is especially noteworthy— though smaller than that for taxes—for royalties and profits, which, on average, make up a small amount of total government take). This provides us with a great deal of variation in our dependent variable (which is to say, there is "noise" in the regressions), which is less than desirable. We previously described the ratio of sunk costs to total costs and competition, which are proxies for MNC bargaining power, and the government's ability to run the business (that is, the inverse of the share of U.S. citizens employed), which is a proxy for the host government's bargaining power. "Nonoperational" takes a value of 1 if the plant was strictly in the exploration stage and so not extracting material: 6.5 percent of the observations are classified as nonoperational.

Fixed Effects Regressions

We estimate equation 3 using a fixed effects regression to remove time-invariant, firm-specific characteristics that would bias our estimation of the effect

---

26. See "Royalty Information Briefing #3: Royalties—History and Description" at the Alberta Department of Energy's Alberta Royalty Review, More Royalty Information webpage (www.energy.gov.ab.ca/Org/pdfs/InfoSeries-Report3-Formulas.pdf).

27. Otto and others (2006).

Table 2. Summary Statistics of Key Variables

Variable	Observations	Mean	Standard deviation
Host country share of benefits	2,046	0.378	0.278
Host country share of benefits from taxes	2,046	0.242	0.219
Host country share of benefits from royalties	2,046	0.056	0.181
Host country share of benefits from profits	2,046	0.039	0.123
Ratio of sunk costs to total costs	2,046	0.564	0.367
Competition	2,046	41.870	51.620
Government's ability to run business	2,046	0.075	0.176
Price of oil[a]	2,046	24.650	12.300
MNC's relative profitability	2,046	0.017	0.460
Nonoperational	2,046	0.065	0.246
Democracy	2,046	0.607	0.385
Political risk	2,046	4.938	2.216
Democratic accountability	2,046	3.712	2.037
Bureaucratic quality	2,046	2.358	1.457
Corruption	2,046	3.249	2.003

Source: Authors' calculations.
MNC = multinational corporation.
a. Price of oil is in real 2006 U.S. dollars per barrel.

of our institutional variables on government take. This procedure decreases the variation in our institutional variables considerably but does not appear to dramatically change our results relative to the ordinary least squares regressions we have run. In table 3, regression 1 shows that an increase in the ratio of sunk costs to total costs results in an increase in government take of 0.056. The other limitation to an oil company's bargaining power, competition, results in a 0.019 increase in government take. An increase of 0.01 in the share of nationals employed by the multinational (which is a proxy for the government ability to run the business) results in a 0.001 increase in the government take. A US$1 increase in crude oil prices results in an increase of government take of 0.006, which confirms the prevalence of contracts that tie host country benefits to prices. An increase in the profit margin of an MNC's project relative to its projects in other countries increases government take by 0.278. We interpret this result as evidence that the multinational is more willing to concede to generous terms when a project is exceptionally profitable. Finally, an affiliate that is nonoperational decreases government take by 0.096. This latter result is consistent with the fact that firms do not pay taxes until they are operational. All of the estimated coefficients are significant at the 1 percent level, and the regression R squared is 0.23, an indication that our regressors have significant explanatory power.

Table 3. Fixed Effects Regressions[a]

Dependent variable is host country share of total benefits.

Variable	(1)	(2)	(3)	(4)	(5)
Ratio sunk costs to total costs	0.056	0.057	0.058	0.057	0.057
	(2.90)**	(2.91)**	(2.97)**	(2.93)**	(2.93)**
Competition	0.019	0.017	0.023	0.018	0.019
	(3.03)**	(2.44)*	(3.56)**	(2.82)**	(2.93)**
Government ability	0.001	0.001	0.001	0.001	0.001
	(3.44)**	(3.77)**	(3.36)**	(3.63)**	(3.50)**
MNC's relative profits	0.278	0.271	0.279	0.276	0.277
	(18.50)**	(17.75)**	(18.59)**	(18.15)**	(18.34)**
Real oil price	0.006	0.006	0.006	0.006	0.006
	(8.88)**	(8.72)**	(8.95)**	(8.69)**	(8.90)**
Nonoperational	–0.096	–0.085	–0.095	–0.090	–0.093
	(3.31)**	(2.95)**	(3.28)**	(3.12)**	(3.21)**
Political risk	0.014				
	(4.19)**				
Democracy		0.010			
		(0.48)			
Democratic accountability			0.017		
			(4.67)**		
Bureaucratic quality				0.011	
				(2.20)*	
Corruption					0.012
					(3.23)**
Statistics					
Observations	2,042	2,042	2,042	2,042	2,042
Number of parent firms	289	289	289	289	289
R^2	0.23	0.23	0.24	0.23	0.23

Source: Authors' calculations.
MNC = multinational corporation.
*Significant at the 5 percent level; **significant at the 1 percent level.
a. The absolute value of the *t* statistic is in parentheses.

When we add political risk to the regression, the coefficient is 0.014 and statistically significant at the 1 percent level. Since political risk varies from 0 to 6 with 6 being the least risky, this result implies that government take varies 1 for 1 with political risk.[28] The ICRG measures of institutional quality (democratic accountability, bureaucratic quality, and level of corruption) all have roughly the same positive effect on government take and are all statistically significant at least at the 5 percent level. When these institutional variables are added, the coefficients and standard errors on the other regressors are largely unaffected. The coefficient on democracy is positive but statistically insignificant so that—at least as measured—there does not appear to be a strong association between political rights and civil liberties and government take.

28. For a description of the academic dataset, see Knack and Keefer (1995).

Table 4. Fixed Effects Regressions[a]

Dependent variable is host country share of benefits from taxes.

Variable	(1)	(2)	(3)	(4)	(5)
Ratio sunk costs to total costs	0.055	0.056	0.056	0.056	0.055
	(3.05)**	(3.11)**	(3.10)**	(3.08)**	(3.07)**
Competition	0.014	0.008	0.016	0.013	0.013
	(2.42)*	(1.26)	(2.67)**	(2.23)*	(2.22)*
Government ability	0.002	0.002	0.002	0.002	0.002
	(5.37)**	(5.86)**	(5.39)**	(5.54)**	(5.48)**
MNC's relative profits	0.196	0.184	0.195	0.193	0.193
	(14.06)**	(13.05)**	(13.97)**	(13.76)**	(13.82)**
Real oil price	0.005	0.005	0.005	0.005	0.005
	(8.13)**	(7.94)**	(8.14)**	(7.96)**	(8.11)**
Nonoperational	–0.067	–0.057	–0.065	–0.063	–0.064
	(2.51)*	(2.13)*	(2.41)*	(2.34)*	(2.37)*
Political risk	0.012				
	(3.93)**				
Democracy		0.027			
		(1.99)*			
Democratic accountability			0.012		
			(3.38)**		
Bureaucratic quality				0.010	
				(2.07)*	
Corruption					0.008
					(2.38)*
Statistics					
Observations	2,042	2,042	2,042	2,042	2,042
Number of parent firms	289	289	289	289	289
R^2	0.18	0.17	0.18	0.18	0.18

Source: Authors' calculations.
MNC = multinational corporation.
*Significant at the 5 percent level; **significant at the 1 percent level.
a. The absolute value of the t statistic is in parentheses.

The fact that democratic accountability and democracy yield different results suggests that the two variables are measuring different things. Indeed, democratic accountability as measured by ICRG appears to capture political stability rather than accountability to the people per se.

Turning to table 4, which uses government take from taxes as the dependent variable, we see that the results are largely the same as with total benefits, but with slightly different magnitudes. Government ability doubles in magnitude compared with the previous regressions, while the magnitude of the multinational's relative profitability falls by about a third. One explanation for these changes is that government ability is known ahead of time, and so it impacts the overall tax deal a firm gets up front, while the firm's in-country profitabil-

Table 5. Fixed Effects Regressions[a]

Dependent variable is host country share of benefits from profits.

Variable	(1)	(2)	(3)	(4)	(5)
Ratio sunk costs to total costs	0.016	0.016	0.016	0.016	0.016
	(1.95)	(1.99)*	(1.94)	(1.95)	(1.95)
Competition	−0.003	−0.001	−0.002	−0.003	−0.003
	(1.16)	(0.53)	(0.87)	(1.19)	(1.09)
Government ability	0.000	0.000	0.000	0.000	0.000
	(2.25)*	(2.43)*	(2.36)*	(2.24)*	(2.29)*
MNC's relative profits	0.005	0.007	0.006	0.005	0.005
	(0.80)	(1.14)	(0.95)	(0.76)	(0.86)
Real oil price	−0.001	−0.001	−0.001	−0.001	−0.001
	(2.10)*	(2.05)*	(2.05)*	(2.09)*	(2.08)*
Nonoperational	−0.014	−0.015	−0.015	−0.014	−0.014
	(1.16)	(1.22)	(1.24)	(1.14)	(1.19)
Political risk	0.000				
	(0.22)				
Democracy		−0.013			
		(1.58)			
Democratic accountability			−0.001		
			(0.90)		
Bureaucratic quality				0.001	
				(0.38)	
Corruption					−0.000
					(0.19)
Statistics					
Observations	2,042	2,042	2,042	2,042	2,042
Number of parent firms	289	289	289	289	289
R^2	0.05	0.06	0.05	0.05	0.06

Source: Authors' calculations.
MNC = multinational corporation.
*Significant at the 5 percent level.
a. The absolute value of the *t* statistic is in parentheses.

ity relative to other projects only becomes known over time. Thus some of the concessions associated with relative profitability may be more closely tied to royalties or profit sharing or both. The magnitudes and significance of the institutional variables are largely unchanged with the exception of democracy, which is now significant at the 5 percent level. This may be because tax rates are typically public knowledge while royalties and profit sharing agreements tend to be private knowledge. The results for the variable democracy in table 5 support the hypothesis that democracy is not a significant predictor of the host country share of benefits from profits.

In table 5, when we look at the results for government take from profit sharing regressed on our set of explanatory variables, the coefficients are generally of smaller magnitude and less statistically significant. The impact of the share of sunk costs on government take is much smaller at 0.016 and only marginally significant. Competition, the MNC's relative profits, the nonoperational dummy, and all of our institutional variables are not statistically significant. Government ability remains statistically significant but only at the 5 percent level and with a miniscule coefficient. The sign on the price of oil changes, indicating that a US\$ 1 increase in the price of oil reduces the host country share of benefits from profits by 0.001. Since taxes and royalties tend to rise with oil prices, this result implies that profit sharing agreements have become less favorable to host countries as oil prices have increased. However, the R squared for these regressions is far smaller than for that in tables 3 and 4. The relatively small share of government take from profits and the smaller variance that we observed in the summary statistics may result in there being dramatically less "signal" for all the "noise" in our data and may disguise any actual significant results. Moreover, it seems a bit ill advised to conclude from these results that these standard explanations do not affect profit sharing behavior.

Discussion and Conclusion

The basic multivariate regressions presented here demonstrate preliminary evidence that the bargaining power of host governments and extraction companies can impact the relative distribution of rents. Moreover, we find an indication that the higher the quality of government institutions and the more democratic and accountable a host country government is, the better the government's take of rents is. Our work represents the first generalized econometric attempt to look at bargaining power in natural resource extraction. The implication of our findings is that, on average, poor countries keep a smaller share of the rents from natural resource extraction compared with the share kept by rich countries. Although the World Bank has been extensively involved in some of these negotiations, the cases of Chad and the Democratic Republic of the Congo suggest that it has not been very effective at protecting host country rents. In addition, this paper provides systematic empirical evidence in support of Vernon's classic theory of the obsolescing bargain. As the ratio of sunk costs to total costs increases, the multinational's share of rents declines.

Whether the relationship between governance and government take we have uncovered is attributable to better governance, meaning lower political risk and thus a smaller demanded risk premium for firms, or whether it is a result of more capable governments being able (or willing) to negotiate better deals for their citizens is unclear and warrants further investigation. We know from Wei and others that risk matters, but could bargaining power matter as much too?[29]

In addition, any correlation between countries that have nationalized a resource extraction industry and the country's level of governance could bias our estimates. A more thorough investigation of nationalized industries and country governance would be useful for further understanding the relationship between bargaining power and rent sharing. In particular, a more thorough inquiry into the nature and variation of rent sharing methods (for example, taxes; production sharing—that is, the host country government getting a share of the raw materials extracted; profit sharing; and royalties) and the distinction between costs of doing business related to rent sharing versus those related to corruption would advance this field of research substantially. Although the relation between rates of return and governance has been better understood in manufacturing industries and in aggregate, the more complicated relationship that occurs in the resource extraction industries certainly warrants as much, if not more, understanding, if only because of its profound effect on how the natural wealth of nations is utilized.

29. Wei (2000a, 2000b).

Appendix: World Bank Country Classifications

High income, OECD

Australia, Austria, Belgium, Canada, Denmark, Finland, France, Germany, Greece, Ireland, Italy, Japan, Democratic Republic of Korea, Luxembourg, Netherlands, New Zealand, Norway, Portugal, Spain, Sweden, Switzerland, Taiwan, United Kingdom

High income, non-OECD

Aruba, The Bahamas, Bahrain, Bermuda, Cayman Islands, Cyprus, Hong Kong, China, Israel, Kuwait, Netherlands Antilles, Singapore, Slovenia, United Arab Emirates

Upper middle income

Argentina, Barbados, Botswana, Brazil, Chile, Costa Rica, Czech Republic, Dominica, Estonia, Hungary, Latvia, Lebanon, Malaysia, Malta, Mexico, Panama, Poland, Saudi Arabia, Slovak Republic, Trinidad and Tobago, Uruguay, Venezuela

Lower middle income

China, Colombia, Dominican Republic, Ecuador, Egypt, El Salvador, Fiji, Guatemala, Guyana, Honduras, Jamaica, Kazakhstan, Morocco, Namibia, Peru, Philippines, Romania, Russian Federation, South Africa, Sri Lanka, Swaziland, Thailand, Tunisia, Turkey

Low income

Democratic Republic of Congo, Eritrea, Ghana, Haiti, India, Indonesia, Kenya, Malawi, Mozambique, Nicaragua, Nigeria, Pakistan, Senegal, Tanzania, Ukraine, Uzbekistan, Vietnam, Republic of Yemen, Zambia, Zimbabwe

Comment and Discussion

Shang-Jin Wei: The objective of this nicely written paper is to uncover determinants of patterns of profit sharing between governments and multinational firms in natural resource extraction industries, with a particular focus on the oil and natural gas sector.

The paper uses firm-level surveys of U.S. direct investment abroad, collected by the Bureau of Economic Analysis, during the course of various benchmark years from 1977 to 1999. A key variable to be explained is the "government's take," which is the sum of taxes and royalty payment that multinational firms pay to the government as well as any profit sharing, if the oil and gas project is jointly owned by the government. The key finding is that the quality of domestic institutions affects the government take. The better the institution, the higher the share of the total rents that goes to the government.

The authors develop a simple model to motivate the empirical specification by a bargaining framework. The model is reminiscent of Dani Rodrik's work on laborers receiving higher wages in a democracy and is fairly transparent. It makes a seemingly intuitive prediction: namely, the size of the government take depends on three things: the bargaining power of the government vis-à-vis multinational firms, the outside options of the government, and the outside options of the multinational firms.

The key variable in this model is "government bargaining power." Although the framework sounds immensely sensible to me, let me note that nothing in the model says that the government's bargaining power is linked to the quality of domestic institutions. That is an added assumption that needs to be made explicit.

Two Views on a Low Government Take in a Corrupt Country

Could there be an alternative interpretation of the empirical findings? Perhaps those bad institutions (corruption for short) just make it that much riskier for multinational firms to engage in business in those countries. If that is true, the multinationals need to demand what I have called a "corruption premium" to operate in such a country. The government take needs to be adjusted downward to generate this risk compensation. In other words, it is possible that the multinational firms simply would get a fair deal, not a better deal, on a risk-adjusted basis.

This has policy implications as well. In particular, one might ask whether the World Bank or the international community should help developing countries strike a better deal with the multinational firms, for example, by restricting the multinational firm's take in any contract in a natural resource industry. Whether this is a good idea or not depends very much on which interpretation is the right one. On the one hand, if the interpretation is really related to bargaining power, anything that could help strengthen developing country governments' bargaining power or outside options would raise the welfare of the people in the countries. On the other hand, if this is an issue of fair compensation for extra risk, then imposing restrictions on feasible contracts may very well make things worse off for the people in these developing countries.

Can we sort out the two competing interpretations? Yes. I suggest a two-step procedure. First, estimate a corruption premium using data on the volume of foreign direct investment (FDI) in sectors outside the oil and gas industry. Second, check on whether the reduction in the government take documented by the current paper is more than what can be explained by a fair compensation for the corruption risk.

Here are a few papers that may be relevant in this context. James Hines found that U.S. multinational firms are discouraged by host country corruption.[1] In 2000 I worked with a matrix of bilateral FDI data from twelve source countries to forty-five host countries and found that corruption deters FDI.[2] Other things being equal, international investors are hesitant about investing in corrupt countries. In a follow-up paper, I explored the implications of host country corruption on the composition of international capital inflows. I found that direct investors are much more adverse to host country corruption than are international banks or other creditors.[3]

In a study with Beata Javorcik using firm-level data on FDI in central and eastern Europe, we examined how host country corruption affects two decisions by multinational firms simultaneously: their mode of entry (wholly owned company versus joint venture) and the size of the investment. We found evi-

1. Hines (1995).
2. Wei (2000b).
3. Wei (2000c).

dence that host country corruption reduces the volume of inward FDI and, for foreign firms in high tech industries, creates a bias in favor of sole ownership.[4] The literature in this field, which includes other papers that I have not cited here, by and large suggests that corruption tends to add risk for international direct investors, and therefore those investors need to be compensated for investing in relatively corrupt countries.

Following the methodology in my paper in *Review of Economics and Statistics*, one can check how much tax and how much host country corruption discourages FDI.[5] The ratio of the two would allow one to estimate a corruption premium in units of tax equivalent. Armed with that estimate, one can then ask in the natural resource sector how much a developing country government with a certain level of corruption needs to reduce its take to compensate foreign investors. This gives an estimate of an "appropriate level of government take" that adjusts for the corruption risk in the country. One can compare this "appropriate level" with the actual government take in the data.

Finding Exogenous Variations in the Bargaining Power of the Multinationals

I have another suggestion. Perhaps the authors can also explore other exogenous variations in multinational firms' bargaining power. In particular, there are two events in 1979 and 1999 that can be useful in this context. I understand that the authors only worked with data from 1982 to 1999, but the sample could be expanded to encompass the first benchmark survey in 1977 and the more recent 2004 benchmark survey.

What happened in 1979? During the Carter administration, Congress passed the Foreign Corrupt Practices Act that prohibits U.S. multinational firms from offering bribes to foreign government officials. None of the other major FDI source countries had such laws at that time. This event potentially altered the bargaining power of U.S. companies compared with that of multinational firms from other countries.

In 1999, the Organization for Economic Cooperation and Development, after two decades of pressure from the U.S. State and Treasury departments, finally enacted a treaty outlawing bribery of foreign government officials by firms from all the signatory countries. In this case, the previous asymmetry

4. Javorcik and Wei (2001).
5. Wei (2000b).

between U.S. and non-U.S. multinational firms was removed. The timing of rectification, however, differed across the signatory countries.

These two events are arguably exogenous from the point of view of any individual company and individual government. Therefore, they offer researchers opportunities to check how a change in the bargaining power of multinational firms affects the government take in the natural resource sector.

Discussion: Laura Alfaro opened the general discussion with two brief comments. First, regarding data and empirics, she remarked that it was somewhat confusing that the variables moved very little over twenty years, with the exception of accountability. Second, Alfaro pointed out that fragile states have difficulties in bargaining and that corruption presents itself in many forms. U.S. companies have the Foreign Corrupt Practices Act that governs the ways in which they conduct business; however, U.S companies do find loopholes to circumvent this. Last, Alfaro commented on the uncertainty of how much corruption is changing because it seems that one cannot be in the oil business without conducting some of these practices.

Beata Javorcik raised three points. First, there is an alternative explanation regarding fragile states being worse bargainers. States that are concerned about their independence may want to give oil companies more lucrative contracts, so that they can create incentives in powerful Western governments to support their independence. Second, these contracts are not only about profit sharing. There is the issue of who pays for infrastructure; it is not just that one needs to build a pipeline, the actual exploration site or activity has to be built as well. Therefore, if the local government is paying for the infrastructure, then they may be getting a higher share. She added that it is important to look at the contracts to understand both components and then to look at the relationship. Javorcik concluded by highlighting Assaf Razin's presentation the day before and the issue of selectivity. The nature of the data is such that only countries with profit sharing agreements are analyzed, which excludes countries that have their own extractive industries. Last, she suggested examining further the direction of causality and offered an example to highlight this point: if a country invites a multinational to help extract resources and they offer a bribe, the country may want to become less transparent, so that its citizens do not know where the money is going.

Theodore Moran applauded the paper and its contributions. He agreed that additional work may be needed but commended the literature review and data on the benefits that come in extractive industries. He suggested finding a way to get data on how capital and how much capital is invested, so that one can get figures on return on investment. In his opinion, this would be highly valuable information.

Raymond Mataloni commented that he had issues with the deep-end variables in the regression, specifically using net income as a denominator. To get better results, he suggested using sales or total revenues as a denominator. Also, he remarked that it was unclear where one can collect information on government ownership share, which is probably not available in the data.

Regarding dynamics, Deborah Swenson was concerned about the dynamics game being played out and offered a suggestion. If one plays too hard at the outset, although a very high share of the rents may be taken now as a result, it is going to come at the expense of not getting the needed investments that will allow one to have higher growth in future years. In addition, she suggested looking at lagging the institutional variables, because although there may not be a lot of variation, it is nonetheless important. She pointed out that to the extent that the returns in the oil industry are very much dependent on the price of oil and capacity at different times, may be reason for dynamic differences.

Susan Collins offered a couple of comments. She noted that the data used, especially on a comparative basis, make it difficult to determine which domestic investments in extractive industries are local. Concerning corruption, Collins stated if one thinks there is a corruption risk premium, presumably in a given country, there are differences across industries, but there has to be a country-specific effect that is important. Collins reiterated a comment made earlier on providing additional information on the nature of the panel being used. This would be helpful because the cross section aspects of it may be behaving differently from what is going on within countries over time.

Margaret McMillan concluded by offering a few brief responses to questions and comments raised by participants. She thanked participants for their suggestions and feedback, which will help take this research even further. She agreed a better job of describing the data is needed and acknowledged that the dynamics component of the paper is a weakness that needs improving. Regarding this, McMillan went on to note that big changes across countries over time are driven by taxes. We know profit sharing of some sort is going on and the only way to measure it with data from BEA is by information on ownership.

References

Adelman, Morris A. 1991. "User Cost in Oil Production." *Resources and Energy* 13, no. 3: 217–40.

Boulos, Alfred J. 2003. "Assessing Political Risk." Supplement. *International Primer*. Washington: Independent Petroleum Association of America.

Globerman, Steven, and Daniel Shapiro. 2002. "Global Foreign Direct Investment Flows: The Role of Governance Infrastructure." *World Development* 30, no. 11: 1899–919.

Helliwell, John F. 1994. "Empirical Linkages between Democracy and Economic Growth." *British Journal of Political Science* XXIV: 225–48.

Hines, James R., Jr. 1995. "Forbidden Payment: Foreign Bribery and American Business after 1977." Working Paper 5266. Cambridge, Mass.: National Bureau of Economic Research (September).

Javorcik, Beata Smarzynska, and Shang-Jin Wei. 2000. "Corruption and the Composition of Foreign Direct Investment: Firm-Level Evidence." Policy Research Working Paper Series 2360. Washington: World Bank (June).

———. 2001. "Corruption and Foreign Direct Investment: Firm-Level Evidence." CEPR Discussion Paper 2967. London: Centre for Economic Policy Research (September).

Karl, Terry Lynn. 1987. "Petroleum and Political Pacts: The Transition to Democracy in Venezuela." *Latin American Research Review* 22, no. 1: 63–94.

Kaufmann, Daniel, Aart Kraay, Pablo Zoido-Lobatón. 1999. "Governance Matters." Policy Research Working Paper 2196. Washington: World Bank.

Knack, Stephen, and Philip Keefer. 1995. "Institutions and Economic Performance: Cross-Country Tests Using Alternative Institutional Measures." *Economics and Politics* 7, no. 3: 207–27.

Moran, Theodore H. 1974. *Multinational Corporations and the Politics of Dependence: Copper in Chile*. Princeton University Press.

Mommer, Bernard. 1998. *The New Governance of Venezuelan Oil*. WPM 23. Oxford, United Kingdom: Oxford Institute for Energy Studies (April).

Newbery, David M. 1981. "Oil Prices, Cartels, and the Problem of Dynamic Inconsistency." *Economic Journal* 91, no. 363: 617–46.

———. 1992. "The Open-Loop von Stackelberg Equilibrium in the Cartel versus Fringe Model: A Reply." *Economic Journal* 102, no. 415: 1485–87.

Otto, James, and others. 2006. *Mining Royalties: A Global Study of Their Impact on Investors, Government, and Civil Society*. Washington: World Bank.

Penrose, Edith T. 1959. "Profit Sharing Between Producing Countries and Oil Companies in the Middle East." *Economic Journal* 69, no. 274: 238–54.

———. 1960. "Middle East Oil: The International Distribution of Profits and Income Taxes." *Economica* 27, no. 107: 203–13.

van Meurs, A. Pedro H. 1981. *Modern Petroleum Economics*. Ottawa, Ontario, Canada: Van Meurs and Associates.

Vernon, Raymond. 1971. *Sovereignty at Bay: The Multinational Spread of U.S. Enterprises*. New York: Basic Books.

Wei, Shang-Jin. 2000a. "Corruption, Composition of Capital Flows, and Currency Crises." Policy Research Working Paper Series 2429. Washington: World Bank.

———. 2000b. "How Taxing is Corruption on International Investors?" *Review of Economics and Statistics* 82, no. 1: 1–11.

———. 2000c. "Local Corruption and Capital Flows." *Brookings Papers on Economic Activity* 62, no. 2: 303–54.

———. 2002. "Valuing Governance: The 'Corruption Premium' in Global Capital Flows." In *Financial Sector Governance: The Role of Public and Private Sectors*, edited by Robert E. Litan, Michael Pomerleano, and Vasudevan Sundarajan, pp. 51–80. Emerging Markets Series. Brookings.

BARRY BOSWORTH
Brookings Institution

SUSAN M. COLLINS
Georgetown University and Brookings Institution

GABRIEL CHODOROW-REICH
Brookings Institution

Returns on Foreign Direct Investment: Does the United States Really Do Better?

O ver the past quarter century, the United States has undergone a striking shift from the world's largest creditor nation, with a net international investment position equal to 11 percent of GDP, to its largest debtor, with a net indebtedness of $2.6 trillion or –20 percent of GDP at the end of 2006 (see table 1). Yet net income from U.S. foreign investments remained positive throughout this transition.[1] This surprising state of affairs is highlighted in figure 1. According to official data, the strong continued income account performance reflects the fact that U.S. investors earn a significantly higher rate of return on their foreign assets than foreigners earn in the United States. But despite considerable recent research, analysts do not agree on whether the United States really does do better and, if so, why.

Some scholars argue that published data are implausible and suggest possible errors in the reported data for either income flows or estimated net asset position. For example, Ricardo Hausmann and Federico Sturzenegger argued that the value of the U.S. foreign asset position is understated, which leads to overstatement of the return on outward foreign direct investment (FDI). In particular, they believe that U.S. trade statistics fail to capture the full amount of U.S. exports of intangible capital.[2] In contrast, Daniel Gros pointed to asymmetries in the data sources used to construct estimates of income and payments on foreign direct investment.[3] He believes that U.S. payments to foreigners, and thus the return on inward FDI, are understated. Pierre-Olivier Gourinchas

---

1. We are indebted to our discussant for alerting us to the substantial upward revisions to net investment income in the June 2007 release of balance of payments. Upward revisions of the investment income, relative to the initial estimates, have been a recurring theme in recent years. In the June 2007 release, the estimates of net income for the period 2001–06 average $40 billion per year above the initial estimates.

2. Hausmann and Sturzenegger (2006).

3. Gros (2006a, 2006b).

Figure 1. U.S. Net Investment Income and International Assets, 1976–2006

Billions of dollars

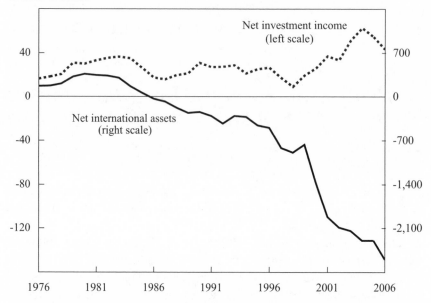

Source: Bureau of Economic Analysis, U.S. International Transactions Accounts and U.S. Net International Investment Position at Yearend 2006 (www.bea.gov/international/index.htm).

and Hélène Rey changed the presentation of the data to emphasize the total return (inclusive of capital gains) and conclude that the United States earns a premium because it acts as an international venture capitalist, borrowing in relative safe short-term liabilities while investing in riskier long-term assets.[4]

The purpose of this paper is to examine in greater detail some of the competing explanations for the apparent differential between the rates of return on U.S. foreign assets and liabilities. In particular, we focus on the rate of return on foreign direct investment. As we show, almost the entire return differential occurs in FDI, where American firms operating abroad appear to earn a persistently higher return than that earned by foreign firms operating in the United States. We first review a number of explanations in the literature for this differential. We then offer some new evidence on the potential role of income shifting between jurisdictions with varying rates of taxation.

In summary, we do not believe that the differential in returns is an illusion of bad data, as alleged by much of the recent discussion. Although the Bureau of Economic Analysis (BEA)—the statistical agency that collects and reports

4. Gourinchas and Rey (2007).

the relevant data—is handicapped by unreliable source data, we believe that the existing accounts that it puts together are superior to suggested alternatives. However, we argue that the current literature places too little emphasis on the potential role for tax-related income shifting. In particular, we find statistically significant evidence of a substantial diversion of income to low-tax jurisdictions, suggesting that the reported earnings on FDI are distorted by efforts to avoid U.S. corporate taxation.

The following section examines the official statistics on the balance of payments (BOP) and the international investment position (IIP) of the United States. The third section discusses the main competing explanations, some of which assert that the official measures are incorrect. The fourth section contains our argument on tax considerations, and the last section concludes.

What Do the Published Data Show?

The official statistics on the U.S. external position are surprising in two respects. First, despite the enormous size of the nation's external indebtedness, the net debt has actually grown more slowly than would have been expected from a simple summation of the annual current account deficits, which are now in the range of $700 billion to $800 billion per year. The cumulation of past current account balances would suggest a net liability position of about –$5.5 trillion at the end of 2006, compared with an actual value of –$2.6 trillion (table 1).[5] Second, as mentioned above, the United States has experienced no deterioration in its net foreign investment income despite the emergence of the large negative asset position.

These two puzzles raise a number of questions that have direct bearing on the sustainability of the U.S. position. Why have the large current account deficits failed to lead to a larger buildup of net liabilities? What accounts for the nearly $3 trillion that is missing? And why has the United States continued to do so well on its net investment income? To some observers, these two puzzling facts seem inconsistent with the gloom and doom that dominates discussions of the deteriorating U.S. trade position and predictions of a near-term financial crisis.

---

5. The asset position data released in 2007 include a new category for financial derivatives, but only for year-end 2005 and 2006. To preserve historical comparability, we exclude the contribution of financial derivatives from the totals that are reported in table 1, table 2, and figure 1 and cited throughout the paper. In 2006 the inclusion of financial derivatives would raise both total foreign assets and liabilities by approximately $1.2 trillion. See BEA (2007).

The Balance of Payments Division of BEA publishes two consistent sets of accounts covering external holdings. The transactions accounts (BOP) provide annual and quarterly data on the normal balance of payments items, including inward and outward investment and the capital income that stems from that investment. The international investment position (IIP) shows the gross asset and liability position of the United States. In principle, all of the items in both sets of accounts are valued at their current market transaction price. A complication arises with FDI, however, because many foreign affiliates are not actively traded and therefore lack a current market price.

The IIP provides two alternative estimates of FDI at current market value: *current cost* and *market valuation*.[6] The current-cost method incorporates market values for the financial components of the IIP but values the tangible asset portion of FDI at current replacement cost using country-specific, capital-goods price indexes. This is consistent with the methodology used to value domestic tangible assets in the Federal Reserve's flow of funds accounts.[7] The market-valuation concept short-circuits all of the underlying adjustments to balance sheets of foreign affiliates by directly incrementing net equity positions in line with country-specific equity market indexes. In contrast to much of the literature, we choose to emphasize the current-cost method in our empirical analysis for two reasons. We find it more consistent with the valuation methods used to compute rates of return on domestic capital. Furthermore, we are uneasy with the assumption implicit in the market-valuation methodology that changes in the value of foreign affiliates parallel changes in the aggregate stock exchanges of the foreign affiliates' host country.

Table 1 demonstrates the puzzle of the missing $3 trillion by contrasting the current-cost valuations of U.S. foreign assets and liabilities with simple summations of the corresponding flows. The top panel of the table shows cumulative foreign investments for the United States of nearly $8.5 trillion in 2006. The 2006 current-cost valuation of these assets abroad was $12.5 trillion, implying that the United States had valuation gains of $4.1 trillion on these investments. In contrast, the middle panel shows that foreign investments in the United States had a valuation gain of just $1.2 trillion on a larger cumulative asset position of $13.9 trillion. These valuation changes arise from a combination of asset price changes in the host country, exchange rate changes, and a miscellaneous category called "other valuation changes."[8]

6. See Landefeld and Lawson (1991).

7. Tangible assets make up about one-quarter of foreign affiliates' net stockholder equity.

8. The category of "other valuation changes" reflects breaks in data series and the gain or loss associated with the sale of the interest in a foreign affiliate at a price different from what had been recorded in the accounts. Although the category is quite large in the aggregate, historical information is not available on its distribution across asset categories.

Table 1. U.S. Investment Position at Current Cost and Cumulative Valuation, 1980–2006

Billions of dollars

	Total assets		Foreign direct investment		Equity investments		Other assets	
	Current cost valuation	Cumulative value	Current cost valuation	Cumulative value	Current cost valuation	Cumulative value	Current cost valuation	Cumulative value
U.S. investments abroad								
1980	930	930	388	388	19	19	523	523
1990	2,179	1,876	617	612	198	53	1,365	1,211
2000	6,239	5,064	1,532	1,685	1,853	756	2,854	2,624
2006	12,517	8,454	2,856	2,638	4,252	1,355	5,410	4,461
Valuation gain		4,063		218		2,896		950
Foreign investments in the United States								
1980	569	569	127	127	65	65	377	377
1990	2,424	2,196	505	488	222	102	1,697	1,606
2000	7,620	6,973	1,421	1,668	1,554	574	4,645	4,731
2006	15,116	13,943	2,099	2,419	2,539	1,043	10,478	10,482
Valuation gain		1,173		-319		1,496		-4
Net investment position								
1980	361	361	261	261	-46	-46	146	146
1990	-245	-320	111	124	-24	-48	-333	-396
2000	-1,381	-1,908	111	17	298	182	-1,790	-2,107
2006	-2,599	-5,489	756	219	1,713	312	-5,068	-6,021
Valuation gain		2,891		537		1,400		954

Source: Computed by the authors from the international investment position at current cost and a cumulative sum of flows as reported in the Balance of Payments. The cumulated flows are benchmarked to their 1980 valuation. As explained in the text, the 2006 valuation data exclude the category of financial derivatives.

It is apparent from the table that valuation effects are larger for equity investments than for either FDI or other assets. The explanation is quite straightforward, reflecting the fact that cash payouts to equity holders (dividends) are only a small portion of the total return. Furthermore, the valuation effects are larger on the asset side both because U.S. investments in foreign equity markets are somewhat greater than are foreign equity investments in the United States and because gains in foreign market prices have been larger. The greater surprise is that U.S. investors appear to have had valuation gains on their other investments (FDI and nonequity), while foreign investments in the United States appear to have had substantial valuation losses.[9] A small portion of the difference can be traced to exchange rate effects, but the differences in the nonequity component are largely due to inconsistencies in the source data that BEA uses to construct the transactions flows and the end-of-year investment positions. In recent years the surveys have shown larger than expected U.S. holdings of foreign assets and smaller liabilities.[10]

The second puzzle is illustrated by combining the BOP capital income data with matching measures of assets and liabilities from the IIP so as to compute rates of return for U.S. investments abroad and for foreign investments in the United States. To begin with, we have divided the data into two categories, FDI and all other investments. Surprisingly, figure 2 illustrates that U.S. and foreign investors have earned nearly identical rates of return on non-FDI assets over the past quarter century. Moreover, those returns appear to have declined in line with observed market interest rates. This close correspondence is unexpected in view of the common belief that foreign portfolio investments are concentrated in short-term U.S. government securities with low yields, whereas U.S. investments are relatively concentrated in equities and other high-yield assets. Part of the explanation is that low-yield foreign official holdings are only about 20 percent of total non-FDI liabilities, a smaller share than typically believed. In addition, equities are a large portion of U.S. assets, and as discussed above, cash dividends are a small share of their total yield. The total return, which includes dividend income and capital gains, is significantly higher.[11]

9. The difference in the valuation adjustment for FDI assets and liabilities may be due in part to divergent trends in capital goods prices. The United States adjusts the price indexes for rapid quality improvements in information technology (IT) capital with the result that the price index for capital goods declines relative to the general GDP deflator. That pattern of relative price change is much less evident in other countries in which IT capital has a smaller role.

10. A particularly large discrepancy arose with the Treasury survey in December 2003 in which U.S. holdings of foreign bonds were reported at $874 billion or 74 percent above the prior estimate based on flow information. See Bach (2005, p. 59).

11. The balance of payments and the national accounts both exclude capital gains and losses from the income flows. We will return to the measurement of total returns in a later section of the paper.

Figure 2. Rate of Return on Non-FDI Assets and Liabilities, 1976–2006

Percent

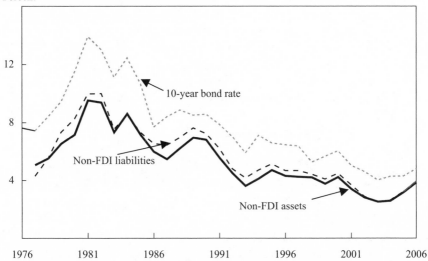

Source: Computed by the authors as the annual income as a percentage of the mid-year estimate of assets and liabilities. The ten-year bond rate is the constant maturity yield on U.S. government securities. All of the data are from the sources listed in figure 1.

Instead, the higher earnings on U.S. foreign investments can be traced to a much larger return reported for the FDI of U.S. resident business enterprises (U.S. direct investment abroad or USDIA), compared with foreign firms operating in the United States (foreign direct investment in the United States or FDIUS). As shown in figure 3, the differential has been large and persistent, averaging 6 percent during the period 1977 to 2006. We have emphasized measures of the rate of return that are based on valuing physical plant and equipment at current replacement cost, but the alternative of adjusting owners' equity in line with country-specific equity indexes (market valuation) yields similar results.

The gap in FDI returns seems to suggest that U.S. firms use their capital more efficiently than do their foreign counterparts. If so, it is interesting to ask whether U.S. firms have made unusually high returns abroad or whether foreign firms operating in the United States have done especially poorly. As a benchmark measure, figure 3 also shows the after-tax return on domestic non-financial corporate capital from 1976 to 2005.[12] It consistently lies between the estimated returns on outward and inward FDI, suggesting both an above-average

12. The rate of return includes profits, net interest, and rent in the numerator to avoid issues of distinguishing between the returns to bondholders and stockholders. The denominator measures mid-year tangible assets at replacement costs, and therefore the return is a real rate free of inflation effects.

Figure 3. Rate of Return on FDI and Corporate Capital, 1976–2006

Percent

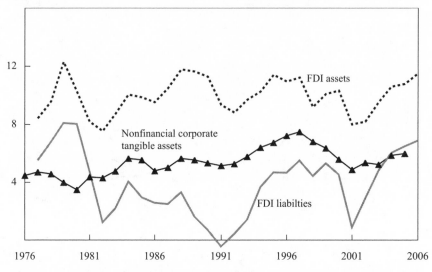

Source: Authors' calculations from sources given in figure 1 and *Flow of Funds Accounts of the United States* (Board of Governors of the Federal Reserve System). The domestic corporate rate of return is for nonfarm nonfinancial corporations, and it is defined as the sum of after-tax economic profits and net interest as a percent of tangible assets.

return on USDIA and a low reported return for FDIUS. Until recently, most of the discussion and research has focused on the perceived low return on FDIUS. A belief that foreign-controlled corporations operating in the United States were shifting their income abroad to avoid U.S. taxation was a significant topic in the 1992 elections, and various explanations for their low returns were frequent topics of research.[13] More recently, the discussion has shifted to put a greater emphasis on the high return on USDIA.[14]

Competing Explanations

The observation that the rates of return on outward and inward FDI differ by a substantial magnitude has been noted by many researchers. The ongoing discussion revolves around five alternative explanations:

—Differing characteristics of USDIA and FDIUS

---

13. Mataloni (2000); Grubert (1997).

14. Hausmann and Sturzenegger (2006); Buiter (2006); McGrattan and Prescott (2006); Kitchen (2006).

—Errors in accounting for exports of U.S. intangibles and a consequent underestimate of the USDIA asset position

—Errors in the reporting of earnings on USDIA and FDIUS

—Alternative measures of the return

—Tax incentives

We discuss the first four below, leaving the role of taxes to be evaluated in a subsequent section in which we offer some new empirical results.

Differing characteristics of FDI

The sharply differing rates of return on inward and outward FDI are long-standing and frequently noted in the research literature. In the 1990s the basic assumption was that the differences were real, and researchers sought explanations in different characteristics of the enterprises. Most frequently, the differential has been attributed either to the fact that U.S. foreign subsidiaries have been in operation for a longer period of time than foreign subsidiaries in the United States have or to the claim that the risks of doing business may be greater for U.S. firms operating abroad than they are for foreign firms operating in the United States.

Steven Landefeld, Ann Lawson, and Douglas Weinberg reported that firms acquired by foreigners had below average rates of return at the time of purchase; and Harry Grubert, Timothy Goodspeed, and Deborah Swenson found that rates of return did tend to rise in the years following an acquisition within a dataset of individual foreign-controlled corporations in manufacturing.[15] Raymond Mataloni also found strong maturation effects for a panel of manufacturing companies from 1987 to 1997.[16] However, the size of the age effect is quite small relative to the total gap in the returns on inward and outward FDI. Furthermore, while U.S. firms were investing greater amounts abroad in the years before 1980, the explosive growth of inward and outward FDI in subsequent years should have rapidly reduced the importance of any initial differences.[17]

The hypothesis that the higher return on outward FDI is due to the greater riskiness of investing in other countries has been evaluated by Juann Huang and Angelo Mascaro.[18] They showed that returns on outward FDI are more volatile and that outward FDI has a considerably higher sovereign risk rating. However, sovereign risk accounts for only about one-third of the observed dif-

---

15. Landefeld, Lawson, and Weinberg (1992); Grubert, Goodspeed, and Swenson (1993).

16. Mataloni (2000).

17. Gros (2006b, p. 9).

18. Huang and Mascaro (2004).

ferences in rate of return, and the correlation between returns by country and sovereign risk is not statistically significant.

Neither of these two explanations seems to us sufficient to account for the magnitude and persistence of the differences between the returns on inward and outward FDI. However, Huang and Mascaro argued that, taken together, these two effects may account for as much as two-thirds of the reported difference.

Unrecorded Exports of Intangibles

Hausmann and Sturzenegger argued that a persistently higher return on outward investment relative to inward investment is implausible.[19] They advanced an alternative viewpoint that the value of overseas assets is understated because of large exports of intangibles to foreign affiliates that go unreported in official trade data. Trade in intangibles includes transfers of patents, trademarks, and financial assets, as well as more difficult-to-quantify concepts such as management and technical know-how. Hausmann and Sturzenegger asserted that these intangibles cannot be directly measured but their magnitude can be deduced by their impact on other flows (for example, income receipts), which is similar to the methods used by astronomers to deduce the existence of dark matter. Thus they capitalized net investment income at an assumed 5 percent rate and compared it with the official IIP.[20] This calculation suggests that the net IIP should be raised by about $3.1 trillion at the end of 2004. A revision of that magnitude would largely eliminate the cumulative current account deficit since 1980.

However, the Hausmann and Sturzenegger assumption of a constant 5 percent return on U.S. assets and liabilities is also implausible. There is no reason for assuming that the return has been constant, much less that it has had a value of 5 percent. Yet, their analysis does draw attention to the difficulties of accurately measuring the flow of trade in intangibles. Intangibles have no geographic location and can only be defined in terms of the residence of their owners. In principle, the balance of payments includes transactions in intangibles between a parent and its foreign affiliates, both as part of services trade and as an element of FDI. Yet in practice, the decision of whether or not to transfer ownership to a foreign affiliate is largely independent of any production process or economic transaction. The output of the intangible capital can be attributed to a specific location almost at will. Robert Lipsey has expressed concern that this

19. Hausmann and Sturzenegger (2006).
20. Cline (2005) performed a similar calculation using the ten-year Treasury bond rate.

"phantom" production and trade could erode the value of the economic accounts.[21]

The historical cost valuation on the investment position consists of the cumulative sum of past FDI flows plus accounting adjustments. Thus any undervaluation of flows would also be incorporated in the firm's balance sheet. In theory, the alternative market valuation of FDI should correct for any systematic undervaluation of the flows. However, most affiliates are privately held and do not trade on organized exchanges. Recall that BEA estimates a market value for U.S. affiliates by applying the ratio of market value to book value for a broad group of traded corporations in the host country. Thus there is no built-in correction of asset levels that would adjust for errors in measurement of the flows. However, critics of the dark matter argument, such as Willem Buiter and Matthew Higgins, Thomas Klitgaard, and Cédric Tille, point out that no evidence has been presented to suggest that intangibles are a larger element of outward FDI than of the investments of foreign firms in the United States.[22] Furthermore, not everyone agrees that the estimates of the investment income flows are better than those for the investment positions.

Mismeasured Earnings

Gros also believes that the finding of a sustained yield advantage on outward FDI is implausible.[23] But in sharp contrast to Hausmann and Sturzenegger, he argued that it is the income data that are wrong. In particular, he focused on the fact that U.S. firms reinvest a large portion of their earnings on outward FDI, whereas foreign firms report little or no reinvestment of earnings. Second, he believes that the low return on foreign FDI in the United States cannot be reconciled with the fact that the average rate of return on foreign portfolio equity investments is nearly equal to that earned by U.S. investors. In effect, foreigners earn a return comparable to their U.S. counterparts until they invest more than 10 percent in a U.S. corporation—the threshold for the definition of FDI.[24]

Gros also rejected tax avoidance as an explanation for the low return on inward FDI. He believes this would imply continuous declines in U.S. export prices relative to import prices and thus a deterioration in the terms of trade that he did not observe to be true. Instead, he points to the inclusion of rein-

---

21. Lipsey (2006).
22. Buiter (2006); Higgins, Klitgaard, and Tille (2007).
23. Gros (2006a, 2006b).
24. The argument is a bit of an overstatement, because, although 10 percent constitutes the dividing line between portfolio and direct investment, the bulk of FDIUS is in majority-owned affiliates.

vested earnings as the source of the difference and favors focusing on dividend repatriation rather than on earnings to compare returns on inward FDI with returns on outward FDI. Eliminating the reinvested earnings component would eliminate about two-thirds of the reported return on outward FDI, thereby substantially narrowing the rate of return gap.

Like Hausmann and Sturzenegger, Gros presented no evidence that the reported returns on FDI are wrong, only that he regards the differential as implausible. Nevertheless, his discussion does highlight an important inconsistency in national reports of FDI. Although the fifth edition of the *Balance of Payments Manual* adopted a measure of income from FDI that includes reinvested earnings, not all countries have done so.[25] However, Gros was not able to resolve the puzzle of large FDI return differentials by simply excluding the reinvested component. The low return on FDIUS is not just a reporting problem, because it is also reflected in the audited tax returns of foreign-controlled U.S. corporations.[26] Furthermore, because U.S. firms pay taxes only on repatriated foreign income, it is not surprising that they reinvest a large portion of that income. More fundamentally, we believe that Gros was too quick to reject tax avoidance as a contributor because he adopted too narrow a perspective on the potential for shifting income among jurisdictions.

Alternative Measures of the Return

The BOP accounts, as with the national income accounts, exclude capital gains and losses. Excluding valuation changes is consistent with a desire to focus on resource use and resource transfers. However, the exclusion seems less relevant for financial transactions in which earnings are often reinvested and incorporated into asset price changes. The resulting interest in valuation effects and in measures of total return explains a large part of the increased focus on the asset and liability positions reported in the IIP.[27] However, the measures of the returns on FDI and other financial assets and liabilities that we described previously exclude those valuation elements.

As discussed earlier in connection with the data in table 1, valuation effects are large and quite favorable to the United States. Table 2 provides a more detailed perspective on the BEA data by separating the total valuation change on the international investment position into three components: asset price

25. IMF (1993).
26. We present the tax return data in table 3 in the section on tax policy and income shifting.
27. See as well the important research of Lane and Milesi-Ferretti (2001, 2003) to create measures of the IIP for a large number of countries. The importance of wealth valuation effects is also highlighted in Tille (2005).

Table 2. Valuation Changes on the International Investment Position, 1990–2006

US dollars (billions)

	With FDI at current cost				With FDI at market value			
	Total	Price	Exchange rate	Other revaluations	Total	Price	Exchange rate	Other revaluations
Net								
1990–95	299	–73	42	330	239	–157	77	319
1995–2000	180	–5	–370	555	–208	15	–563	340
2000–06	2,235	924	311	1,000	2,905	1,604	470	832
Outward								
1990–95	464	169	57	237	663	331	94	237
1995–2000	582	840	–419	161	1,416	1,867	–607	156
2000–06	2,593	1,281	408	904	2,690	1,324	561	804
Inward								
1990–95	165	243	15	–93	424	488	17	–81
1995–2000	402	845	–49	–394	1,625	1,852	–43	–184
2000–06	358	357	96	–96	–216	–280	91	–27

Source: Bureau of Economic Analysis, changes in selected major components of the international investment position, 1989–2006. As explained in the text, the 2005 and 2006 data exclude the category of financial derivatives.

changes, exchange rate changes, and other valuation changes due to coverage changes and inconsistencies in the basic source data on stocks and flows. We have consolidated the data for the period from 1990 to 2006 into three comparable subperiods. As shown, the combined revaluations have consistently favored the asset side of the accounts. A large portion of the net change, however, can be traced to revaluations that are due to the "other revaluations" category. The effect of exchange rate changes was negative during part of the period and is highly variable. It is also noteworthy that the net effect of price changes varies substantially between the versions with FDI at current cost and market valuations. Thus we infer that the greatest differences revolve around the question of how to value FDI, a category for which we have no direct market measure. An important shortcoming of the BEA data is that it is not possible to disaggregate the valuation changes at the level of individual asset categories.

Gourinchas and Rey address these issues by constructing their own measures of the U.S. external position that emphasize the total return (inclusive of capital gains and losses) instead of nominal receipts and payments.[28] Particularly for the years after 1980, their measures of aggregate investment flows and

28. Gourinchas and Rey (2007).

stocks are very similar to those of BEA.[29] However, they use a methodology for calculating the returns on assets and liabilities that is quite different. Instead of supplementing the official estimates of capital income receipts and payments with estimates of capital gains and losses, they fully replace the income flows with their own estimates of total return, which are based on the performance of country-specific market indexes and the country composition of U.S. investments. Similarly, on the liability side, U.S. payments to foreigners are based on the total return estimates of U.S. market indexes.[30]

For FDI, Gourinchas and Rey exclude the income reported by BEA on both inward and outward FDI and replace it with their measures of the total return derived, as explained above, from the country-specific equity market indexes. In effect, they switch the focus from a debate about the sources of a differential rate of return on inward FDI compared with outward FDI to a focus on the simpler question of whether or not foreign equity markets outperform those of the United States.

In their version of the accounts, the United States earns a slightly higher return on its FDI, but the advantage is substantially smaller than that of non-FDI assets. In striking contrast to the returns shown in figure 2, the Gourinchas and Rey data show that the United States' advantage lies outside FDI, since the United States substantially outperforms other countries in its investments in each of the categories of equity, debt, and bank credit. However, we cannot compare their measure of returns, excluding the capital gain or loss, with the income and payments data from BEA because only the total return is reported in their published paper.

The alternative set of international accounts constructed by Gourinchas and Rey reflects an argument similar to that of Gros in that Gourinchas and Rey reject BEA's FDI income data and replace them with a series that largely eliminates any difference between the returns on inward FDI and outward FDI. The resulting focus on the relative performance of equity markets assumes away the possibility that affiliates may do better or worse than the average firm in the host country. They posit instead an alternative puzzle of why the United States does so well on its non-FDI investments.

We agree with Gourinchas and Rey about the importance of developing effective measures of the total return on international financial investments. However, we do not understand why they go so far in rejecting the BEA data on capital

29. The capital flow data are virtually identical to those of BEA, with some reclassification; and except for FDI, they benchmark their asset positions to those of BEA in the fourth quarter of every year. The FDI flows are identical to those of BEA.

30. We were unable to obtain the Gourinchas and Rey data for direct comparison with that of BEA, but the appendix to their paper provides a very thorough documentation of their methodology.

incomes. In addition, Stephanie Curcuru, Tomas Dvorak, and Francis Warnock, using a methodology similar to that of Gourinchas and Rey, conclude that the United States does not earn substantially higher returns within the two categories of bonds and stocks.[31] We favor a less extreme approach in which BEA would publish the three components of the official valuation measure—price changes, exchange rate changes, and statistical discontinuities—for each of the major asset categories. Researchers could then use either the nominal or the total return, depending on the specific circumstances.

Tax Policy and Income Shifting

The influence of taxation on decisionmaking by multinational corporations has long been a major topic of economic research. A survey by James Hines highlighted the wide range of those studies and the consistent evidence that taxes do have important consequences.[32] However, most of the studies have focused on the effects of taxation on the location of investments. Less attention has been paid to the issue of greatest interest in the present context: Do firms shift income from the United States to jurisdictions of relatively low tax rates?[33] We are not only concerned about the extent to which tax incentives affect the placement of FDI but also about whether those incentives lead firms to disproportionately assign income to low-tax jurisdictions beyond an amount implied by their investment decisions.

There are two important mechanisms by which firms might shift reported net income. The first, which has attracted most of the attention, relies on the adjustment of cross-border transfer prices among affiliates within the same corporation. Governments try to control tax-induced transfer price adjustment by requiring the use of prices that are based on comparable arm's-length transactions. However, this process involves substantial ambiguities. The second similar mechanism involves the transfer of intangible capital between a parent corporation and its affiliates. The use of the capital, in the form of manufacturing or marketing knowledge, is allocated to affiliates in low-tax jurisdictions at a price below the appropriate arm's-length royalty.

Although it is within the U.S. customs union, Puerto Rico is a striking example of the potential for income shifting. Until recently, section 936 of the Tax Reform Act of 1976 made income earned in Puerto Rico completely exempt

31. Curcuru, Dvorak, and Warnock (2007).
32. Hines (1997).
33. Huizinga and Laeven (2006) conducted such an analysis for European multinational firms operating within Europe and found evidence of substantial tax-related profit shifting.

from U.S. taxation. The provision was intended to encourage U.S. firms to establish manufacturing facilities on the island—but it also created strong incentives for income shifting. Mainland pharmaceutical firms, for example, correctly reported a low value for raw materials exported to the island and a high value for final products exported from the island. Much of the difference between the two reflected the rent the companies earned on research and development (R&D) for new patented drugs, the whole of which was attributed to the Puerto Rican affiliates. In effect, R&D expenses were recorded in the United States where the tax rate was high, while the returns were recorded in Puerto Rico where the tax rate was zero. This income shifting is estimated to account for a 17 to 31 percent overstatement of Puerto Rico's GDP in 2004.[34] Grubert and Joel Slemrod reported rates of return in excess of 100 percent on tangible assets for the Puerto Rican affiliates of corporations in pharmaceuticals and electronic equipment.[35]

Patrick Honohan and Brendan Walsh found comparable evidence of extraordinary returns by multinationals with large amounts of intangible capital operating in Ireland, another foreign low-tax jurisdiction.[36] Microsoft provides a particularly good example, as it operates an affiliate in Ireland that receives much of its revenue from sales outside the United States. In 2004 the Irish affiliate reported assets of $16 billion and profits of $9 billion.[37]

Existing Literature

Grubert and John Mutti provided broad evidence of income shifting by U.S. multinationals.[38] Their analysis of the profitability of U.S. affiliates as a function of host countries' statutory tax rates for 1982 found a significant and large negative correlation, implying that firms declared more income in low-tax countries. Similarly, Hines and Eric Rice analyzed the reports of U.S. nonbank majority-owned affiliates in 1982 and found a negative relationship between local tax rates and profits, controlling for the capital and labor inputs.[39] In the early 1980s, however, the U.S. corporate tax rate was not particularly high relative to those of the countries in which its FDI was concentrated. Thus it was uncertain whether tax shifting would result in a net reallocation of income away from the United States.

34. Bosworth and Collins (2006, pp.23-29).
35. Grubert and Slemrod (1998).
36. Honohan and Walsh (2002, pp.39–44, appendix).
37. Glenn R. Simpson, "Irish Subsidiary Lets Microsoft Slash Taxes in U.S. and Europe," *Wall Street Journal*, November 7, 2005, p. A1.
38. Grubert and Mutti (1991).
39. Hines and Rice (1994).

A link to the U.S. parent was provided by David Harris and others who reported that the parents of U.S. multinationals with affiliates in low-tax jurisdictions had lower U.S. tax ratios.[40] In addition, Andrew Bernard, Bradford Jensen, and Peter Schott used a new dataset that included customs records of exports and export prices that distinguished between sales to foreign affiliates and arm's-length transactions.[41] They found that exporters consistently charged lower prices to affiliates and that the difference varied inversely with the tax rate in the destination country. They estimated a loss of $15 billion in the trade balance for 2004, or about 6 percent of U.S. FDI income.

Related research that has focused on foreign-controlled corporations operating in the United States has not found evidence that income shifting is a major contributor to the low reported return on inward FDI. Foreign firms do appear to have consistently earned a below average rate of return over the past quarter century (see figure 3). However, Mataloni found no significant negative correlation between the returns earned by foreign-controlled corporations and their reliance on intra-firm trade.[42] Grubert used data from U.S. corporate tax returns to examine the behavior of foreign-controlled corporations from 1987 to 1993.[43] He concluded that a large portion of the difference between the returns of foreign-controlled and domestic corporations can be accounted for by non-tax factors. Furthermore, he found that firms with less than 50 percent foreign ownership also had low relative rates of return. Since income shifting would seem to be more difficult in the presence of other stockholders, he viewed this finding as a significant argument against the hypothesis.

In table 3, we present more recent information on the income of domestic and foreign-controlled corporations, as shown in the Statistics of Income data of the Treasury.[44] One interesting characteristic is the much higher incidence of negative or zero income among foreign-controlled corporations than among domestic corporations (30.2 percent compared with 12.7 percent). This fact plays a dominant role in accounting for the overall difference in the rate of return on net worth between the domestic and foreign-controlled firms (see columns 3 and 6). Notably, if the comparison is restricted to firms with positive net income, domestic and foreign firms have roughly equivalent rates of return (columns 4 and 5). However, this is not true if firms in the financial sector (FIRE) are excluded, as shown in panel B. Thus restricting the sample to

40. Harris and others (1993).

41. Bernard, Jensen, and Schott (2006).

42. Mataloni (2000).

43. Grubert (1997). The paper is an update of an earlier article by Grubert, Goodspeed, and Swenson (1993).

44. See Hobbs (2006).

Table 3. Rate of Return, Domestic and Foreign-Controlled Firms, 1995–2003

Percent

	All firms			Firms with positive net income		
	Domestic controlled (1)	Foreign controlled (2)	Differential (1 – 2) (3)	Domestic controlled (4)	Foreign controlled (5)	Differential (4 – 5) (6)
Panel A. All sectors						
1995	7.1	4.0	3.1	9.8	10.1	–0.4
1996	6.9	3.7	3.3	9.5	9.2	0.3
1997	6.6	4.1	2.5	9.0	8.6	0.4
1998	5.2	2.3	2.9	7.9	8.3	–0.3
1999	5.0	2.8	2.2	7.7	8.5	–0.8
2000	4.4	2.3	2.1	7.9	8.2	–0.3
2001	2.8	–0.8	3.6	6.8	7.1	–0.3
2002	2.7	–0.6	3.2	6.4	7.6	–1.1
2003	3.4	0.8	2.6	6.3	6.4	–0.1
Panel B. All sectors excluding FIRE						
1995	10.8	5.1	5.7	15.8	10.9	4.9
1996	11.0	3.5	7.5	16.0	9.1	6.9
1997	10.8	3.6	7.2	16.3	8.6	7.7
1998	8.1	2.3	5.8	13.9	8.9	5.0
1999	7.1	2.5	4.6	13.3	9.3	4.0
2000	5.4	2.1	3.3	12.4	8.3	4.1
2001	3.2	–1.1	4.3	11.1	7.3	3.8
2002	3.1	–0.5	3.6	10.9	8.3	2.6
2003	4.9	0.5	4.4	11.1	7.2	3.9

Memo: 1995–2003 average share of total net worth in firms reporting zero or negative income (all sectors).

Domestic controlled   12.7
Foreign controlled   30.2

Source: U.S. Department of Treasury, Statistics on Income, and authors' calculations.
FIRE = financial services, insurance, and real estate.

firms with positive net income has the greatest impact on the comparison between domestic and foreign firms in the financial sector in which the rate of return of foreign firms is substantially higher. The differential between domestic and foreign firms for firms with positive net income remains negative in industries such as manufacturing and wholesale trade.

New Results

We reexamine the issue of income shifting using more recent data from BEA's survey of U.S. multinational corporations. For the years 1999 to 2004 we have income and balance sheet data for U.S. majority-owned foreign affiliates in fifty-one countries. We constructed effective tax rates for each country, smooth-

Figure 4. Correlation between Effective Foreign Tax Rate and Top Domestic Rate[a]

Effective foreign tax rate (percent)

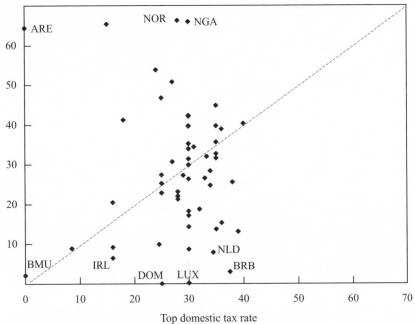

Top domestic tax rate

Source: Authors' calculations based on Bureau of Economic Analysis, Financial and Operating Data, tables III.E 5 and III.E 6, various years; University of Michigan World Tax Database.

a. Effective foreign tax rate is computed as total taxes paid divided by the sum of taxes paid and net income, averaged over 2001–03. Top domestic tax rate is for year 2002.

ARE = Argentina, BMU = Bermuda, BRB = Barbados, DOM = Dominican Republic, IRL = Ireland, LUX = Luxemborg, NGA = Nigeria, NLD = Netherlands, NOR = Norway.

ing the data by taking three-year centered moving averages.[45] We then estimated simple gravity-style equations in which the log of income from country *i* was related to the log of the country's GDP; the log of its distance from the United States; the ratio of total trade to GDP, as a measure of openness; and the effective tax rate.

As shown in figure 4, the effective tax rate on foreign firms often is quite different from the top statutory domestic tax rate in the host country.[46] These differences reflect other aspects of the tax law, such as depreciation allowances and the common practice of granting preferences to foreign investors. For

45. The calculation was suppressed in those situations in which the net income was negative. For 1999 (respectively, 2004), the tax rate was set equal to the centered three-year average for 2000 (respectively, 2003).

46. The statutory tax rates are from the World Tax Database compiled by the Office of Tax Policy Research at the University of Michigan (www.bus.umich.edu/OTPR/otpr/introduction.htm).

Figure 5. Average Effective Tax Rates, 1999–2001 and 2002–04ᵃ

Percent

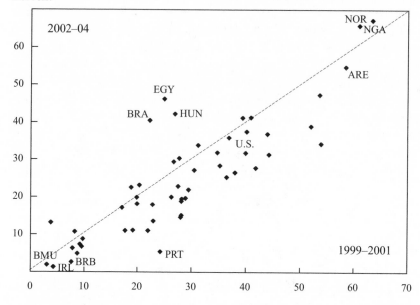

Source: Authors' calculations based on Bureau of Economic Analysis, Financial and Operating Data, tables III.E 5 and III.E 6, various years.

a. Effective tax rate is based on total taxes paid and total income earned over years 1999–2001 and 2002–04, respectively.

ARE = Argentina, BMU = Bermuda, BRA = Brazil, BRB = Barbados, EGY = Egypt, HUN = Hungary, IRL = Ireland, NGA = Nigeria, NOR = Norway, PRT = Portugal.

example, the effective tax measure more clearly highlights the low tax applied to FDI in the Netherlands (NLD in figure 4) and Luxembourg (LUX), for example. At the same time, it indicates the importance of excluding oil-exporting countries where the effective tax is very high.[47] We also find a consistent pattern of decline in the effective tax rates between the two subperiods: 1999–2001 and 2002-04 (figure 5). Countries have reacted to the international competition by reducing the taxation of corporations.

How do tax rates abroad compare with those in the United States? Table 4 reports the average effective tax rate across the sample of countries, weighted by the stock of FDI. As shown, the U.S. tax rate was roughly 15 percentage points above the weighted foreign rate from 1999 to 2001. The 2002 tax reduc-

47. We believe the high effective tax rates reported in oil-producing countries may be due to firms' grouping royalty payments in with foreign taxes. Such payments are conceptually quite different from tax payments, and we therefore exclude the three oil-producing outliers in figure 4 (United Arab Emirates or ARE; Norway, NOR; and Nigeria, NGA) from the regressions reported below.

tion lowered the gap slightly, but the United States tax rate has remained considerably above the average of the countries in which its multinational corporations invest.

The basic regression results for exploring cross-country differences in FDI income are reported in table 5. The first three columns report the results for FDI income of the U.S. parent companies. The first two of these use annual data for the period 1999–2004 giving a total of 290 observations, with the caveat that the tax rate is a centered moving average as described above.[48] In column 1, the estimated coefficient for tax rate is negative and highly significant, a result that is very much in line with the previous finding that U.S. corporations are sensitive to tax considerations in the allocation of their investments.

Column 2 reports the same specification but with the country-specific stock of direct investment included as an explanatory variable.[49] An important result to note is that the tax rate coefficient remains negative and statistically significant even when the accumulated investment stock is controlled for. We interpret this finding as reflective of income shifting, since firms seem to go beyond the simple redistribution of their investments to reallocate income to low-tax jurisdictions. The last three columns repeat the regressions using total affiliates' income and equity, with no adjustment for the U.S. parent's share. The results appear quite robust to this alternative formulation.

We used the regression results of column 2 in table 5 to estimate the magnitude of net income shifting. Thus we show in column 1 of table 6 the level of FDI income that would be predicted each year using each country's effective tax rate, summed over the fifty-one countries in our sample.[50] The same calculation is repeated in column 2 but with every country assumed to have the U.S. tax rate instead of its own effective tax rate. Since the U.S. tax rate consistently exceeds the average tax rate abroad (see table 4), the predicted income in column 2 is consistently below that for column 1. The difference between the two values is our estimate of the net income shifted out of the United States, shown in column 3. The fifty-one countries accounted for 81.5 percent of FDI income receipts in 2004 (column 4).[51] We find that U.S. firms reported an

48. Because of concerns about correlations of the error term across years but with a common country, columns 3 and 6 report the same specification as columns 2 and 5 but with all of the data converted to two nonoverlapping subperiods.

49. Direct investment is measured here at historical cost, as BEA does not provide a geographical breakdown of direct investment position at either current cost or market value.

50. Because of data limitations, the number of countries included was below fifty-one in some years.

51. The geographical distribution of direct investment income is reported without a current-cost adjustment and net of withholding taxes. In 2004 these adjustments reduced aggregate income earned on direct investments abroad by $23 billion.

Table 4. Weighted Average Corporate Tax Rates

Percent

	Rest of world[a]	United States[b]
1999	26.3	39.5
2000	25.9	42.2
2001	24.7	37.9
2002	22.8	31.4
2003	19.0	32.8
2004	18.8	31.0

Source: Authors' calculations based on data from Bureau of Economic Analysis, Financial and Operating Data, tables III.E 5, III.E 6; National Income and Product Accounts, table 1.14.

a. Weighted annually by foreign direct investment stock in each country. The underlying tax rates are three-year centered moving averages.

b. Annual average.

Table 5. OLS Regressions of Foreign Income[a]

	Log direct investment income			*Log foreign affiliate income*		
	Annual *(1)*	*Annual* *(2)*	*3-year average* *(3)*	*Annual* *(4)*	*Annual* *(5)*	*3-year average* *(6)*
Tax rate	−0.032	−0.015	−0.016	−0.045	−0.018	−0.014
	(6.84)	(4.78)	(2.92)	(9.80)	(5.90)	(3.55)
Log GDP	0.78	0.12	0.09	0.83	0.23	0.20
	(19.28)	(2.79)	(1.28)	(22.47)	(6.15)	(3.75)
Trade/GDP	0.009	0.003	0.002	0.007	0.001	0.002
	(8.48)	(3.93)	(1.69)	(6.95)	(1.88)	(1.64)
Log Distance	−0.57	−0.15	−0.02	−0.49	−0.04	−0.07
	(5.77)	(2.14)	(0.19)	(5.33)	(0.59)	(0.76)
Log direct investment stock		0.77	0.83			
		(19.52)	(13.26)			
Log equity					0.73	0.75
					(21.16)	(15.09)
Constant	2.48	−0.27	−1.47	2.37	−1.46	−1.08
	(2.79)	(0.45)	(1.58)	(2.94)	(2.75)	(1.38)
Adjust R^2	0.63	0.85	0.87	0.70	0.88	0.91
Observations	290	285	97	284	284	100

Source: Bureau of Economic Analysis, Financial and Operating Data, tables III.E 5, III.E 6, and III.B 1-2, various years; U.S. Direct Investment Abroad Historical Data, tables 11_9905 and 13_9905; World Bank, World Development Indicators; and authors' calculations.

a. The *t* statistics are reported in parentheses.

Table 6. Income Earned on U.S. Outward FDI

Millions of dollars

	Predicted income, country tax rate[a]	Predicted income, U.S. tax rate[a]	"Extra" income[b]	Share of total income covered (percent)
1999	83,414	66,698	16,716	86.4
2000	91,760	72,826	18,934	86.4
2001	97,615	76,059	21,556	81.7
2002	115,322	98,176	17,145	87.1
2003	131,371	106,703	24,667	86.4
2004	146,737	118,185	28,552	81.5

Source: Authors' calculations.
FDI = foreign direct investment.
a. Figures are based on regression coefficients from column 2 of table 5.
b. Totals reflect rounding.

"extra" $28.5 billion earned abroad in 2004, or an average of 15 percent of total receipts over the course of the six years. Thus income shifting on outward FDI could account for as much as 1 to 1.5 percentage points of the return on FDI assets shown in figure 3, equal to about one-third of the gap between the return earned on outward investment and the benchmark return of nonfinancial corporate capital.

Conclusion

Whether the United States can continue to earn positive or near-zero net investment income will have a direct impact on the size of the current account imbalance over the short to medium term. The fact that the United States has done so to date, despite a large and growing net international indebtedness position, has provoked a stream of research on the sources of the rate of return differential. Such explanations have focused on observable characteristics of firms, data quality issues, and the importance of including valuation changes in the measure of the return.

We argue here that tax-induced income shifting is an important part of the story. Using country-specific income and tax data, we find that about one-third of the excess return earned by U.S. corporations abroad can be explained by firms reporting "extra" income in low-tax jurisdictions of their affiliates. We caution, however, against more extreme attempts to reconcile the return puzzle by restating the official balance of payments figures. The official data may exaggerate the U.S. FDI premium, but its size and persistence suggest that the return differential is quite real.

We conclude by stressing the importance of BEA's expanding the accounts to document the separate contributions of price changes, exchange rate changes, and revaluations at the level of individual asset categories. At least three research papers have produced unofficial measures, but only BEA can produce consistent estimates that would facilitate analysis based on both nominal and total returns.[52]

---

52. Curcuru, Dvorak, and Warnock (2007); Gourinchas and Rey (2007); Tille (2003).

Comment and Discussion

Cédric Tille: The U.S. external account shows a striking disconnect between the stock of external liabilities and the stream of associated dividends and interest payments. At the end of 2006 the market value of net U.S. liabilities to foreign investors amounted to 16.6 percent of GDP, while the United States earned a net capital income *surplus* equal to 0.3 percent to GDP during the year.[1] This discrepancy primarily reflects a yield gap in foreign direct investment (FDI) holdings, with U.S. investors earning a better return on their FDI holdings abroad than foreign investors earn in the United States.

The paper by Bosworth, Collins, and Chodorow-Reich reviews possible explanations for the yield gap and focuses on the role of different corporate tax rates between the United States and the rest of the world. If the tax rate is relatively high in the United States, multinational firms can shift their profits to their foreign affiliates through the pricing of intra-firms transactions and the allocation of expenses such as research and development. The authors find that differential taxation can account for a sizable share of the yield gap.

My comments are structured as follows. First, I show that the yield gap is also observed for overall returns. I then discuss another potential explanation and present additional evidence on the relevance of taxation issues. The final section discusses the implications for the sustainability of the current account.

Yield and Total Returns

The evidence presented by the authors focuses on the yields on FDI, that is, the streams of earnings (retained and distributed) divided by the corresponding

The views presented are those of the author and do not represent the views of the Federal Reserve Bank of New York or the Federal Reserve System.
1. The net capital income is from the revised balance of payments data released on June 15, 2007, which show a substantially larger surplus than in the preliminary data.

Table 7. Average Gaps in Yield and Total Returns, 1983–2006[a]

Percent

	Yield gap	*Return gap*
FDI (current cost)	7.0	8.7
FDI (market value)	5.7	7.6
Non-FDI	–0.4	2.6

Source: Bureau of Economic Analysis and author's calculations.
FDI = foreign direct investment.
a. Yields are computed as the stream of earnings and interest in a year, divided by holdings at the end of the previous year. Total returns also include the valuation change (change in holdings net of financial flows). The gaps are the differences between the yield (return) on asset and that on liabilities.

stocks. Such flows are not the only source of return, however, and capital gains also play a sizable role.[2] Including the valuation gains, nonetheless, does not change the pattern of a large gap between FDI assets and liabilities, with a limited gap in other categories (table 7). Over the last twenty years, the yield on FDI assets exceeded that on FDI liabilities by between 5.7 and 7.0 percentage points, depending on the exact measure, with essentially no such gap outside FDI. The pattern is the same for overall returns, with FDI assets earnings between 7.6 and 8.7 percentage points more than FDI liabilities. Although a gap is also observed outside FDI, its magnitude is much smaller.[3]

Another Potential Explanation: The Vintage of FDI Liabilities

The paper provides an extensive review of factors, other than differential taxation, that could account for the yield gap. These factors include the possibility that foreign FDI holdings in the United States have only been established recently, while U.S. FDI assets have been established decades ago. This raises the possibility that U.S. affiliates of foreign multinationals are still getting established in their market, leading to a temporarily low profitability.

This vintage channel is especially noteworthy as the yield gap reflects a very low yield on foreign FDI holdings in the United States. Furthermore, the yield on FDI liabilities shows sizable fluctuations (figure 6). Over the last twenty years, the yields were especially low in the early 1990s and the early years of the twenty-first century. An obvious factor for this is the U.S. business cycle, as these periods were recessions. However, low yields also followed waves of

2. See, for instance, Gourinchas and Rey (2007); Lane and Milesi-Ferretti (2006); Tille (2005).
3. The absence of a return gap outside FDI is consistent with Curcuru, Dvorak, and Warnock (2007).

Figure 6. Yield on FDI liabilities

Percent

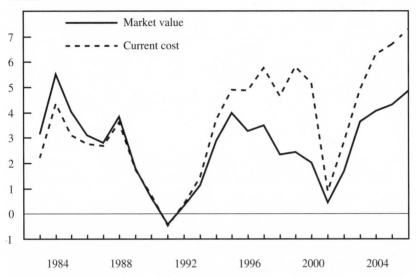

Source: Bureau for Econonic Analysis.

foreign FDI in the United States (figure 7).[4] FDI flows from foreign countries into the United States were especially large in the late 1980s and the late 1990s.

A simple regression analysis suggests that large FDI inflows are followed by low yields, even accounting for the business cycle (table 8). The yield on FDI liabilities in a given year is well explained by GDP growth in that year and FDI inflows in earlier years. The first regression shows the results with FDI inflows for the current and the last four years, while the second regression considers only the inflows three years before, which are the only ones with a statistically significant impact.

The second regression in table 8 shows that one percentage point of GDP growth boosts the yield by 39 basis points, while additional inflows of 1 percent of holdings lower the yield three years hence by 16 basis points. FDI inflows also play a substantial role in driving the fluctuations of yields. Based on the second regression, FDI inflows account for 56 percent of the variance of the fitted yield, with GDP accounting for 26 percent.

The above evidence is clearly limited as we only consider aggregate yields and flows with no breakdown by sectors. Nonetheless, it indicates that unusually large FDI inflows in the United States tend to be followed by unusually low yields.

4. The FDI inflows are scaled by the stock of FDI liabilities at the end of the previous year, at market value.

Figure 7. FDI Inflows Scaled by Lagged Holdings (Market Value)

Percent

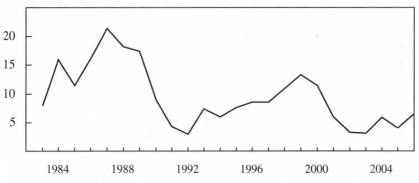

Source: Bureau for Econonic Analysis.

Table 8. Impact of FDI Inflows on Subsequent Yield, 1983–2006[a]

Dependent variable: Yield on FDI liabilities in time t (market value)

Item	Regression 1		Regression 2	
	Coefficient	t *statistic*	*Coefficient*	t *statistic*
Constant	**0.035**	2.81	**0.030**	3.25
GDP growth in year *t*	0.231	0.73	**0.390**	2.02
FDI inflows in year *s* / FDI holdings at the end of year *s* – 1				
Contemporaneous (*s* = *t*)	0.036	0.37		
One lag (*s* = *t* – 1)	0.018	0.14		
Two lags (*s* = *t* –2)	–0.036	–0.28		
Three lags (*s* = *t* – 3)	**–0.142**	–1.52	**–0.164**	–3.73
Four lags (*s* = *t* – 4)	–0.039	–0.55		
Adjusted R^2	0.51		0.60	
Variance of yield (percent)				
Actual yield			0.021	
Fitted yield (total)			0.014	100
Due to FDI inflows				56
Due to GDP growth				26

Source: Bureau of Economic Analysis and author's calculations.
FDI = foreign direct investment.
a. Statistically significant figures are in bold.

The Sensitivity of Earnings to Taxes

The authors focus on the impact of different tax rates on the yield on U.S. FDI assets. They document that the U.S. effective corporate tax rate exceeds that of other countries. U.S. multinationals can take advantage of this differential and shift their profits to their foreign affiliates by setting the transfer prices for goods and services traded between the parent and the affiliates accordingly. A similar effect can be obtained through the allocation of intangible assets. For instance, research and development expenses can be allocated to the parent, while the resulting intangible capital is used in affiliates. If the royalties for the use of intangible capital are set below market rates, profits will be shifted from the parent to the affiliates. The authors present evidence of such transfers for the cases of Puerto Rico and Ireland. A regression analysis confirms that the yield on U.S. FDI assets abroad is affected by tax differentials.

Developments in FDI outflows through 2005 provide a clear illustration of the relevance of tax issues. In 2005 U.S. multinational companies benefited from a temporary tax break on earnings in foreign affiliates that were repatriated in the United States. This led to a sharp swing in the allocation of FDI earnings between reinvested and distributed earnings (figure 8). Reinvested earnings usually account for the bulk of the total. Starting in the first quarter of 2005, reinvested earnings decreased, and sharply fell in the last two quarters of 2005, before surging back to more usual levels in the first quarter of 2006. The pattern was mirrored in distributed earnings, with little impact on the overall receipts.

Implications for External Sustainability

The paper makes a strong case for a role of tax differentials between the United States and foreign countries in accounting for the yield gap in FDI. The magnitude, while sizable, is however limited relative to the overall gap. The authors point out that the differential taxation can account for between 1 and 1.5 percentage points of the yield gap, which represents between a fifth and a third of the overall gap.[5]

The sizable yield gap observed between FDI assets and liabilities is then likely to be driven by several factors, of which tax considerations are a relevant one. Ultimately, understanding the drivers of the yield is relevant to a sustainability analysis. If the yield is likely to persist, the United States can

5. The yield gap in FDI currently stands at 3.9 percentage points when using holdings at market value and 5.4 percentage points when holdings are assessed at current cost.

Figure 8. Earnings on FDI Assets

Millions of dollars

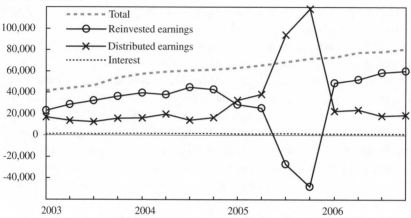

Source: Bureau for Economic Analysis.

keep earning more on its external assets than it pays on its liabilities, allowing it to sustain a relatively large current account deficit. If, however, the yield is likely to narrow soon, the United States could be faced with a substantial deterioration on its capital income balance, requiring a prompt adjustment in the trade balance to prevent a widening of the current account deficit.

The sustainability of a yield differential stemming from different tax rates across countries ultimately reflects the persistence of these tax gaps. Should the United States bring its corporate tax rate in line with foreign ones, U.S. multinationals would loose their incentive to report profit abroad and the yield gap would narrow. It is important, however, to bear in mind that profit shifting would primarily alter the split of the current account between the trade and capital income balance, as opposed to the current account itself. Consider the case of a U.S. firm that charges royalties to its affiliates that are below market rates. If the firm decides to raise these royalties, its affiliates' profits would be reduced. However, the higher royalties would represent a service export that would boost the trade balance, largely offsetting the reduction in the capital income.

Other possible explanations for the yield gap have different implications. In particular, if the low yield on U.S. affiliates of foreign firms represents a vintage effect as these firms are still building up their profitability, the yield gap is likely to narrow in the future. Higher profitability of the affiliates in the U.S. domestic market would then translate into a deterioration of the capital income balance.

Discussion: Jane Ihrig began the general discussion by commending the paper and the issues it addresses. Regarding data collection, she pointed to her own work at the Federal Reserve Board, noting that at the FRB, data are collected, made available to the public, and given to BEA to use in their flows. Commenting on errors in the flow surveys, she added that as surveys have become more regular (that is, annual) errors are easier to detect and the flow surveys are asking more questions. In addition, Ihrig suggested that what we have seen are the valuation adjustment corrections, things that have been corrected over time. Ihrig also raised the issue of tax rates and their effects on the rate of return "puzzle," which can be frustrating because it seems like it should be there, but we cannot seem to find it. She concluded by commenting that seeing the results today in the anecdotal cases that were brought up made her hopeful.

Raymond Mataloni commended the paper for its original contributions and for the doubts that the authors raise about some of the alternative stories out there. Commenting on Cédric Tille's comment to the paper, Mataloni found intriguing the decline in the pattern of effective tax rates, found in pre-2001 and post-2001.

The session concluded with brief responses from Barry Bosworth to the questions and comments raised by the participants. Regarding the break in 2002, Bosworth alluded to a possible similarity with the tax cuts that occurred in the 1980s under President Reagan. Along these lines, he pointed out that during this period there was a lot of tax competition when other countries began to try and match the United States. On a similar note, Bosworth noted that on the econometric analysis side of things, variation was due to weighting up. The tax rates in the two subperiods are absolutely constant and that what is making it appear to change a bit over time is just the weights. Gabriel Chodorow-Reich briefly interjected by pointing out that when looking at the annual data there is a lot of noise in what is happening because firms have low incomes or high incomes. This is why things were smoothed out. Bosworth added that one reason we did not find what we wanted with tax effects was because we kept using the official tax rates rather than the effective tax rates, which makes a big difference in what we conclude. Last, Bosworth commented that he found the information about the increased frequency of surveys very useful and interesting and that they will try to incorporate several of the comments raised by participants.

References

Bach, Christopher L. 2005. "Annual Revision of the U.S. International Accounts, 1991–2004." *Survey of Current Business* (July): 54–67.

Bernard, Andrew B., J. Bradford Jensen, and Peter K. Schott. 2006. "Transfer Pricing by U.S.-Based Multinational Firms." Working Paper 2006-33. Dartmouth College, Tuck School of Business.

Bosworth, Barry P., and Susan M. Collins. 2006. "Economic Growth." In *The Economy of Puerto Rico: Restoring Growth*, edited by Susan M. Collins, Barry P. Bosworth, and Miguel A. Soto-Class, pp. 17–69. Brookings.

Buiter, Willem. 2006. "Dark Matter or Cold Fusion?" Global Economics Paper 136. London: Goldman Sachs (16 January).

[BEA] Bureau of Economic Analysis. 2007. "U.S. Net International Investment Position at Year End 2006." News Release BEA 07-31. Washington: U.S. Department of Commerce (www.bea.gov/newsreleases/international/intinv/2007/pdf/intinv06.pdf).

Cline, William. 2005. *The United States as a Debtor Nation*. Washington: Institute for International Economics and the Center for Global Development.

Curcuru, Stephanie E., Tomas Dvorak, and Francis E. Warnock. 2007. "The Stability of Large External Imbalances: The Role of Return Differentials." NBER Working Paper 13074. Cambridge, Mass.: National Bureau of Economic Analysis. Also as International Finance Discussion Papers 894. Board of Governors of the Federal Reserve System (April).

Gourinchas, Pierre-Olivier, and Hélène Rey. 2007. "From World Banker to World Venture Capitalist: US External Adjustment and the Exorbitant Privilege." In *G7 Current Account Imbalances: Sustainability and Adjustment*, edited by Richard H. Clarida, pp. 11–55. University of Chicago Press.

Gros, Daniel. 2006a. "Foreign Investment in the US (I): Disappearing in a Black Hole?" CEPS Working Document 242. Brussels: Centre for European Policy Studies (April).

————. 2006b. "Foreign Investment in the US (II): Being Taken to the Cleaners?" CEPS Working Document 243. Brussels: Centre for European Policy Studies (April).

Grubert, Harry. 1997. "Another Look at the Low Taxable Income of Foreign-Controlled Companies in the United States." Paper 74. Washington: U.S. Treasury Department, Office of Tax Analysis (October).

Grubert, Harry, and John Mutti. 1991. "Taxes, Tariffs and Transfer Pricing in Multinational Corporation Decision Making." *Review of Economics and Statistics* 73, no. 2 (May): 285–93.

Grubert, Harry, and Joel Slemrod. 1998. "The Effect of Taxes on Investment and Income Shifting to Puerto Rico." *Review of Economics and Statistics* 80, no. 3: 365–73.

Grubert, Harry, Timothy Goodspeed, and Deborah Swenson. 1993. "Explaining the Low Taxable Income of Foreign-Controlled Companies in the United States." In *Studies in International Taxation*, edited by Alberto Giovannini, R. Glen Hubbard, and Joel Slemrod, pp. 237–70. University of Chicago Press.

Harris, David, and others. 1993. "Income Shifting in U.S. Multinational Corporations." In *Studies in International Taxation*, edited by Alberto Giovannini, R. Glenn Hubbard, and Joel Slemrod, pp. 277–98. University of Chicago Press.

Hausmann, Ricardo, and Federico Sturzenegger. 2006. "Global Imbalances or Bad Accounting? The Missing Dark Matter in the Wealth of Nations." Working Paper 124. Harvard University, Center for International Development.

Higgins, Matthew, Thomas Klitgaard, and Cédric Tille. 2007. "Borrowing without Debt? Understanding the U.S. International Investment Position." *Business Economics* 42, no. 1 (January): 17–27.

Hines, James R., Jr. 1997. "Tax Policy and the Activities of Multinational Corporations." In *Fiscal Policy: Lessons from Economic Research*, edited by Alan J. Auerbach, pp. 401–45. MIT Press.

Hines, James R., Jr., and Eric M. Rice. 1994. "Fiscal Paradise: Foreign Tax Havens and American Business." *Quarterly Journal of Economics* 109, no. 1 (Feb.): 149–82.

Hobbs, James. 2006. "Foreign-Controlled Domestic Corporations, 2003." *Statistics of Income Bulletin* (Summer): 67–112 (www.irs.gov/taxstats/article/0,,id=162576, 00.html).

Honohan, Patrick, and Brendan Walsh. 2002. "Catching Up With the Leaders: The Irish Hare." *BPEA*, no. 1: 1–57.

Huang, Juann H., and Angelo Mascaro. 2004. "Return on Cross-Border Investment: Why Does U.S. Investment Abroad Do Better?" Technical Paper 2004-17. Washington: Congressional Budget Office (December).

Huizinga, Harry, and Luc Laeven. 2006. "International Profit Shifting within Multinationals: A Multi-Country Perspective." Economic Papers 260. Brussels: European Economy, European Commission, Directorate-General for Economic and Financial Affairs.

[IMF] International Monetary Fund. 1993. *Balance of Payments Manual*. Washington: IMF, Statistics Department.

Kitchen, John. 2006. "Sharecroppers or Shrewd Capitalists? Projections of the U.S. Current Account, International Income Flows, and Net International Debt." Washington: Office of Management and Budget (February).

Landefeld, Steven, and Ann M. Lawson. 1991. "Valuation of the U.S. Net International Investment Position." *Survey of Current Business* (May): 40–49.

Landefeld, J. Steven, Ann M. Lawson, and Douglas B. Weinberg. 1992. "Rates of Return on Direct Investment." *Survey of Current Business* (August): 79–86.

Lane, Philip R., and Gian Maria Milesi-Ferretti. 2001. "The External Wealth of Nations: Measures of Foreign Assets and Liabilities for Industrial and Developing Nations." *Journal of International Economics* 55, no. 2: 263–94.

———. 2003. "International Financial Integration," *IMF Staff Papers* 50 (Special Issue): 82–113 (Washington: International Monetary Fund).

———. 2006. "The External Wealth of Nations Mark II: Revised and Extended Estimates of Foreign Assets and Liabilities, 1970–2004." Discussion Papers 5644. London: Centre for Economic Policy Research (April).

Lipsey, Robert. 2006. "Measuring International Trade in Services." NBER Working Paper 12271. Cambridge, Mass.: National Bureau of Economic Analysis.

Mataloni, Raymond J., Jr. 2000. "An Examination of the Low Rates of Return of Foreign-Owned U.S. Companies." *Survey of Current Business* (March): 55–73.

McGrattan, Ellen R., and Edward C. Prescott. 2006. "Technology Capital and the U.S. Current Account." Working Paper 646. Federal Reserve Bank of Minneapolis, Research Department (November).

Tille, Cédric. 2003. "The Impact of Exchange Rate Movements on U.S. Foreign Debt." *Current Issues in Economics and Finance* 9, no. 1. (Federal Reserve Bank of New York).

_____. 2005. "Financial Integration and the Wealth Effect of Exchange Rate Fluctuations." Staff Report 226. Federal Reserve Bank of New York (October).